RIDING SHOTGUN

The Autobiography of the
Original Wizard of Oz

RIDING SHOTGUN

The Autobiography of the
Original Wizard of Oz

ANDY BERNAL

With a contribution from Russ Gibbs

FAIRPLAY

PUBLISHING

First published in 2021 by Fair Play Publishing.
Second Print 2022

PO Box 4101, Balgowlah Heights, NSW 2093, Australia.

www.fairplaypublishing.com.au
sales@fairplaypublishing.com.au

ISBN: 978-1-925914-23-8
ISBN: 978-1-925914-24-5 (ePUB)

Front cover original painting by Christopher Paul Toth.

Front cover design and page layout by Leslie Priestley.

All photographs are from the personal collection of Andy Bernal.

All inquiries should be made to the Publisher via sales@fairplaypublishing.com.au

NATIONAL
LIBRARY
OF AUSTRALIA

A catalogue record of this book is available from the National Library of Australia.

DEDICATION

To the three most important ladies in my life – my mother Margaret, my daughter Isabella, and my wife Jaynie. My guardian angels who have inspired, empowered and looked over me in their very own different ways. I would not be here to tell my story without their unconditional love and support. There are not enough words to describe my adoration for them and I hope that once they have turned the final page of this book, they are as proud of me as I am of them.

To every young kid out there – shoot for the stars and follow your dream, whatever that may be. If my story inspires you a little or helps you stay strong in times of need, then sharing it will have been worthwhile.

'Truth is stranger than fiction,
but it is because Fiction is obliged
to stick to the possibilities;
Truth isn't.'

Mark Twain

The Line-Up

FOREWORD

Andy Bernal was a pioneer who paved the way and created a belief that not only could you become a Socceroo, but also play many years of club football in Europe and the United Kingdom. Many of us played with or against him during our careers and he was the toughest of the tough, could play several positions and was a fantastic man-marker.

He captained the Australian Institute of Sport in 1983/84, the place many of us later attended, again one of the early pioneers of that programme. His journey is an incredible story of unbelievable heights, to the very depths of human darkness, but to be here telling it is a testament to his mental fortitude, desire, passion, discipline and will – the exact traits that enabled him many years ago to become the first Australian to play in Spain, one of the greatest football nations on the planet.

Andy's experience also reminds us that the game needs to address the often-forgotten human element that goes with being a professional player. The game impacts all of us in different ways. The need for greater mental health awareness is of prime importance. If addiction, depression, anxiety and stress disorders can almost destroy one of our very toughest warriors, then we are all at risk. Implementing educational processes and programmes is a must to help players who need it.

Thank you, Andy, for sharing this amazing journey. I am sure it will inspire, empower and educate our future stars.

Craig Moore
April 2021

CHAPTER 1

WELCOME TO MADRID

It was early morning in Sydney, June 2003, when I was woken by a phone call that would begin one of the most surreal chapters of my life.

The call was from my London boss, Tony Stephens of SFX Sport Group UK, with instructions to get to Madrid immediately. Why? The highly anticipated transfer of football superstar David Beckham to the most famous and successful club in the world, Real Madrid.

Beckham was to be presented to the world as a Real Madrid player, the final piece of the Galactico jigsaw puzzle that Madrid President Florentino Perez was assembling. Perez's dream was to build a 'super team' with Beckham the latest addition based around what arguably was, at that time, the world's top five players, the best of the best: Zinedine Zidane, Ronaldo (the Brazilian one), Roberto Carlos, Luis Figo, and now David Beckham.

Known only to a few of us on the planet, and highly secret in the football world, this move of Beckham's had been a year in the making. Twelve months earlier I had met with Jorge Valdano the winner of the 1986 World Cup Final with Argentina, along with the former Spanish international goal scorer, Emilio Butragueño, a member of the famous 'La Quinta del Buitre', a quintet of players that had gone down in Real Madrid history. The purpose of that Madrid meeting was to advise the pair, who at the time were the club's joint directors of football, about the potential transfer of some of England's best football talent that we managed at SFX. The three names I gave them were Beckham, Michael Owen, and Leeds United defender Jonathan Woodgate.

Real Madrid were interested and would eventually sign all three, but it was Beckham they were after first. Not only was he a prodigious football talent, but a sports marketing dream.

Many months later, and shortly after the now famous dressing room bust up between Beckham and Sir Alex Ferguson, I also met with Barcelona legend Carlos Rexach, who at the time was pulling the strings at FC Barcelona, Real

Madrid's biggest rivals. He asked me if the Beckham-Real Madrid deal was complete, and I said "no". It didn't need a degree in rocket science to understand the SFX position either. A Barcelona offer increased our bargaining power and leverage with Real Madrid, and competition between Spain's two biggest rivals for the one player was a perfect position for the agency.

Shortly after that meeting, Barcelona agreed to a world record transfer fee with Manchester United for the signing of Beckham, something that Joan Laporta, who was running for the President's role at the club confirmed in 2003.

"We said we would put Barcelona on top of the football world and that we would incorporate Ronaldinho or Beckham or Thierry Henry," Laporta told Sky Sports in the UK. He continued: "We talked to Manchester United to find out the possibility of incorporating Beckham and we reached an agreement with them at Heathrow Airport. We had to wait for an answer from his agent, which arrived after our elections and, by then, Beckham had already signed for Real Madrid."

Instead, Laporta had to settle for Brazilian superstar, Ronaldinho, a very special player in his own right.

That set the scene for my new Spanish adventure, a plan discussed previously in London with both Stephens and David that I was the man to manage the superstar in Spain.

The boxes were all ticked. I spoke both English and Spanish perfectly. I also had family throughout the country, one of whom was a senior undercover police officer in Madrid assigned to the anti-terrorism unit. Importantly, my existing relationships with former and current Real Madrid players, coaches and staff were reassuring and comforting to David. He knew his was in good hands.

But what exactly would I be doing? It was never really specified or defined so I rolled with whatever the occasion required. Every day brought a different challenge, but my personal constants never changed. In me, David had an interpreter, personal manager, driver, bodyguard and, most importantly, a friend.

It was the day of David Beckham's arrival into Madrid and I was waiting for his arrival at the Torrejon de Ardoz Military Air Force base. A private jet bearing David and his entourage was coming into land. A hot day awaited the Beckhams; for the official signing David would be accompanied by his wife, the Spice Girl Victoria Beckham – but unknown to us all much more heat lay ahead.

I was on the tarmac early, and had been there for half an hour, alongside the eagerly awaiting Real Madrid officials. Waiting with us was also an assistant sent by SFX in London, Rebecca Loos. To this day, I am not clear why she was there.

The aircraft landed, and with that Real Madrid's most valuable asset had arrived safely on Spanish soil. I greeted David and Victoria at the bottom of the impressive jet stairs, both looking a billion dollars as I introduced them to the club officials. Vehicles were at the ready, we jumped in and the England captain was on his way to the team hospital for the obligatory medical exam.

I sensed Victoria wasn't happy when she saw Loos amongst the welcoming party. This was confirmed later that evening, when Victoria made it clear to me that she was under no illusion about the type of person Loos' was, and I agreed. Loos was not my type at all; she was definitely no Posh or Baby Spice, trust me. But she had the type of game that could infuriate every wife on the planet, something that those of us in the industry were well aware of.

Quite simply, she was surplus to requirements in Madrid. Her presence upset Victoria and yet Tony Stephens would always tell me to make sure Victoria was happy, whatever it took. Victoria was a star in her own right and her light was not to be dimmed, Stephens would say. Having Loos in Madrid must be one the dumbest decisions made by a sports management company in the history of sport. The culprits, Stephens, and Holmes had scored an own goal and we hadn't even commenced pre-season.

It was also the beginning of the end of a long relationship between David Beckham and SFX.

Our security detail for this first event comprised one Real Madrid security officer and two bodyguards from the UK. The main one was Merrick MacDonald, the Beckham family's most trusted bodyguard, a former Royal Marine Commando and UK Police tactical response officer who was trained in anti-terrorism and bodyguard duties. These would range from elite driving tactics through to kidnap and extortion threats. Little did I realise that all of Merrick's skills would be put to use in the coming months. Early in the piece he pulled me aside and said words which kind of still haunt me today. "Andy, listen carefully. I've done my homework, you're a warrior like us, you'll be needed, so I'm going to teach you everything I know, a fast-track SAS course. Whatever you do, do not deviate from what I say. This business is not a game. People die."

A few years later Merrick was dead, killed in Baghdad when a roadside bomb blew up the vehicle that he was travelling in.

Whilst I learnt a lot from Merrick, he couldn't speak or understand Spanish, so in my own way, I quickly became important to him. His first port of call on anything said around us was me.

He could be childish at times, dishing out Chinese burns or poking you somewhere that would disable you for several minutes, laughing all the time and taking joy in saying, "you know I could have killed you with a bit more pressure!" Looking back, it's evident that this was his way of escaping the complete madness of looking after the Beckhams.

Merrick was a good man and protective of us all. It was ironic that one of the toughest and most professional soldiers on the planet had been taken from us, blown to bits, most probably by a kid using a mobile phone. It doesn't seem real. He was like Rambo or the Terminator – those guys aren't supposed to die.

Back to the day itself and we were off to the medical exam. These are the parts of the day that can drag on for footballers but are important for the club. They are spending millions so they must be assured the asset they are purchasing is in pristine condition and fighting fit. Generally they are a formality, but sometimes players can fall foul and underlying medical issues can arise which prevent deals from being completed. However, these are rare at this level, and in this case Real Madrid had already received David's complete medical history from Manchester United.

The boom gate went up and we exited the military base. Immediately upon turning onto the freeway we entered a different world. Motorbikes and cars came from everywhere, lots of them, lenses pointed at us, their constant flashing lights blinding us at times. Lying in wait, they obeyed no road rules, and it was like nothing I had ever seen before. Inside the car was the footballer known as 'Golden Balls', and he was their golden ticket. A good quality photograph brought big money, but in their desperation to get the money shot, it brought even bigger danger. Like seagulls chasing and fighting over that one potato chip you throw away, you can suddenly have hundreds of birds around you. French football legend Eric Cantona said it better, and I now felt his pain, "welcome to the world of the paparazzi!"

On the motorway, our Guardia Civil motorbike and vehicle escort couldn't believe it either. Outnumbered, they too had seen nothing like it. Extraordinarily little respect, if any, was shown towards the police by the paparazzi and they were forced to call for back-up. More motorbikes and a police chopper eventually joined the party, hovering above us, itself in a battle with helicopters from national and international news corporations.

Bedlam and insanity ensued, a madness which I somewhat understood growing up around Speedway and loving NASCAR, with Spanish DNA that innately pushes us to want to be Fernando Alonso or Marc Marquez every time we hit the road! This lot though were a completely different level, off the chain Moto GP pilots with cameramen riding pillion.

As we approached the hospital, Princess Diana came to my mind. Her death in a car crash precipitated by a similar paparazzi frenzy had me thinking of possibly dying in a car crash with David Beckham. This was my first taste of the paparazzi wars, and it wasn't hard to imagine that dying was a real possibility!

Upon arrival we were met by Real Madrid's Chief Medical Officer, Dr Del Corral, who would conduct the medical exam. By this stage, every single nurse on duty was out to greet the world's most popular sportsman. Never had I seen so many nurses dolled up, starstruck, silent but internally screaming, their faces lit up with emotion and adoration, the like I had only ever seen on film and directed at Elvis and the Beatles. This was my reality now, and I couldn't help thinking I might get lucky with some Spanish senoritas running off DB's coat tails ... hey there are worse things in life.

The medical at which I was present throughout, went much as expected and when all tests were completed the doctor told the eagerly awaiting press, "*David esta como nuevo, fisicamente esta perfecto*", which I loosely translated for David as "you're all good mate, in perfect knick".

We then headed to the team hotel for lunch and a short rest before departing to the Estadio Santiago Bernabéu for the official contract signing.

On the way to one of football's most iconic grounds, it was the same deal as earlier that day. Once again, we would be chased by the paparazzi, and it did not cease, ever. It was at this point that our security team began discussing the creation of a 'circle of steel' around David and his family.

My mind processed many options, the most immediate and basic need being a requirement for more security personnel, as paparazzi and journalists were already camping outside the hotel and infiltrating it, masquerading as chefs, waiters and room service attendants. All connected, an army of them, it seemed like they were on every corner of Madrid.

We arrived at the stadium and were greeted by the Head of Marketing Jose Angel Sanchez and Jorge Valdano who took David, Victoria, their eldest son Brooklyn and myself straight to the home dressing room. It was a special place, a black shiny floor made of what seemed like Pirelli rubber, life size pictures of each player on the locker doors blending perfectly with ocean blue and white tiled walls in Mondrian type patterns, giving the room a warm, vibrant and empowering feel.

Little 'Buster' (Brooklyn's nickname) couldn't take his eyes off a few footballs lying around and before you knew it, the kid, his dad and myself had an impromptu kickabout on the hallowed turf of the Santiago Bernabéu as the Spanish sun slowly departed the sky. The moment ended when Jose Angel shouted that El Presidente had arrived, so we moved upstairs to a boardroom with a perfect and majestic view overlooking the pitch.

With only a select few people in the room, and with the swoosh of a pen, David Beckham became a Real Madrid footballer. It was a four-year deal that was lucrative personally for David, with Manchester United receiving a £24.5m transfer fee. There were hugs and handshakes everywhere, but my eyes were focused on the pitch below, flashing back 17 years to when I played on the very same pitch I was now staring at. The first Australian player to grace it, I was lost for a moment until, in the words of Eminem, I snapped back to reality.

This unbelievable day continued back at the hotel where, at a dinner to mark the occasion, would have me sitting at his request next to World Cup winner, Jorge Valdano. Flanked either side by Real Madrid Board members, we sat opposite David and Victoria. It was an exclusive club, in which I felt more than comfortable.

We talked football, Jorge's words so eloquent that you couldn't fail to fall more and more in love with the game as he spoke. Quickly, the conversation moved to my favourite player of all-time, Diego Armando Maradona. He was a player that Jorge had had won the Mexico 1986 World Cup with, both part of an amazing Argentine side captained by the genius that was Maradona. Jorge's face would light up telling me his Maradona stories and you could feel the genuine warmth and love for his compatriot and teammate. In Jorge's words 'Diego won him a World Cup.'

The chat reverted to Beckham talk, and I thanked him for trusting my football assessment of David that I had first given him a year ago, and for then making the move happen. He said, "Please tell David later that I won the World Cup alongside Diego Maradona, and for me David's right foot is the equivalent of Diego's left foot, they both were born with a magical wand." Compliments don't come bigger than that.

The evening came to an end, the expensive Cuban cigars capping off what was an amazing, insane day. I had lived my first day of superstardom. It felt surreal, like I had been Bond in a James Bond movie.

Tomorrow would bring the official unveiling of David Beckham as a Real Madrid player. It would also bring another paparazzi frenzy, now already a constant.

Sure enough, morning came, and the hotel was surrounded and besieged by an ever-growing army. We departed for David's presentation and after another crazy car chase, the convoy of vehicles eventually arrived at the Ciudad Deportiva, Real Madrid's training complex at the time, located on the famous Paseo de la Castellana. The unveiling would occur in the club's basketball stadium and as you would expect with a signing of this magnitude, the world press were there in numbers. Shining bright, David stood between one of football's all-time greats, Alfredo Di Stefano, and the president of Real Madrid, Florentino Perez.

David read a short speech that had been prepared for him by Tony Stephens who ran it past me for final approval. It was short, sweet and to the point, it needed no more in my opinion. David masterfully delivered it to the packed room and global television audience.

It was now time for David to change into his new playing kit; he then performed a few tricks to the applause of the thousands of fans surrounding the training pitch. The England captain again delivered with his usual style and aplomb.

Valdano turned to me, smiled and gave a nod of approval. Excited about the football talent he was building at the club, he let me know about another prodigious talent the club was looking at, a young boy whose very name would light up Jorge's face. Only a few years later, he would be introduced as a Real Madrid player. Today, amongst the excitement and general fanfare of another Galactico presentation, the boy's name could easily have been lost on me, but it was not. Valdano does not entertain time wasters, he knew he could trust me and valued my opinion. He whispered, "The boy is a special talent, who will one day captain Real Madrid and Spain." Well he wasn't wrong – the kid in question was a 16-year-old prodigy from Seville named Sergio Ramos.

The glitz and the glamour, in tandem with ultimate professionalism and a burning desire for greatness, was deeply embedded throughout every department of the club. From day one, it was abundantly clear, and I felt privileged to be shown the working mechanisms from within by important staff members. I now fully understood the global enormity of the giant powerhouse that is Real Madrid.

You may well be asking yourself, how does a boy from Canberra end up here? Easy really, you just need to know the formula and then adjust to the levels expected of you. I'll show you how, grab your seat belt and buckle-up for the ride of your life!

CHAPTER 2

THE EARLY YEARS

I have often wondered how and why I ended up experiencing situations and events in my life that to most humans would seem not only incredible but incomprehensible, unbelievable, not possible, and only the stuff of dreams. The ride is not free, you pay in many ways and one thing is for sure; hard work and determination are key, but the most defining is the DNA passed on, in essence your human genetic makeup at birth. In my case, my parents passed on DNA that in many ways mirrored their own courage, strength, fortitude, and willingness to live life as a wonderful adventure.

My mum, Margaret Arranz Antolin, and dad, Andres Bernal Rodriguez, arrived in Australia on the migrant ship Monte Udala, which docked in Melbourne on 21 January 1961 carrying 462 passengers. on what was a 30-day trip departing from Santander in Spain and stopping for a few days in Cape Town, South Africa. Ironically, while they were both on that ship, they were travelling independent of one another; my mum with her parents, my dad riding solo.

A month at sea travelling to the other side of the world would bring a multitude of emotions ranging from excitement, exhilaration and fear. Many times they would question the decision itself and question what lay ahead in an unknown land, a place they would arrive at, without understanding one word of English. Their bravery astounds me, warms me, and has always empowered me.

My dad came to Australia of his own choice and for him this was an adventure of a lifetime. Mum, on the other hand, had no choice. She was happy living and studying at a Catholic Convent in Burgos, cared for by the nuns and paid for by a wealthy friend of the family. It was the only alternative, as she was the eldest sibling and there was simply not enough food for all the family. Even though she lived away from her family to help with this, her family still suffered much hunger and lived in abject poverty. Yet to this day, Mum continues to pine for her homeland, like many other immigrants I suppose.

My future parents' paths didn't cross on the ship. Upon arrival in Melbourne they were put on upgraded cattle trains to the immigration camp more than 300 kilometres away in Bonegilla in rural Victoria. It would be five years later in Queanbeyan, the New South Wales border town with the nation's capital Canberra, where they would meet for the first time.

Mum was working in a milk bar and dad was in town for a wedding. His first port of call on arrival was a hamburger and a vanilla milkshake and, by fate, he called into the milk bar where mum worked. They got talking and realised they both had my grandfather, Honorio Arranz, in common. He was of course, mum's father, and on the trip over he had become good friends with my dad, but they had lost contact when dad went north to the cane fields.

So that's how mum and dad began their romance; a chance meeting at a milk bar in Queanbeyan. Two beautiful souls who gave my sister, Raquel, and myself love, love and more love.

Mum was living with her parents Honorio and Angelines in the garage of a house owned by the Marina family, Spanish immigrants who had arrived a few years earlier and settled in Queanbeyan. My good friend and someone I really looked up to as a kid, was their son Angel Marina who played for the Canberra Raiders in the club's first ever season in the National Rugby League in 1982.

My dad loved Australia and was a proud Aussie. He especially loved telling us about his adventures in North Queensland. Even when he returned to Spain many years later on holiday, he would tell everyone that Australia was the best country on the planet.

He was a sniper in the Spanish military during his compulsory national service. A standout in unarmed combat and as a rifleman, on guard duty one night he heard a noise about 50 metres away from the guard tower. It was pitch black, the middle of the night, and he could see no more than ten to twenty metres from the barracks wall. A small flickering light at about 6ft height was the only observation he could make.

As instructed in training, he shouted his first command, "who goes there?" There was no answer, so he repeated the command twice more. Again, there was no answer. Raising his rifle, he fired at the tiny shining flash of light, he reckoned was probably the size of a 5-cent piece. A heavy thump followed and soldiers with torches headed towards the target, only to shout out in shock that it was one of General Franco's favourite horses! My dad had shot it right in the middle of the head, under the eyes, the flashing light a piece of the metal on the bridle. Under the Franco dictatorial regime, it was possible to be killed for less, and dad's worst fears realised when he was summoned to the General's offices for a debrief.

Two months prior he had been in the very same spot defending himself after throwing a bowl of boiling soup into another soldier's face, burning it severely, and leaving him forever scarred. The reason? At dinner one evening, the soldier next to him called him a son of a bitch, not appropriate when you've lost your mother at the age of three! Dad had his head shaved completely as punishment and was sent to military prison, locked up in darkness for a month as his sentence. He would fondly recall that he was never called a son of a bitch again.

However, he was now in a lot more bother and the repercussions for shooting dead General Franco's horse genuinely scared him. But to his surprise, he was awarded a commendation and a promotion to Franco's team of special guards.

After leaving Bonegilla immigration camp, he spent five years cutting sugar cane in Ingham, Tully and Mareeba in Far North Queensland, getting through 25 tonnes a day, chopping and loading it all onto sugar trains. This was tough, hard, and dirty work in torturous heat and humidity where you were potentially only one bite of a taipan snake away from death.

Queensland, known as the Sunshine State, was a tough place in the 1960s but my dad loved it.

On Fridays after work, they would head to the local pubs, and speaking no English at all, they would attempt to woo the local girls with their good looks and Spanish charm. The nights out nearly always ended in a street fight against the white boys and the Aboriginal boys for money and for fun! I remember watching the old western movies with dad when I was younger, and he would always say that Far North Queensland back then was wilder than anything in the American west.

With the influx of European immigrants who began arriving in significant numbers after the Second World War, came racial abuse. It impacted him deeply and it would not be long before he experienced in Australia what he had witnessed in Cape Town on the stopover.

At the request of some local Aboriginal fellas, he bought them some beers, exiting the pub and handing them over with a smile, only to find himself a few minutes later, cuffed and savagely beaten by two police officers. Unknown to him, it was illegal at the time to buy beers for Aboriginal people. When the local interpreter arrived, my father was released but the event hurt him, not for the beating he took, but the fact that social injustice was alive and real in this new country that had been sold to him as a beautiful tropical paradise.

Not long after on a Friday evening after a week-long sugar cane cut, dad and two mates headed into the town centre for a few beers.

A few kilometres outside of Tully, the lads' Holden picked up a tail. Five cars full of young Australian men looking for a bit of fun with three wogs. What they didn't know was these three wogs were not to be f***ed with. Cane cutting kept them fit and strong, the job turned them into weapons, and the deadly Taipan snakes kept them focused and alert. Dad could street fight, whilst the other two Spanish lads had joined the French Foreign Legion back in the day, and they were two very loose humans, highly skilled trained killers.

They quickly hatched a plan. They would turn around at the city roundabout and head back towards the cane fields. They wanted open countryside with little chance of any police around. Pedal to the metal they needed distance from the pack.

The way dad told it, it was reminiscent of a scene out of the film '*Mississippi Burning*'. A lynching, a bashing, in fact, anything was possible, but the trio remained calm. This was boys against men. The decision was made to get approximately one mile ahead, stop and get out, each one quickly grabbing a machete from the boot and simply waiting for the ensuing cars to arrive.

When they did arrive, they came to a screeching halt, their headlights shining brightly onto the three Spaniards waiting with machetes at the ready. Approximately twenty men jumped back into their vehicles quicker than they had jumped out, a very smart decision as one swipe of the machete could cut a man in half and these three were not who you wanted to be testing. They were never followed again!

The sugar cane days led dad to hunting crocodiles in the Daintree Forest, north of Cairns. It was proper 'Rambo' territory. Four-wheel drive jeeps, sleeping in hammocks between the trees, avoiding snakes and spiders that could end your life with one bite. They would pick out and shoot the crocodiles as they exited the water on the river's edge. These reptiles were massive, three to four metres long and you needed to hit them between the eyes, anywhere else and you lost money on the skin. They would go into the forest for a fortnight or so and come back out with thousands of dollars worth of crocodile skin to make jackets, shoes, handbags, watchbands, the lot.

It was a lucrative business, but it was dangerous and you would have to get close to execute that minimum damage shot; miss and you were in deep trouble. Not only that, there was the constant thought of what could come at you from behind while you were focusing on the crocodile. There were a million other things in the forest that could have your ass like a wild dog or even a wild pig.

In New York about ten years ago, these adventures would once again be told by dad, this time to a stranger he met while visiting my sister and her family. Downstairs from my sister's apartment by the Hudson River in Battery Park, he told his stories to a very handsome man, wearing a baseball cap and puffing on an e-cigarette.

Intrigued by my dad's Spanglish, with a delivery reminiscent of Paul Hogan in 'Crocodile Dundee', they began chatting, comfortable in each other's presence. They introduced themselves as Andy and Leo.

Dad finished the conversation wanting to purchase the e-cigarette that Leo was smoking. Leo directed him to a tobacconist not far away and said, "tell the man Leo sent you, he will look after you!"

'Looked after' is an understatement!

While this was happening, my sister Raquel had been notified by a friend that dad had been chatting to Leonardo Di Caprio, who is rarely caught for a chat. But my dad wasn't your average cat. Walking through the apartment door, my dad was fully focused on his new high tech e-cig when he was greeted with, "Papa, do you realise you were talking to Leonardo Di Caprio?"

"Who the bloody hell is Leonardo Di Caprio?" he asked. He hadn't seen any Leo movies, lost interest towards the end. His favourite actors were still Clint Eastwood and Charles Bronson, but now after watching a few Leo movies at my sister's house over the coming days, Mr Di Caprio had joined Dad's top three!

While dad roamed the Sunshine State, mum was in Canberra living with her parents. She was put to work at 14 years of age cleaning houses for the wealthy, telling me it was better than the torture of attending school and being laughed at every day for looking and speaking differently. She prided herself on being the best cleaner and would eventually, with no formal education, end up working in a government job as a secretary for a Minister at Parliament House. I'm enormously proud of her for that achievement, getting that job with English as her second language, and with no formal education was simply an incredible feat.

A lot of my friends reckon I get the killer instinct from her. Dad was a weapon, but she has the killer mindset.

I was born in Canberra in 1966. My childhood was exciting, thrilling, dangerous and fun for the most part. Hours and hours were spent playing sport of every type, summer and winter non-stop. During these times, my brain would play footage of me playing for the Socceroos, Kangaroos or the Australian cricket team on famous stages around the world.

I never had a doubt in my mind that I would play on those stages. However, many happy childhood memories were also unfortunately tainted with racial abuse over many years which impacted me a whole lot more because I could feel the hurt in my parents, and especially my grandparents, when they were laughed at and humiliated because of their accents, what we ate, and our traditions.

My *Abuelo* and *Abuela* (grandparents) could understand no English. I had been raised by them since birth and in their company, we only spoke Spanish. I was a young boy, so how did I answer them when they would ask me, "why are people laughing at us or so nasty to us?" Their pain created confusion, anger, and resentment in me for years to come. We just wanted to be Aussies too!

Mum and dad did their best to create a normal household, ensuring that both my sister Raquel and I had a good upbringing in a beautiful home environment. We did most things together as a family and spent lots of time watching any sport shown on TV with the World Cup and Olympic Games our favourites. Add into the mix classic old school TV programmes such as '*Happy Days*', '*Hogan's Heroes*', '*Bewitched*', '*I Dream of Jeannie*', '*Lost in Space*', '*Little House on the Prairie*', '*The Waltons*', and a bloke called Kung Fu!

Like many families of that era we weren't considered well off, but as kids we also never wanted for anything. Mum and dad worked hard, often doing two jobs at times so we could prosper. Looking back there were more good times than bad, but to this day one horrible recollection still haunts me.

At an early age I remember waking up in the middle of the night with my left leg in a steel and leather brace. It was a continuous excruciating pain, as the steel bars twisted my leg towards a normal shape. Like the brace Forrest Gump wore, it had been strapped onto my leg while I slept and upon awakening it sent me into a horrible panic.

From birth my left leg wasn't classified as normal. It was not as physiologically straight as it should be and the knee itself was deformed. A normal existence would be problematic with doctors telling my parents that playing sports would be a miracle. The patella did not sit right, did not track as it should, and when

I walked, I felt the excruciating pain of bone-on-bone. Years later, surgeons at the Australian Institute of Sport would confirm this, a handicap for life and there was no fix.

The brace was uncomfortable and unsightly. The doctors wanted me to wear it to school, but I had enough abuse coming my way being a wog so that was never going to happen. Some kids had seen me wear it once and already the cruel voices shouting 'cripple' and 'spastic' were tormenting my soul.

Over time and subsequent years, I would straighten it slightly by strengthening the surrounding muscles, but despite all the efforts, the passage of time and constant unmonitored loading would compound the damage. Strangely, it hurt less when I ran, but this created faster wear and tear, so I couldn't win. Fusing the knee straight would eradicate pain but I would never run again. Replacement knees were only figments of medical imagination back then, and even if possible, that would also end any sporting dream I had.

A lifetime of knee operations, seven in total, where surgeons would drill into the bones stimulating hyaline articular cartilage growth. Ingesting thousands and thousands of anti-inflammatory tablets that rot away your stomach lining and now cause a different pain just one of many side effects. The pain was a constant every day; it would not cease, but neither would my will to keep playing. It has mentally and physically traumatised me all my life.

Canberra in the 1960s, 1970s and 1980s was white man's land, white Australia. Local rugby league, rugby union, AFL and car races, like NASCAR speedway ones, dominated the sporting landscape with 'wogball' a thing new Australians played. However, my dad was relentless in his mission to be accepted into this landscape and the Australian sporting culture. So off we went to all these sporting events, the car races being our favourite, and if we came across drama then a street fight '*mano a mano*' would fix it all.

For me at school it was always 'wog, choc, or dago' and all through primary school I was bestowed 'gollywog'. The occasional Aboriginal kid at school would cop it worse, but for me this provided an escape as the wogs were relegated to a less important target when a blackfella showed up. It was a war every day, but despite all the racial torment we survived. We knuckled down, copped the racism, gave back as good as we got and created millions of migrant success stories.

In the midst of all the excitement and madness, would come my Holy Communion and Confirmation at the local Catholic Church. The priest would tell us to say a prayer at night before going to sleep. I did for a while, mostly asking God if he could stop everybody calling us wogs, stop all the hate, but then I stopped because the message didn't seem to be getting through. With time, integration became easier and then a group of 'wogs out of work' made a comedy series that made it cool to be a wog and that's how it is today. So maybe my prayers did work!

As a kid my dream was not football. I wanted to play rugby league or cricket for Australia. Playing football wasn't cool in those days.

Former Socceroo and evangelist for the game, the late Johnny Warren famously titled his autobiography 'Sheilas, Wogs and Poofters'. Johnny was spot-on. If you played the round ball game in Australia back then you'd be called one of those rather charming names, or in my case many times, all three!

I ended up playing for the Socceroos, but I was probably a much better rugby league player, a fullback in the Billy Slater mould. I loved the position; it was much like being a sweeper in football, the whole picture was yours, right there in front of you. I loved the physicality of it, the big hits, stuff that you couldn't get away with in football. I was kicking round the corner goals while rugby league stars of the day – Mick Cronin, Graham Eadie, and a bit later on, Mal Meninga – were doing their best with the toe punting method. Unfortunately, my Canberra Raiders, State of Origin and Kangaroo dreams remain exactly that – just a dream.

My uncle, Luis Arranz, was an accomplished footballer who played for one of the top local sides, Woden, which was supported by one half of the Spanish community and played in Atlético Madrid colours, while the other half of the Spanish community supported another suburban club, Lyons, which played in a Barcelona strip. This is when football began taking importance in my life, tagging along with my uncle at every opportunity to watch his game, watching his every move.

My weekends were spent playing junior football for my local club Belsouth, then watching my uncle play. Crowds of between 500 and 3,000 were the norm for local Canberra football with most of the sides made up of European or South American immigrants. Most of the players and supporters couldn't speak much English, so the escape from reality back to their roots in Spain, Croatia, Greece, or Italy, was a local football match full of passion; fights on and off the pitch, then back to their respective clubhouses for a feast of traditional food, drink and music. In our case, the Spanish club displayed an Australian and

Spanish flag on the outside, while inside, football, flamenco and bullfighting posters created a Spanish like atmosphere.

I learnt a lot from these players, many of whom were exceptional talents back in their homelands. Their stories would not only inspire me but educate me in the finer arts of trickery in the game. In Argentina they call it '*viveza*', the literal translation is cleverness, or perhaps more appropriately, cunning. These were good times with our communities, a relief from the usual weekly racial tirade.

There was no Fox Sports, Optus, or PlayStation around in those days. In fact, like many who grew up in Australia at the time the only football games I remember being televised were the FA Cup Final once a year and '*The Big Match*' on Monday afternoons, which showed English League highlights.

It was while watching these highlights that I fell in love with Leeds United. I loved watching those players in pristine white shirts, mixing silky skills with an unbelievable work rate and fighting spirit.

I would sit in school at Belconnen High dreaming of playing for the great Leeds team of the 1970s with legends of the club such as David Harvey, Frank Gray, Eddie Gray, Terry Yorath, Billy Bremner, Johnny Giles, Trevor Cherry and Peter Lorimer. To me they were the Real Madrid of Britain, and just to catch a glimpse of my heroes on the ABC's highlights programme, inspired me. Hours after the show had finished, I would still be kicking a ball around in our backyard, trying to replicate what I had seen earlier.

Who would have guessed at that stage that I would one day grace that same turf at Elland Road, Leeds' famous stadium, in the colours of Reading and come away with a League Cup victory? That night I enjoyed what can only be described as a wonderful battle with the superbly gifted Jimmy Floyd Hasselbaink. Not long after that, Stuart Gray would become a Reading FC teammate of mine. He was the son of Leeds legend Eddie Gray, one of my favourites as a kid. What a small world it is!

I would always be selected for the ACT Schools football, cricket, athletics and rugby teams, but there came a point where I had to choose between the sports. Mum and dad wanted my choice to be football and it was easy to understand why. It was their culture, their sport, the world game. I knew that they would back me 100 per cent with that choice.

Around this time, playing for the ACT in an U-15 game, I was approached by a gentleman who introduced himself and told me to keep working hard as the

Socceroos needed players like me. This was the first time I ever met the legend Johnny Warren.

In time, we became good friends, ending up living not far from each other near Bronte Beach in Sydney after I had returned from England. I vividly remember as an eight-year-old watching him play for the Socceroos in the 1974 World Cup in Germany and his kind words on our first ever meeting, still resonate with me today. That was a major turning point for me and from that moment there would be no stopping me as I pursued my dreams.

My parents' experiences before I arrived on the scene, and then being by their side during my formative years, went a long way to shaping my childhood and beyond. Dad was involved in all my sporting ventures and I spent much of my childhood just hanging next to him.

We had many wonderful encounters and adventures, but somehow trouble was never far away, a constant companion that we never invited but more often than not showed up.

My Aunt Angela's wedding at Saint Christopher's Cathedral was one such time. As the bridal party exited for a big group photo at the end of the service, a couple of cars full of 'bodgies' rolled up shouting, 'wog this, wogs that, go back to your own country', standard racial abuse for the time.

My dad was having none of it, jumping from the group and running down the stairs, picking out the driver of the lead car who had his window slightly down, leaving just enough gap to put your hand and arm through. Dad did just that, grabbing the guys Adam's apple and proceeded to rip it out of his neck. I recall him telling me, "I had it in my fingers and was going to pull it out of his neck, but I could see in his eyes that he was dying on me. I could have killed him, but I let him go and said, if I ever see your face again, I will kill you."

Fast forward 20 years and Mum and Dad were on a day out at the Catalina Golf Club on the South Coast of New South Wales, a favourite holiday spot for landlocked Canberra people.

As fate would have it, Raquel's godfather, Alfonsito Gonzalez, also from Spain who was now a Canberra panel beater and my Belsouth junior coach, walked into the club with a work colleague who he wanted my parents to meet. However, even before Sito had opened his mouth my dad went into kill mode, focused like a tiger, before launching at its prey. It was a face he had never forgotten.

"Hello mate, I think I know you from somewhere and it's not a very good memory..." Dad said.

At this point, the bloke was going pale, his memory taking him back to that long gone wedding day. His panic was further enhanced when suddenly Dad said, "Saint Christopher's Cathedral." At this point Sito's mate had mentally crumbled, probably shat himself too, but Dad offered an olive branch. "We have two choices," he said. "One, you go buy a few schooners and we drink to friendship, or two I finish what I told you I was going to do, if I ever saw you again." The bloke wisely, and quickly, decided that the afternoon's drinks were on him!

Sito Gonzalez took over our junior football team because all the other parents had declined. He had a good CV I suppose! He talked religiously about Deportivo de La Coruña and Celta Vigo. He was also the drummer in a fantastic Latin band that rocked the Spanish club on weekends, so that tipped the scales in his favour and he got the job with no coaching badge or courses in sight. We won the league every year playing good football on shit pitches and only training twice a week. Training consisted of five against five, and shots at goal to finish, nothing else, but always fun.

Recently at the AIS, I watched a young Socceroos warm-up drill, which had me confused just at the sight of the football pitch covered in flagpoles, cones, bibs, beacons and 20 or 30 balls. The whole set-up was so complex and busy that it could have been Hong Kong Airport in the middle of the night. Funnily enough, the kids performed the warm-up drills with world-class precision, like seals and dolphins at Sea World, only to be hit with reality the following day when, in a game, they lacked 'viveza', the street smarts, the kind that Sito Gonzalez would pass on; learnt as a kid on the streets and ghettos of La Coruna and Vigo in northern Spain.

Was he a good coach? He was a good man, he loved the beautiful game and he loved me. His smile would light up our weekends and light up the whole Spanish community. From U-7 onwards I would proudly put on the Captain's armband and lead his troops into battle, his only instructions to the team were, "play like Spain"! We won everything we played in, so hell yes, he was a good coach. When I left Belsouth, he too walked away, joining my uncle and me at the Spanish club team Narrabundah FC.

At the Spanish social club, Sito was the host of fiestas, the event organiser, and the community comedian. At Christmas he would dress up as the black King of the Orient, handing out presents to all the children of Spanish immigrants all paid for by the Spanish Embassy. I can only imagine the woke crowd these days, they'd go nuts with his black face make-up day. The irony of it all, was that he was the most non-racist man you would ever meet and all the little kids loved the Black King. Sito just enjoyed making others happy, a trait that transferred to his son Christopher who on weekends these days, masquerades as the Brumbies rugby union mascot Brumby Jack!

The greatest gift I received from Sito was that he encouraged me to dream. His parents had split up and his father ended up in Rio de Janeiro becoming a good friend of Joao Havelange, the FIFA President from 1974 to 1998. Sito had travelled to Rio where he met Havelange and Brazilian icon Pelé after a game at the Maracanã Stadium.

Pelé gave him a pair of his boots on that visit, which he kept in his tin garage out the back of his house in suburban Spence! Out he went into the Canberra winter one night and came back in like Santa Claus carrying the greatest gift ever, Pelé's boots. They were all black and, when I touched them, adrenaline fuelled energy instantly ran through my body while inside my head I could hear Brazilian football commentary, while seeing Pelé playing in old black and white clips. I didn't lift my head, just stared at them, too afraid to ask if I could try them on despite knowing they were too big anyway.

All through this, Sito would be recounting his trip to Brazil to my parents. The Maracanã, the beaches, and the girls in bikinis. He told it with such passion and joy that I was right there on Copacabana Beach with him. I swear, on the way home sitting in the back of our car, I could even hear the drums of Carnival. The day I met Ronaldo Nazario and Roberto Carlos, I hugged them, and I thought of Sito. I knew he was looking down, smiling.

Peter Desmond was my partner at Belsouth and together we tormented the city and won everything that there was to win in our age group. The Spanish kid and the Pommy kid were an unbeatable double act. Peter and his Dad would regale me with stories of Arsenal, London, and British football in general and I couldn't get enough. Somehow, I knew even then that I would one day play in those famous stadiums lining up against the likes of Arsenal, Tottenham Hotspur, Chelsea and West Ham United.

Peter was a great mate, and it was one of the worst days of my life when I heard that he had died of a brain haemorrhage at the age of just 17. The news hit me hard like a lightning bolt. How could this happen at his age? Life was just so unfair, I was devastated. He had just won the National Schoolboys title with the ACT and had been training with his beloved Arsenal while Watford were keen on looking at him as well. Peter's loss shook me a for a long time and taught me to chase my dreams harder, with no regret, because tomorrow we may not be here.

Before his death I would go in depressive states over having what was basically only one perfectly functioning knee, so now I would always default to "one knee is a far greater option than not being on the planet at all". At his funeral I made a promise to him that I would either play for Arsenal, or play against them at the famous Highbury Stadium, their home ground before they moved to the palatial Emirates Stadium.

Many years later the football gods obliged and playing for Ipswich Town, I ran onto the Highbury turf for a midweek clash. The Arsenal side that night was full of international stars such as England's Lee Dixon, Paul Merson and Michael Thomas, who would score a title winning goal at Anfield in 1989. Also in the line-up were the classy Paul Davis, defensive titans Martin Keown and Steve Bould and beanpole Republic of Ireland striker Niall Quinn. Not too shabby that line-up I told myself as thoughts of Peter came into my head. I carried his memory with me in every game I played in England.

Away from football, the daily racial tension always surrounded our family, maybe because we wouldn't sit back and take it. One series of events over a month rocked the Belconnen area also known as 'Belcompton'. Tensions had escalated in the street and my sister and I had now been attacked physically so the family was going to war. I would try my best to fight them off, but every day I was outnumbered by much older boys who were much bigger than me and in a pack. It was just a hopeless mission. Dad hated bullies, disliked violence, and his message was always never to pick fights. In fact he would tell me to walk away, to be the bigger man, but if you have no option you fight to the death and now the commander had given the signal!

To open the month of madness, his first intervention certainly put the panic up our neighbours at the time, as he went into military mode. Our bashing was the straw that broke the camel's back, and it had been coming a long time.

Dad loaded one of the double-barrel shotguns that we used on hunting trips and off he went, headed next door with me in tow. I was super excited, this was the big show. Mum was screaming at him to stop, but he was on a mission, destination neighbours house, and nobody was stopping him. Up the porch stairs he went and started banging the gun barrels on the door, and yelling "come out you f***ing c***!" Unsurprisingly, no one took him up on his offer, but I can vividly remember my mate Stuart Harris who lived behind us, saying he'd seen the kids and their dad scooting out the back door and over the fence towards some form of safety. They certainly weren't sticking around for the mad wog next door who was back in military mode, with shotgun in hand. Duck season was officially open, and lucky for them they did not return.

It wasn't over yet though, as five police cars rolled up into our street and soon after had dad in handcuffs with me standing right by his side. They asked him if there was anything he wanted to say and he responded cool and calm "Yes, if this happens again, you will need to send five ambulances, never mind five police cars!" The neighbours never again even looked at us, eventually selling up and moving out.

Only a week later, I was ambushed at Hawker shops by three older 'skips', escaping after smashing a hard plastic milk crate into one of their faces, splitting it in a straight line about 1cm wide from the top of the eyebrow to the bottom lip. It was a perfect pick up and smash, you could see the facial bone through the cut, and it left the other two in shock and frozen. It gave me time to escape on my bike and head home to wait with dad, guns in hand, locked and loaded, but the chasing racists did not follow that night. Dad's shotgun episode the week before had put the 'hood' on notice and now we had the local hospital stitching people up.

A few days later, Dad demolished the national parks depot where he was stationer, after a new worker criticised the smell of my mum's Spanish meals three days in a row. Strike three came when the new guy said "that bloody wog food is stinking the place out". Once Dad had left the bloke in a pool of blood, he began trashing the depot piece by piece, eventually pouring tractor fuel over the place and threatening to set the whole place alight unless the new man was removed from the depot, never to return.

Government bosses along with the police arrived to find the bloke searching for his teeth amongst the destruction, with Dad at the ready with lighter in hand. It ended well with the new guy given his marching orders. Dad came home happy, continued taking his wog food to work, while his boss and friend, Dominic Cantazariti, another wog and coincidentally Jaynie's godfather, was chuffed also.

Instances like that never ceased, so that Christmas I asked my parents if I could have a new, bigger hunting knife. Now this wasn't an unusual request from me as we used to go on hunting expeditions looking for rabbit, deer, or pig. Indeed hunting days were a large part of my formative years growing up and, until the massacre at Port Arthur in Tasmania in 1996, it was not unusual to have a couple of shotguns and rifles in the house with plenty of rounds in the wardrobe ready to go.

We often undertook night raids to the south coast where we would frequent a couple of rubbish tips in the early hours of the morning. These places were surrounded by rainforest and were exactly where the big wild pigs would go to scavenge for food. We could hide in empty 44 gallon drums, or behind vehicles, waiting patiently for the wild animals to arrive. It was exciting but scary at age 11 or 12. I would be as quiet as mouse as the pig noises became louder on their approach, then suddenly one of the guys would hit a switch and the spotlights would light up an area the size of a football pitch's 18 yard box. From that point on, the shooters went into 'American Sniper' mode.

We would take the pigs home and eat them. They were delicious, especially the head and snout which my grandfather taught me to pick apart. He ate anything that moved, except for a bat – that was probably the only thing I never saw him eat! The gun noise in the forest would echo like a bomb blast, and that gun powder smell still brings back evocative memories for me. I love that smell.

While hunting for rabbits we would pick up a few of dads' Spanish mates along the way and head to farms at Captains Flat, Cooma and Yass. When the guns went off, I took the role of a retriever hunting dog, making sure I got the go ahead from dad so as not to get hit by friendly fire. I could see what he was aiming at and would go flying after it to collect the bounty, a process that I also found was good training for me, sprinting flat out across all kinds of terrain, pretty much the perfect athletic development.

If you got to an animal and it wasn't dead, you had to finish it off. There were different methods for different animals of course, but in most cases my trusted hunting knife through the animal's heart or throat would end its life. Most times it was easy, no pressure and methodical. Other times, especially when wild dogs were involved you had to approach with caution. They are vicious, cunning beasts and can grow to the size of large wolves so in those cases, it was waiting for the gun to arrive and then, end its life with a bullet to the head. Super exciting when you are a young boy.

Once the animal was dead, I would pick it up or drag it back to my dad, like a dog pleasing its owner. Big deer hunting was a different kind of thrill, and illegal in some parts of the country. A big stag required time, stalking and waiting maybe for days for the right shot. It was all a bit too slow for me, although nailing the right beast felt like an imperious achievement.

Anyway, back to the knife I wanted for Christmas. Truth is, it was for more than just hunting, it had a greater purpose. I had moved onto high school and the route there was a daily hell until I showed my 'little buddy' to a waiting posse and told them what I would do to them. Again, these were older boys in a big group that were looking to bash the little wog football star. Word soon spread and I never again encountered the wog bashing brigades, as they thought I would have no hesitation piercing them with holes. Both my parents knew I was taking the knife to school only to be used as a last resort and if attacked by a large group. I never had to use it, but the message from dad was clear: "If you use it, open them up like a watermelon."

I had only a few individual heroes, apart from the great Leeds United side that I adored. Their poster, along with Mike Tyson, West Indian cricketer Viv Richards and Diego Maradona adorned my walls. They were icons and idols who empowered me.

Viv Richards was amazing, I loved cricket and the West Indies were the best team on the planet. He strutted around like Mike Tyson in his prime, the complete cricketer, a great brave attacking batsman who never wore a helmet. A magnificent fielder, he could also roll the arm over with some quality spin bowling if required. He faced the likes of Dennis Lillee and Jeff Thomson when they were at their peak, the scariest of the scariest fast bowlers, proper head-hunters and Viv with no helmet showed no fear, casually chewing gum and slaying the ball to all parts of the field. He would always look in total control with his beautiful balance and movement. He was elegant and smooth like a black panther.

Diego Maradona was my idol, my inspiration, who along with Johnny Warren kept me on the football path. He debuted for the Argentina national team at just 16, which immediately caught my attention, and after that I followed his every move. A football genius, he won the U-20 World Cup and then the senior World Cup in 1986 when he single-handedly guided his country to the major prize. He was on a different planet to any other player I had ever seen, and his story out of poverty to worldwide fame was inspiring. Off the pitch he was a little crazy - sounds familiar - but with a big heart that he would use to give great joy to his nation and many others.

In the summer months, along with our traditional six-week holiday to Batemans Bay on the south coast of New South Wales, I would focus on Little

Athletics and cricket. It didn't get more Aussie than that, and both helped me become a better athlete for football.

They say a child's first live sporting events are key in the desire to want to live them yourself. Strangely, the first big live events I ever went to, were far removed from any type of football, but they had me hooked on a life of sports entertainment. Dad liked World Championship Wrestling which was a big deal in those days.

The ABC would televise events Australia wide, and at the very first one that we went to watch live at the police boys club, a giant appeared. His name was Andre, and those who follow wrestling worldwide undoubtedly have heard of this 7ft 4, 236kg man mountain. The global wrestling champion spent the whole night throwing Australian icons clean over the top ropes and crashing into chairs and tables ringside. It was amazing and so exciting to watch. I was immediately hooked on sports entertainment, and what would become the monster global production that is the WWE.

After the show we would sit in the boxing area of the gym waiting and attempting to get an autograph from one these superheroes. While we were there, dad would bring up names like Lionel Rose, Cassius Clay aka Muhammed Ali, Tony Mundine, Carlos Monzón, Joe Louis and Rocky Marciano. He loved the fight game, studied it religiously, and that created my love affair with it, and something else I would eventually pour my heart and soul into. Eventually Andre the Giant appeared, and I ran towards him, touched him like he was from another planet, from a land of giants, but to my surprise he was real, a giant amongst normal men. He was so big that my head came up to his knee and I was standing on tippy toes! He bent over and shook my hand which must have seemed like a little marble within his huge palm, but I felt no fear, he was gentle and kind. A special human, one of a kind.

Every second Saturday of the month was motorsport at Tralee Speedway. The smell of burning rubber and ethanol got you hooked in an instant. Speedway on dirt is how NASCAR began, and over the years it has been a breeding ground for the greats, Jimmie Johnson, Dale Earnhardt, Dale Earnhardt Junior, Carl Yarborough, and of course, Richard Petty, they all started in speedway.

Our favourite driver was a bloke called David Wignall who was a loveable rogue. His style was fearless and ruthless, much like his heroes, the motorsport legends Richard Petty and AJ Foyt. Once a year, Team USA would come out to Australia and it was the most exciting thing I had ever seen. David Wignall would go onto become Australian speedway champion in 1973/74 and as fate would again strike, in 2016 he would become my father-in-law when I married his youngest daughter and the apple of his eye, Jaynie. I was now married into motorsport royalty and to this day I still spend weekends in his speedway garage reminiscing about the past. Not long after I met him, he gave me his shotgun and said if you can't hit a few targets in the backyard you can't be part of the family! Luckily for me it wasn't my first rodeo!

My football was progressing well. At 15, I went for Belconnen United U-20 trials, where after general opinion I had run riot at training, the coach decided I "wasn't quite ready". He had his favoured group of boys and I don't really think that he could work me out. To be fair, I was a nasty little prick, but I could play as well, but for someone who was a volunteer coach by night, he wanted the team to be as easy as possible. Being ever the diplomat, I told him to go f*** himself and my dad would tell him the same in the car park. I left with one last jab, "You'll watch me play on TV one day!"

After that, I joined my uncle Luis who was coaching the Spanish club Narrabundah U-20 and we won the league, beating Belconnen United home and away, a precious memory in which I can still see myself chasing around and kicking lumps out of anything that moved in a light blue shirt!

At 16 I joined the Canberra Arrows who were playing in the National Soccer League (NSL) and played for their U-20 team. It was a fantastic time for football in Canberra. We had a national league team since its inception in 1977, and like many kids who played the game, we had a team to aspire to play for. Our home ground was Bruce Stadium now home to the Canberra Brumbies and the Canberra Raiders and fans would flock there in thousands. For me, it would be the highlight of the week, playing in the curtain raiser then heading up into the stands to watch many great Socceroos, thinking I wanted to be out there with them, not playing the curtain raiser crap.

A year later in 1983, I was selected to join the AIS to train and play at their facility based in Canberra, my hometown. This was basically the best U-18 players in the country and it was only the third year of the football program. I knew at this point that I was going places. Jimmy Shoulder, who was Head Coach, came to our house and promised my mum and dad that he would look after me and make sure that I finished school, which I did at Dickson College, before going to the University of Canberra for one year. That was always just a stop gap in my journey as I had my mind set on European football.

Amongst those I attended the AIS with, Frank Farina, Tony Franken, George Kulcsar, Robbie Hooker, Lou Hristodoulou and Warren Spink who would all become Socceroos as I did. In the years after, the AIS really cranked into gear to become a quality production line of Australian international talent that included Mark Bresciano, Steve Corica, Brett Emerton, Craig Foster, Vince Grella, Lucas Neill, Craig Moore, Luke Wilkshire and the legendary Mark Viduka amongst many others.

Our coaches were two Englishmen, Jimmy Shoulder and Ron Smith. These two were hands-down two of the best coaches I have ever had anywhere on the planet. Jimmy had played for Sunderland and was also a decent cricketer, donning the pads for Darlington, whilst Ron was with Tottenham as a junior and was a brilliant educator.

Whilst at the AIS I captained the side to a National Youth League title and was named captain of the Australian Schoolboys, although disappointingly we never toured anywhere. I also wore the armband for the Australian youth team that qualified for the 1985 World Youth Cup in Russia and became the youngest player at age 18 to captain an U-23 Australian side in one of our matches at the Merlion Cup in Singapore.

On the negative side, Jim and Ron had booked me into the AIS sports psychologist Jeff Bond, who much later helped Pat Cash with his Wimbledon triumph. I was getting yellow and red cards for fun, and for some reason I wanted not only to win all my battles, but to inflict maximum pain and damage on opponents. Maybe it was because I was always in pain, which in turn made me angry, so I wanted others to be handicapped by injury too. I felt hard done by, already knowing that the knee would eventually stop me playing for the biggest teams on the planet, feeling almost resigned to second place but mentally knowing I was better than that. Good old Jeff Bond, as best he tried, was unable to fix me.

Months earlier, while touring Europe with the AIS, we would play the final of a German youth tournament at the home stadium of Borussia Dortmund against a quality Real Madrid outfit. Real's youth side were coached by Vicente del Bosque, who would go onto much success with Real Madrid and Spain, leading La Roja to FIFA World Cup glory in 2010 in South Africa before adding the 2012 European Championship to his trophy cabinet for good measure.

During that tournament I would befriend a young goalkeeper called Julen Lopetegui who was playing for Real Sociedad. Julen, years later in Madrid, would be a great help to both David Beckham and myself. He went on to play for Real Madrid, Barcelona and Spain, and would eventually manage the national team and Real Madrid. He most recently won the Europa Cup with Sevilla.

Off the back of that tournament in Germany, Del Bosque invited me to train at Real Madrid but a friend of mine who was working at the Spanish Embassy in Canberra, and was originally from Gijón, found out and within weeks, I was pretty much signed by Sporting Gijón without even having to attend a trial.

Unfortunately, this led to me being ineligible for the Youth World Cup in Russia because the Spanish club wanted me to be classed as a Spanish citizen, at a time when each La Liga club could only have two foreigners registered, a rule that was standard across most of mainland Europe.

So off to Spain I went, back to the country my parents left many years before in search of a better life. The irony that I was heading in the opposite direction to try and achieve exactly that, a better life, wasn't lost on me. Vamos!

CHAPTER 3

IF YOU'RE NOT FIRST, YOU'RE LAST

Off to sunny Spain I headed, the land known for its world class football and the home of Real Madrid and Barcelona, arguably the two greatest and most iconic football institutions in the world. On top of that there was bullfighting, beaches, tapas, sangria, wine, flamenco, dancing horses, beautiful senoritas and last but not least, my bloodline. It felt as if my destiny had been written from up above, something I had envisioned for many years.

I had heard many migrant stories and despite all these people leaving their homeland for a better future, in a beautiful country that is Australia, they all pined and longed for a reunion with their Spanish motherland. What was it about Spain? Its flavour, its street vibe or 'la movida' as they call it, or was it something in the air that is almost indescribable? It has a magical attraction that once experienced is never forgotten, that somehow stays with you forever.

As a kid I would read 'El Pais' at the Spanish club in Canberra, one of Spain's premier newspapers, look at the football tables and read the match reports. My imagination took me to those stadiums, while many club patrons would often whisper between themselves, "he will never play there, they have the best players in the world, it's impossible, players like him in Spain are a dime a dozen." Well, it was now time to walk the walk and show them that this dime got you a lot more than the standard dozen! Their ignorance and jealousy wouldn't even let them remember that I was the product of two special Spanish nationals, and I was in effect going home.

This all came about after our AIS European tour, from which I also received offers from a couple of clubs in England, namely Ipswich Town and Nottingham Forest, who were big names in world football at that time. Ipswich had won the FA Cup in 1978, the UEFA Cup in 1981, and were runner's-up in the First

Division, the forerunner of the Premier League, in successive seasons in 1980/81 and 1981/82. They had some serious pedigree back then and later down the track I would join them too.

Forest was even better known in that period. They had won the League in 1977/78, the League Cup in 1977/78 and 1978/79, and against all odds, had won the European Cup in 1978/79 and 1979/80 led by a charismatic and bold manager in Brian Clough.

In Australia, three National Soccer League (NSL) clubs were chasing my signature including my hometown club Canberra City, Sydney Olympic and South Melbourne but my mind was already made up, I was going to Spain.

I wanted the big stages. Why do something if your target is not the very top? As always, the mindset was rolling the dice, always believing that if you are good enough, with a bit of luck that you make yourself, you will end up exactly where you want to be. I was not really interested in playing in the NSL back then, unless forced upon me as eventually would happen. The same mindset would apply today with the A-League options. For me, it was Europe or bust, but you must have the ability, not just a vivid imagination and a delusional view of where you sit in the football landscape.

I hadn't spent my whole childhood dreaming of England and Spain, obsessed with becoming an international footballer, to settle for a minor league in Australia. The quicker a young kid can get into a European or UK set up, the better footballer he will end up for a multitude of reasons. There are levels in every sport and the quicker you understand them, the quicker you can acknowledge where you sit, and the quicker you can get on with your career. Some fantastic Socceroos have played in these lower leagues and gone on to become excellent footballers in Europe but at that time it just wasn't for me. In the end, and not by choice, I did play NSL for several seasons before transferring to Reading FC from Sydney Olympic at age 28, an adjustment very few Australian players would be capable of making for numerous reasons, so it probably said more about me than the actual competition I was playing in.

I had a tantalising trial and training offer from Real Madrid, courtesy of Vicente Del Bosque, but Sporting Gijón was a done deal. All I had to do was get on a plane, land in the city and sign the paperwork, so understandably I went for the sure bet. The fact that I had family living in the city made the move a whole lot easier. The city was well known to me as dad had spent a couple of years in Gijón working in the mines and shipyards of Asturias. Prior to jumping on the ship that brought him to Australia, he had worked hard and played hard in Gijón, enjoying the San Lorenzo beach culture, while indulging in the refreshing Sidra, an alcoholic cider that is synonymous with the region.

My mum, dad and sister drove me to Sydney Airport along with our great family friends Sito Gonzales, his wife Tina, and their kids Jacqueline and young Christopher. It was a quiet, and in many ways a sad trip to Sydney Airport. I was seriously trying hard not to cry, my mother was a mess, and most of the trip I just sat silent in my own world, somewhere in between excitement and unbearable sadness.

At the airport we discussed how we would communicate with each other. Back then, there were no mobile phones or social media so all we had was a pen and piece of paper. The young ones reading this might well wonder how we survived at all!

By now, I just wanted to get through customs and border control as the wait was killing us all. I've never ever seen my mother so upset in her life and it broke my heart. It hadn't occurred to me until that point, that chasing my dream was in a way destroying my family.

When you get a lot older and you look back and reminisce about those times, a part of you does question if it was all worth it. After finally freeing myself from mum's long embrace, I couldn't look back. I was crying like a baby, in floods of tears that did not cease until the plane departed. A soul-destroying moment, the football dream was not meant to be like this!

The take off in an old JAT Yugoslav airlines plane knocked me back into the reality of possibly dying shortly after we rose into the air, and with the plane shaking violently, it felt as if all the bolts and rivets holding it together, were now about to come apart! Once the seat belt sign went off, 99% of the plane lit up a cigarette and ordered a whisky. Oh, the good old days of plane travel!!!

As the plane approached Madrid Barajas airport many emotions were running through me, the first was a feeling of being home, which may seem ridiculous to some, as I had never been to Spain before. It's hard to explain in words the last leg of that flight, it was of course full of mainly Spanish people, nobody speaking English, but I felt secure, and I felt like one of them. I looked like many of them and for the first time in my life I had no fear or trepidation of being called a 'wog'. That single word had caused me, my family, my community, and all migrants so much pain, anguish, and heartache.

Luckily for me it wasn't a complete step into the unknown. Aside from my family who lived in Gijón, there were two, very familiar and special faces to greet me at arrivals in Madrid. My grandparents had returned to live in Spain and were outside the pick-up point to collect me before we headed to Palencia, their hometown located some three hours north of Madrid.

I had grown up with my grandparents in Canberra whilst my parents worked two jobs each, trying to get ahead. They knew no English, so from birth to age 5, I only learnt Spanish, never knowing just how handy that would be in the years to come! I distinctly remember my first day of school in Australia when I did not understand a single thing, absolutely zero English.

The train ride to Palencia was a genuine tourist experience for me, but also had a deeper meaning. As the train rattled through towns and little villages, I was consciously aware that these were the places that my parents had spoken about when I was growing up in Australia. Places where hunger and poverty were the norm. With little work or even less opportunity for it, there appeared to be no future for them, in a land where only the wealthy landowners and the military generals enjoyed the finer things in life.

The feared dictator General Franco was no longer alive, but the Guardia Civil remained, and they gave me an uneasy feeling, probably stemming from my grandfather's and father's stories of their violence and cruelty when they were better known as Franco's version of the SS. Years later, I would encounter them on many occasions with David Beckham as they had developed into the highway patrol and were much less scary!

When I arrived in Palencia, a city north of Madrid with a population nowadays of around 80,000, I tried to sharpen my focus by going for an early morning run alongside the river, getting myself mentally prepared for the evening train ride that would take me 270km to the north coast and the beautiful city of Gijón.

Despite knowing I had family there, I had never actually spoken to any of them. Communication was a lot more difficult in those days. On the final approach to Gijón train station it dawned on me that I had only ever seen an old photo of my uncle, a military picture of him in his younger days, but how would I recognise him now?

When the train pulled to a halt, I was excited and nervous as I had been told my uncle would be waiting for me. Towards the exit I walked alongside many other passengers and coming towards me, against the traffic flow, I saw what I thought was my dad but it was obviously not my dad, it was my uncle, and what a wow moment that was. He was the spitting image of dad. He greeted me warmly with a big hug before saying, "Vamos, your Aunty has dinner ready!"

I met the rest of the family shortly afterwards and was told endless stories of my dad in his youth before he left for Australia. It became readily apparent that he had been some sort of Casanova and had left a trail of broken hearts behind!

I fell asleep early that night, feeling comfortable with family but admittedly nervous ahead of a big day. In the morning I was due at the Escuela de Fútbol de Mareo, Gijón's training complex, located in the mountains of Northern Spain. There was no expectation from me that I would be training with the first team yet, but I had a curiosity, naturally, to see them all, as many of them were stars of the game.

I had diligently done my homework and knew the club were fourth in La Liga and due to play German side FC Cologne in a UEFA Cup tie later in the week. The captain was Antonio Maceda, a Spanish international centre-back of some repute, who would not long after gain a transfer to Real Madrid. Leading the side from the front was the superstar centre forward Enrique Castro Quini, who had just returned from FC Barcelona, and was known affectionately as Quini.

He was some finisher, the epitome of goalscoring excellence and one of the best strikers in world football ever, in my opinion. He was about 5ft 10, quick and powerful, super intelligent and had impeccable finishing quality with both feet and his head. Quini was a five times 'Pichichi' winner, the top goalscorer in La Liga. For good measure he also won the award twice more when playing in the Segunda Division!

During his first campaign at the Camp Nou, Barca's historical home stadium, he was kidnapped by the Basque Separatist Organisation ETA and held captive for months, eventually being rescued unharmed by the police. He was a god of Spanish football and I would soon meet him!

My first training session was with the U-20 team. The kitman handed me my Sporting Gijón training kit and out I went for my first session, a 9 vs 9 game. I played it safe, didn't go mad as I certainly didn't want to create any enemies on my first day.

The dressing room was not welcoming though. They rarely are at top level and it takes a while to gain approval and respect. The torture continued through the game as even those on my own team, would not pass me the ball. They all had their position and status within the team, the changing room and even the showers. So I just waited until last and showered alone. It brought home the reality that being Australian youth team captain meant absolutely nothing at all to them; it wasn't worth one ounce of respect! I was a genuine threat to their future, a persona non grata so I just went with the flow, which I can tell you was not the best of feelings. It can destroy most footballers even before the football comes into play. These dressing rooms are not for the fainthearted, only the strong survive.

Only one player spoke to me that day. His name was Marcelino, a Spanish U-20 international at the time. We became friends and he is now a world class manager in charge of Athletic Bilbao. Nobody else spoke to me or acknowledged me, it was almost as if I didn't exist at all!

I understood Spanish, I spoke the language, but it obviously wasn't as crisp as theirs. There was more awkwardness in opening your mouth, so I kept mine shut. I left the dressing room and noticed that the first team were doing shooting practice, so I stationed myself about twenty metres away, leaning on a fence, and watching intently, my focus on the legendary Quini.

His first connection was a magical header, that began with a perfect leap, judging his jump to perfection, connecting with the ball, the result a pinpoint header that thundered off his brow and into the goal. I was lost in a moment of magic and all the sadness that I had felt earlier, just evaporated as I saw this Spanish goal god doing what he did best. To this day I maintain that I have never seen such natural finishing quality in front of goal.

Quini was just the absolute perfect goal scoring machine. Take a moment and think about how hard it is to be the top scorer in La Liga and then remember that this maestro had done it five times in the top division, it is simply crazy. Only two players have won that award more times than Quini; Telmo Zarra, a Spanish striker in the late 1940s and early 1950s, and Barcelona legend Leo Messi.

Quini's five successes as the top-flight leading scorer sits him alongside the incomparable Alfredo Di Stefano and Mexican superstar Hugo Sanchez. That's more than Hungarian Ferenc Puskas and Cristiano Ronaldo, to put it all into perspective. He was 35 or 36 at this time, but it was no handicap as he continued to put on a masterclass in finishing during that session with finish after finish past all three Gijón goalkeepers who rotated through the drill. Quini would end his club career with 302 goals in 567 games and have El Molinón Stadium named in his honour.

My uncle wouldn't be picking me up from training as he was working, which meant that I either needed to hitch a lift or walk the 10km down the mountain.

It was starting to rain – it always does in Gijón – and the light was fading rapidly. In all it had been a horrible first day for me, I had expected it to be tough, but not to suffer such unfriendliness and disdain towards me. I decided that walking was the best option, hoping that maybe a bus would come past.

Many of my U-20 colleagues drove past me as I made my way down the road, they saw me and just kept on driving. Humiliated and upset, I remember upping my pace just willing this nightmare to be over. No mum and dad to speak to, not even able to text them a message, my only comfort ahead was a lonely peace in the small room provided by the club above the Bar Altillo.

Halfway down the mountain, in what felt like a walk of shame, a final car approached. I just put my head down, continued to walk, I didn't want to be humiliated one more time by another car full of young players who would look at me and just keep on driving. This car slowed down slightly as it passed me, travelled on a little, then pulled over to stop. It was a beautiful sports car with blacked out windows. When I came alongside the car, the driver's window came down, it was Quini. He had stopped to offer me a lift! The famous legend, the football maestro, the Spanish goal scoring machine, was also the one with the biggest heart, the humblest, most caring of them all, the very reason he was adored by fans all over Spain.

As he drove me home he could tell that I was upset, he gave me some words of wisdom which I still treasure. I recall him telling me "tomorrow you have a match. A few of the boys are pissed that you are here," he said.

"Same happened to me at Barcelona. It's the life we choose, hate comes with it, so you go and show everybody that you belong here. There is no other way."

It was just what I needed to hear, and coming from someone I admired so much, lifted my spirits and ignited a burning desire to be the best on pitch the following day.

The match that Quini was talking about was a clash with a team from the Spanish Second Division, a test for the young U-20 squad against a team of seasoned professionals. The game was played in typical Asturias conditions. The pitch was a mud bath, not a blade of grass to be seen anywhere, and the rain which hadn't relented from the day before, continued to come down in bucket loads. It was like a war in mud, three or four inches deep, I loved it. Pure long ball stuff, the famous Spanish tiki taka football as far away from this as was the moon.

I was in mud heaven, sliding in for tackles left, right and centre, involved in everything, and to cap it all off, scoring our second of the match in a 2-0 win with a trademark header. Maybe watching Quini the day before had paid off?

The boss of the U-20 side picked me out in the dressing room after the match saying "El mejor hoy campéon," translated as, "The best player today". I was ecstatic and from that match on the players were all great with me. How the world changed in 90 minutes, that trademark saying and feeling that lives by your side as a footballer for all your career.

Quini was proven right and I was accepted into the group. Soon after, I would be promoted to join the first team training sessions, kitting up and training alongside Spanish internationals that I had only been reading about in the newspaper at the Spanish club in Canberra, and on TV watching the 1982 FIFA World Cup that Spain hosted.

It got even better for me when after many training sessions, I would see Quini, Cundi, and a few other of the Spanish internationals pull shotguns out of their cars and head off into the mountains on quail and rabbit hunting missions, still in their training kit! That was my game, so I joined them, and life started to shine a little sun my way.

But it wasn't all plain sailing after my goal scoring debut. My registration and ITC (International Transfer Clearance) ended up being a bureaucratic nightmare, as the Australian youth team matches in World Cup qualifiers that I had played in, now categorised me as a foreigner in Spain, despite having a Spanish passport and national ID document! I was only allowed to train and play practice matches as foreigners were not allowed to play in the Segunda B division. Gijón's best U20s played there, so I was not ready to play in the first team and it wasn't likely, whilst occupying a foreign import spot, I was left in a holding pattern waiting for a loan deal to come.

Even if I was allowed to play as a Spaniard, I was never going to play for the Sporting Gijón's first team at this stage of my career. Both their central defenders were current Spanish internationals and their number 6, the defensive midfielder Joaquin, was a former international and one of the best players I've ever seen, let alone shared the same pitch. A super player very much in the mould of Paul Pogba.

The ITC debacle took a year to sort itself out, but finally they got the registration through, albeit as a foreign import, my first loan opportunity came up. I knew something would come up, so I made sure I did plenty of extra work on top of normal Gijón training, just to be closer to some sort of resemblance of match fitness. My opportunity came in the way of Albacete Balompié, a new club in the grander scheme of things, having only been founded as late as 1940. They're probably best known as the club at which Andres Iniesta, the dynamic and skilful Barcelona and Spain star, began his career ascendancy. They wanted me to play in the number 6 role. The dream was coming true, my Spanish debut was not long away.

Albacete's coach was the ex-Real Madrid defender Enrique Perez Diaz, known in the football world as Pachin. This legend had won seven La Liga titles and two European Cups with Real Madrid, and he was now my boss! My dad had spoken to me about Pachin many times, remembering him as a feared enforcer who took no prisoners, it was nice when Pachin paid me the ultimate compliment, telling me that I reminded him of himself when he was a 19-year-old.

His instructions to me were always simple. "Son, your job is to stop the opposition playmaker, their number ten," Pachin told me. "I don't care how you do it, just do it, I want no excuses after the match. Win the ball and then give it to players, who are far greater footballers than you. If you do this, you will play four or five hundred games in Europe and become an international."

He wasn't wrong. His party piece storyline was that while at Real Madrid, when he won the ball he immediately gave it to Gento, Puskas and Di Stefano. The conversation ending in how many medals he had at home, it all made perfect sense to me.

My Spanish league debut was for Albacete against Sabadell FC, making me the youngest foreign import in the country at that time. A remarkable feat given I was a defensive player. I enjoyed a formidable battle with Pichi Alonso, the former Barcelona and Spain midfielder and father of Xavi Alonso. I became a regular in that team at 19 and had a thoroughly brilliant time playing 34 matches in the team coached by the Real Madrid legend.

My second loan spell was at Xerez CD, a wonderful town in Southern Spain, not far from Seville, known for its world class sherry production, dancing horses and bullfighting. I was again a regular that season playing 38 matches, more than any other player at the club, against the likes of Real Madrid, Barcelona, Valencia, Deportivo de La Coruña, Celta Vigo, Sevilla, Real Betis, Espanyol, and Bilbao Athletic, and was regarded as one of the best man-markers in the top 40 sides in Spain.

For those more familiar with UK football, my time in Spain was the equivalent of being signed by Chelsea, Arsenal or Tottenham and loaned out to say

Nottingham Forest and Reading, playing nearly every single game, with distinction at age 19 and 20. All while occupying a much prized, and valued foreign import spot. It will be a long time before another Australian does that in Spain, if ever.

Three of my most memorable matches were against Bilbao, Valencia and Real Madrid B.

The fixture against Bilbao was a great occasion as another of my uncles, Angel, lived in the City. The stadium, San Mamés, was reserved solely for the gods of the Basque country and visiting teams. To watch his little brother's son play in that stadium, as he told me after the match, was one of the best days of his life. He was beaming and told me he would die happy after that experience. It really moved me emotionally to think of how much joy this had brought him.

It was a truly a wonderful day for me as well, an occasion where both my parents, and my sister were present, at the home of my father's favourite team, the same team he did not have money to buy a ticket to watch at this ground many years ago. That evening, my father was unusually quiet. I knew he was happy and proud, he told me so, but I'm not sure he could take-in what he had just experienced. He would often rattle off the first 11 of his era, tell me they were gods, sadly he was so poor he was never able to watch them live at La Catedral. I recall when I gave him his ticket and he just stared at it for ages and then stared at me. He couldn't speak so I gave him a hug, said 'I love you' and went to the change rooms. I have wondered many times what array of emotions went through his head that day.

I have been lucky enough to achieve a lot in my career, but the highlight for me was the first match my parents watched me play in Spain, which took place at a packed Mestalla Stadium vs Valencia. My parents hadn't been back to Spain, their homeland, in 25 years and I had not seen them for a year. Our only communication were the letters I would send and the occasional phone call via an international operator.

It was a very emotional occasion for our family, the son of Spanish immigrants was playing in the very country they left to find a better life, and they were now back watching him play at the Mestalla and sitting in VIP seats. What are the chances of that happening in any global sport I ask myself over and over?

Third, but not last on the memorable matches, was playing against Real Madrid B at the Santiago Bernabéu stadium. The thought of their son playing at the Bernabéu, and being there to watch me play was something my parents probably never imagined possible, but I do know they were immensely proud. It's a pretty big thing when you think of them having to leave Spain. I suppose I couldn't have given them a bigger thank you, than a day out at Real Madrid, the sun shining and in beautiful seats.

I spent two seasons on loan in Spain. Gijón were keen to welcome me back into the fold after my successful loan spell at Xerez. Being loaned out was all part of furthering my football development and had all been mapped out by Gijón. I also had offers from Sevilla and Real Betis, but only if I could play as a Spaniard, so not to occupy a foreign import spot.

Around this time, I also received notification from the Spanish government that I had to do my national military service, compulsory for all Spanish citizens. This is where things became rather murky and did not sit right with me. I held a Spanish passport, which made my compulsory military service not negotiable, while the Spanish FA considered me a foreigner as I had played for the Young Socceroos.

Back then Spanish teams wanted both of their allocated foreigner slots to be taken up by attacking players, the best ones in the world, so the fact I had even managed to get regular game time over the past two seasons was remarkable if not insane. To remain in Spain long term, I couldn't continue as a foreign import. With this in mind, dad and I went to see the region's military general just outside of Xerez. We told him I was more than happy to do the military service if the Spanish FA would classify me Spanish for football. Unfortunately, he had no control over Spanish FA regulations, but he reminded me I would be joining the army in a few months.

I pleaded with the Spanish FA but they wouldn't budge. From their perspective, they had no choice but to adhere to FIFA's antiquated rules and regulations.

On the way home I told my dad that I'd had enough and knew in my mind I would not be doing military service, something I would have actually loved doing but , and it was a big but, we both agreed that I was either Spanish for everything or nothing at all, so the end of my football journey in Spain, was coming to an end.

Escaping was a risky move. If I was caught by the Military Police, I would have to spend two-years compulsory service in an Army prison, but it was a point of principle to me. Spain was happy for me to go to war for them but wouldn't let me play football for them. It made no sense; it broke my heart and suddenly all my thoughts were on England.

The departure went smoothly. I flew out of Madrid on the national airline IBERIA, oh the irony of that. It was a scary process, one wrong answer to Customs officers meant it was game over. A couple of weeks later the Military Police rolled up at my grandmother's place in Palencia looking for me. She told them I had gone never to return. They asked, where to? She said, "the moon".

Seriously though, it was quite a sad end to my time in Spain, which was possibly the best two years of my life, while playing the best football of my entire career. I ended up captaining Reading FC and being signed by Brian Clough at Nottingham Forest, so I know I could have played for Sporting Gijón's first team. It's something that still saddens me today, as it would have been something incredibly special for my family in that city, but hey that's football.

Spain is a beautiful country with contrasting regions, a lot of sun, Mediterranean beaches and wonderful food. I felt at home and was fully prepared to spend the next ten or twelve years playing there. The football passion was just simply intoxicating and people's lives revolved entirely around the game. As a footballer, it's a very special country to play in, arguably the greatest in the world. The emotions instilled are difficult to capture in words and even more difficult to forget.

It's hard to describe exactly what it felt like to play in those legendary stadiums and live that life while still young. It was an utterly amazing couple of years in which I was fortunate to see every beautiful city in Spain. I hung out with beautiful senoritas, bullfighters, brothers and bandidos, all that sadly cut short by bureaucratic bullshit.

Internally I was devastated, broken, and it certainly impacted me for a long time, but looking back now, my adventure in Spain brought much joy to my family and inspired my young cousin Rafa Bernal to pursue a coaching career. He loved football but never made it to the top level as a player. He is now currently the Head Coach of the Sporting Gijón Ladies' team, and one of the youngest coaches ever to attain the Spanish Pro Licence. In my opinion, in time and given the opportunity he could manage any club in Spain, male or female.

Aurelio Vidmar, John Aloisi and Mat Ryan would all later play in Spain, but as Ricky Bobby, played by Will Ferrell in 'Talladega Nights' famously said, "If you ain't first, you're last."

I said adios to Spain, confident in my football ability and onto the next adventure. London calling.

CHAPTER 4

ESCAPE TO VICTORY

England may have only been a short flight from Spain, but it came with its own unique set of challenges. I had escaped doing my military service, the process not quite as epic as the film 'The Great Escape', but just as daring and dangerous in its own way. Ahead of me, and of major importance, was manoeuvring through British Customs with the sole purpose of obtaining a UK working visa, on the premise of being an Australian tourist, supplementing my trip with part time work in bars and hotels.

In Canberra as a teenager, I had prepared for this eventuality placing the process in a holding pattern for an occasion such as this one. Upon arrival in England, I would be met by my good friend Peter Morgan, who I had played with at Canberra Arrows and who was now studying Politics at Nottingham University.

England was at the top of a list of countries that I always wanted to play in and not getting a visa was simply not an option for me. The problem, or roadblock for want of a better word, was that I was not yet a senior international player, making it impossible to get one. I had not yet won a Socceroos cap. That would come later, the national team coaches were obviously not watching Spanish football! Without regular international appearances, it was impossible to get a Football Association approved work permit, but I would find a way in, I would not be denied!

In Canberra I found that way, discovering that Commonwealth citizens under the age of 23 could be granted a two-year work visa on arrival into the UK. This particular visa was created for young travellers to Britain and meant only for part time work in bars and pubs. However, with no specific wording on the stamp, it was my opportunity.

The only task now was to play the tourist part well, only at this stage of my life I had not yet attended acting classes, so this scene would have to be improvisation at its most real and reliant on natural talent.

Once off the plane I headed for Customs feeling confident that I would soon be on the train to Nottingham. I had played at the Santiago Bernabéu, there was no greater pressure than that, so I felt this would be a walk in the park. The Customs official began with all the standard questions, mostly centred on my financial situation but I had prepared and just like that, bingo! The kind gentleman obliged with a beautifully stamped UK working visa.

I had been through many experiences in my still young career but perhaps the most daunting and difficult mission of my life was to come. I decided that I would ask Brian Clough, arguably the greatest British football manager in history, for a trial with his world-famous Nottingham Forest, a daunting and impossible mission most of the world would think. You just didn't ride your bike into the City Ground and ask Cloughie for a trial, but I had played under Real Madrid legend Pachin, so Clough, whilst having my upmost respect, held no fear.

I rang the club anonymously and after a little persistence found out that Forest were starting pre-season training in eight weeks time. So I created my own pre-season before the team pre-season, so I would arrive fit and raring to go, capable of being in the lead bunch for any task that was set, assuming I could get in the front door that is!

I decided on using the world famous Sherwood Forest for my fitness and ball work. I figured that if the majestic forest was good enough for Robin Hood and his band of merry men, then it would work just fine for me.

As always, my knee was a constant handicap, but my brain almost like magic, would in most cases anaesthetise the pain. By the end of my time in Spain, my knee was on the way out, already bone-on-bone and already three operations down. From this point in my life it, was all mental strength, willpower and mind over matter for me. I was on a mission and several weeks later, after hours of sprints, long runs, ball work and games against myself, I was ready and raring to go.

Now for the tricky part, getting an opportunity, and for that to happen, I needed to see you know who!

Peter lived in a terraced house near the university, a 20-minute bike ride from the City Ground, Forest's Stadium which was located on the banks of the picturesque River Trent, the home of the former European Champions who had won the Cup twice under Clough. In 1979, they defeated Swedish side Malmo 1-0 in Munich; a year later they retained the Cup with another

1-0 win, this time against Hamburg in a game that was played at the Estadio Santiago Bernabéu.

Getting to see 'the gaffer', would not be easy, but as they say in Britain, "he who dares wins", so it was time to man up and dare.

The bike ride to the City Ground on a beautiful summer day had me cycling over the bridge spanning the River Trent, and the sight of the famous cricket ground, Trent Bridge, raised my excitement levels. For a moment, I allowed my imagination to drift off onto the wicket, hitting shots to every boundary point, dressed in white and wearing a baggy green cap!

I arrived at the ground around 9am and the car park was already full. The first day of pre-season always brings excitement, almost as much as my excitement when Archie Gemmill, the ex-Scotland international who had famously scored a winning goal for his country in the 1978 World Cup Finals against Holland in Argentina, agreed to ask the gaffer if he would meet with an Australian lad from Spain who had turned up on a bicycle, and wanting a trial.

It was a nervous wait; the fear of hearing NO was nerve-racking. I had initially told Gemmill my football story. He seemed impressed because without hesitation he went in search of Clough. Minutes later, the gaffer's trusted lieutenant returned with good news, "He will see you now!".

Clough's office was quite an imposing place to be in, not many footballers were brave enough to cross that line, but I knew that being respectful, honest and confident would go a long way, or at least I hoped it would. I knocked on the door, and in that familiar, nasally, Yorkshire accent, Brian Clough said, "Come in young man. Archie tells me you've been playing in Spain and had a problem with military service? I said, "Yes gaffer", quickly explaining my situation and threw in the names of the coaches I had played under.

One in particular got his interest: 'Pachin', the Real Madrid enforcer. Clough continued, "Well if he liked you then I'll bloody like you," and with that, Cloughie picked up the phone to tell Archie Gemmill to get me a kit and introduce me to Des Walker and Neil Webb, who would look after me. Both Walker and Webb were England U-21 internationals and would soon become full England internationals. It had all gone far more smoothly than I thought; Pachin, and my games in Spain carrying a fair bit of weight. I would now be trialling with the two-time European champions.

Clough hadn't finished with me yet though. "You Australians travel a bloody long way just to kick a ball," he continued.

"I had Alan Davidson here. He was a good lad, fantastic player, but a different kind of Aussie to you though, he was a Chinaman." Then out of the blue he asked, "Do you like cricket?"

"I love it gaffer," I replied, then I told him what I had imagined while cycling over the bridge earlier, which made him chuckle.

And with that, it was time to train. "Thank you gaffer," I said, and as I left his office he said, "Young man," I turned to face him again, he continued, "You've got some balls coming in off the street and asking me for a trial."

"Thank you gaffer, I won't let you down," I replied then turned around and walked out the door as fast as I could before he changed his mind.

From the first day of pre-season, I just hung off Des Walker everywhere he went, learning the ropes and getting used to my new environment. Walker was a superb footballer, he had everything you would want in a central defender. His positioning was excellent, his anticipation superb and his pace was something else. Forest fans would chant "You'll never beat Des Walker!" In a foot race there were very few who ever could.

I must have been doing all the right things as within a few weeks, Clough pulled me aside and offered me a rolling contract, so I became a full-time Nottingham Forest player. The second Australian ever to sign for the club, after Alan Davidson. Three months further on from that, I had cemented myself in the reserve team, playing every match in the number 6 shirt, as a holding midfielder.

Clough liked me, he told me I was too good for his reserves, but he had Webb and Walker in those positions. At the time, they were two of the best players in England so it would be difficult to break into the first team. Clough went on to explain that if a first team opportunity came up elsewhere, he would help facilitate it for me.

Brian Clough was a mad genius, in the opinion of many, the greatest British football manager ever. I agree.

He would often tell me top-level football management has absolutely nothing to do with football. I learnt this first hand while playing in a reserve team match against Derby County at the City ground. He pulled me up in the tunnel as I was about to run onto the pitch for the second half and said "Do you like ice cream?"

"Yes of course I do gaffer," I told him, to which he replied "What flavour?". I love vanilla ice cream, but stupidly for some reason "banana paddle pop" came out of my mouth.

He then asked me for more effort that would inspire the rest followed by "I haven't got a clue what a paddle-pop is, but win tonight and I'll get you a banana ice cream in the morning."

I replied "OK gaffer," - what else do you say? I gave him a world of effort for an ice cream that I couldn't get out of my head in the second half. We won, and the very next day while doing my recovery in the gym Brian Clough handed me, not one, but a whole box of banana flavoured ice creams. I still think about that ice cream today!

Try as I might, I was unable to shift Webby or Des Walker from the starting line-up and break into that first 11, so that's when Cloughie made a telephone call to a friend of his, John Duncan, the Ipswich Town Manager and told him to sign me. Ipswich apparently needed a number 6 who could also fill in at the back. They wanted me to play in a reserve match the following day against West Ham. In another kind twist of fate, Ipswich had been keen on me after I had played well against them in a youth tournament in Amsterdam years earlier. Peter Trevivian Ipswich's youth coach at the time, was still with the club, so he would pick me up at the station.

This was a superb chance for me, and I was excited by the opportunity. I had grown up in Australia watching Bobby Robson's Ipswich side dominate the English First Division, winning the UEFA Cup as well. Names such as Mick Mills, Terry Butcher, Russell Osman, Eric Gates, Brian Talbot, Arnold Mühren, Frans Thijssen, Paul Mariner, John Wark and Alan Brazil already had my attention, so I didn't need asking twice. Suddenly, another team that I had dreamed of playing for was now a very real proposition.

It was great to see Peter again when I arrived at Ipswich station. He drove me to my new lodgings so I could settle in, and he would pick me up early the next morning to head to Portman Road.

It was evident that the place had history, a special history. Pre-game I was hanging around in the club gym doing some stretches when I had a bizarre encounter with the Ipswich club kitman who also doubled as the team's bus driver. Back then, the backroom staff did multiple jobs and this winner came with a Del Boy look and cockney accent so everything he said, even if not politically correct was very funny !

"So, you're the Aussie lad that Cloughie sent us," he said. When I confirmed his statement, he followed up with the memorable, "You don't look like an Aussie do you? My wife and I watch 'Neighbours' every afternoon and you don't look like any of them."

'Neighbours' was massive in the UK back then, when Jason Donovan and Kylie Minogue were making their mark, beginning careers that would take them to stratospheric heights as the blonde-hair and blue-eyed couple next door, Scott and Charlene. There were no wogs on 'Neighbours' back in those days so he had a point!

I told him briefly of my family background and that I was born in Australia. "That's it!" he said triumphantly. "I knew you must have had some sort of wop or dago in you, but don't you worry son, we've got a few darkies around the place you'll just add a bit more colour!" And with that off he trotted pleased as punch with himself.

Not long after, we played away to Aston Villa away in Birmingham, a large city with many immigrants from India and Pakistan, some of whom worked at our hotel. I had finished eating my pre-match meal, and was heading upstairs when 'old mate' , noticing I had left my tracksuit jacket behind, shouted "Andy, don't be leaving that lying around here my son, this lot will turn it into a curtain quicker than you can blink!"

There was no malice in his banter. It was commonplace then, a part of the fabric of British society that reached as far as Australia, and where the British TV sitcom, 'Love Thy Neighbour' was one of the most popular shows on the box. So this form of racist banter was nothing new to me.

I had a good game in the trial against West Ham, and the following morning I was called in to the office and signed for Ipswich Town. It was a quickfire introduction as I went straight upstairs from the offices to join the first team squad for an indoor session of five-a-side. Heavy snow had fallen on the Suffolk town, making the outdoor training facilities unplayable. I didn't care where we trained because I did all conditions and all terrains. These games were hard-fought affairs and the squad of twenty was split into four teams of five players who would all witness my grandiose humiliating introduction to the team!

The four 'captains' stood out in front, picking players for their teams, a bit like what it used to be like in schoolyards all around the world. Players were being selected left, right and centre and it wasn't looking good for me! We were down to the final two, it was me and a staff member who was making up the numbers. England U-21 international Mark Brennan, a decent player with a beautiful left foot, had the first pick of the last two and picked the staff member so I had the honour of being the last man picked. Trust me, humiliation doesn't come much greater than that.

As fate would have it, the first game we played was against Brennan's team and two minutes in, my world lit up. The sports hall was a rudimentary building, a brick wall enclosing the four sides of the playing arena which had a synthetic playing surface that was as hard and unforgiving as an old thin carpet on a bed of concrete . Brennan received the ball facing the wall, placing his foot on it while attempting to shield it from me. That would be the wrong decision as I had already made up my mind the minute I was picked last, that at some point he would be hit. Opportunity came knocking like an early Christmas present. Maybe it was a sign from above as the heavy snow falling seemed the perfect weather for Santa Claus and his reindeers. It had been my only thought, no other thought in my brain, other than to inflict maximum damage on him.

I nailed him with a rugby league shoulder charge, slamming man and ball into the brick wall, leaving him in a world of pain. I bent over him and whispered in his ear, "Never pick me last again."

We never spoke while I was there, he was higher in the pecking order, but he stayed right away from me after that morning. To this day, I do wish I had inflicted more hurt on him, like Keane on Alf-Inge Haaland, as he made it personal. Ironically, years later he joined my old club Sydney Olympic and I bet you he never told the lads that story.

John Wark was the big star at Portman Road. The accomplished Scottish midfielder had just returned to Ipswich after top scoring in the First Division (now known as the EPL) for the wonderful Liverpool side of that era. Making a beeline to the manager after my tackle he quickly informed him that I was to be his new roommate and on top of that, he always made sure that I was on his team in training sessions. John and I had great chats as roomies. He had also played with my friend Craig Johnston at Liverpool. John also had his own little bit of Hollywood fame playing a prisoner of the Nazis, alongside Sylvester Stallone, Michael Caine and Pelé in the film 'Escape to Victory'!

Three weeks after joining Ipswich I was in the team and made my English league debut away to Birmingham City at St Andrew's, as a substitute. Less than seven days after that, I made my starting debut in the League defeating Hull City 2-0 at Portman Road. The local newspaper compared my performance to one the club's greats, Brian Talbot who was a key figure in Bobby Robson's team until he was transferred to Arsenal, so it was a great honour to be mentioned in that company. Cloughie had been proven right again.

There were some tough nuts who played the game in those days. One I met was the famous Vinnie Jones. We were playing a reserves friendly match at the old Plough Lane, where Wimbledon, aka 'The Crazy Gang', used to play. Early in the game I went in on him hard, always looking to make my mark and stamp my authority on the game, even more important when the hit is on the opposition's general in order to set the tone for the match.

It had been raining all day and like everybody else I was wearing the longer studs, the longer the better in my case. I went in and nailed him, my studs dug in at the top of his thigh and slid down to the knee. The tracking was visible, but the studs hadn't cut his skin open.

A tackle like that would normally have seen most men stretchered off, or at least limping around for the continuation of the match, but not Vinnie Jones. He bounced straight back up and got right in my face. He was taller than me and ended up about an inch away from my face, looking down straight into my eyes with intense, but controlled anger. Like an ice-cold methodical killer, a white pointer, the eyes spoke of a horrible east-end gangland death. "Nice tackle son, just the way I like it," he growled, just before the referee came over, jumping between us, and saying something that both of us ignored. As we parted and ran off, another Wimbledon player came over to me and laughingly said, "Good luck son, you'll f***ing need it!"

I spent the next 85 minutes dodging incoming heat like I have never seen before! I just about survived Vinnie's attempts at payback, but all's fair in love and war. We shook hands afterwards, like recognised like, and the next time I saw Vinnie he was in the movies. He became a genuine Hollywood star portraying cockney gangsters and there wasn't much character acting for him to learn, he was the real deal, a natural on screen and a player I respected immensely, a genuine leader of men.

I loved playing for Ipswich Town, the team supported by one of my great mates, Horry Money. At the end of the season, John Duncan offered me a three-year deal which I gladly accepted before heading back to Australia for a six-week break, secure in the knowledge that I had made the breakthrough and was now a professional in the English game.

My accommodation was sorted, I was staying with a great family not far from the ground and they treated me as one of their own. Ray East and his wife had a beautiful house on Norwich Road and Ray was assistant manager of Essex County Cricket Club at the time and a fine cricketer for that club in his day. I was looking forward to more BBQs, beers, and backyard cricket on summer afternoons at Easty's. However, what lay ahead was far from plain sailing. My plan to be playing at Portman Road for many years to come would soon end in a second crushing blow.

Fast-forward those six weeks of an enjoyable visit to see friends and family in Australia, I arrived back at Heathrow ready to commence a new stage of my career. Proudly handing my Australian passport to the Customs official, who began flicking through the pages, his facial expression and body language suddenly changing, and something was telling me I was in a lot of bother.

His information screen told him that I had been playing professional football on a visa which was only meant to be valid for part-time work. Remember when I had outfoxed the system with my loophole? Well, it all came crashing down around me and was a sad end to my Ipswich Town adventure. I left behind a few good pals, men such as Chris Kiwomya, who went on to join Arsenal, Jason Dozzell, Canadians' Craig Forrest and Frank Yallop, and Simon Milton. Milts and I still laugh at the fact that my deportation led to a great Ipswich Town career for him, culminating in a testimonial.

United Kingdom Customs subsequently modified their visa rules so that my little trick wouldn't be repeated by future travellers, but my immediate concern was that I had 24-hours to go to Ipswich, pick up everything that I owned and return to Heathrow to be deported.

I was placed on a Qantas flight home and officially became a United Kingdom Home Office deportation statistic, joining Mark Bosnich as the only two Socceroos ever to be deported from 'Mother' England.

CHAPTER 5

BACK HOME

Heading back to Australia was, in my mind at least, a failure and a career killing nightmare of epic proportions. It felt as if everything that I had worked so hard for, playing on the world's biggest stages, against some of the world's best players, had come tumbling down around me. The most important thing was readjusting a mind that was locked into full time elite professional sport, readapting, and somehow understanding the part time national soccer landscape I would have to fall back into.

While this was a setback, it was certainly not the end of my dreams, but it would not be easy in an environment and a city with a million other distractions. The one thing that kept me going was the desire to continue improving and eventually be recognised by the national team, the Socceroos. I wanted to play in a World Cup, but first I needed to find myself a National Soccer League club and play in the league that I never wanted to return to – and all because of bureaucratic red tape that had nothing to do with my football ability. It was a complex combination of government immigration policies and FIFA regulations that effectively meant Europe and the UK were not a possibility, for a while at least.

By the time I had been back home in Canberra for a few weeks I was beginning to feel the first signs of what was probably acute depression. Life felt empty and my every thought took me back to Europe. Fortunately, a lifeline and a new beginning of sorts came quickly from cities boasting wonderful football clubs, Sydney Olympic and South Melbourne. Both clubs had a loyal and fantastic following stemming from their Greek origins, and it would be a tough choice.

I was drawn towards Sydney for two reasons. The first that it was closer to my family in Canberra and the second was that Eddie Thomson, who was the Sydney Olympic coach at the time, was also the Socceroos Assistant Manager.

I knew of Eddie from a few of my AIS teammates who had played for him at Sydney City when they ruled the NSL. I also knew he was a fantastic defender who had played for Aberdeen in Scotland, and was a good friend of Sir Alex Ferguson. 'Thommo', as he was affectionately known, was building a fantastic side at Sydney Olympic and was in line to be the next Socceroo manager, so it just felt right.

Unfortunately my first season at Olympic in 1988 wasn't the best and we finished fifth, knocked out in the elimination final by Marconi, who would also beat us in the 1989 Grand Final, a 1-0 loss in the 91st minute at Parramatta Stadium. The next season, we would go all the way, exacting revenge on Marconi, becoming the best team in the nation with wins over Adelaide City and South Melbourne to put us into the grand final, winning it 2-0. By then Thommo had left to become Head Coach of the Socceroos, and Mick Hickman, his trusted lieutenant, had taken over as the boss.

Marconi and Olympic had a big rivalry in the NSL. It was the biggest match in Sydney, like today's Western Sydney Wanderers vs Sydney FC rivalry. Marconi were known as the Rolls Royce of Australian football with the biggest clubhouse in the western suburbs of the city. It had a Vegas feel about it, poker machines as far as the eye could see and world-famous guests like Ricky Martin rocked the place on weekends. Adjacent to this mecca, was their lovely football stadium.

Sydney Olympic by comparison, had nothing. Well not exactly nothing; we had spirit, passion, club history and one of the best supporter bases I have ever played under. What we lacked was our own stadium and training facilities, two very important requirements for a football club! After winning the grand final, I famously said on national TV in a post-match interview, "Marconi may be the Rolls Royce of Australian football, but we are the Ferrari, albeit without a garage."

Thommo was living in Maroubra at the time I joined the club and he kindly offered me his house to stay in until I found my feet in Sydney. After agreeing on personal terms over the phone, I made my way to Sydney. An easy trip these days, but it was much tougher with no satellite navigation, just a Gregory's Road map to guide you through an unfamiliar, sprawling city.

My first pre-season was something else and totally different from anything I had previously experienced. Twice a week we would run from Bondi Beach to Clovelly and back, followed by beach sprints and 5-a-sides ending with a swim and a surf. Truth be known, I loved it! It was hard but enjoyable work, at one of the planet's greatest and most iconic settings.

Two or three football sessions a week were held at Little Bay, next door to Long Bay maximum security prison. Through prison bars, bank robbers, murderers, rapists and serial killers watched us train on sun-drenched rock hard cricket ovals with little grass on top, and absolutely no give underneath. An absolute nightmare for a knee with no meniscus and next to no articular cartilage!

We would lose the occasional ball into the prison exercise yard during the shooting drills, the stray shot cheekily sending a few prisoners a chorus of "You're shit, and you know you are!" Great banter that I had left behind in England, that made me even more depressed.

Training sessions at Sydney Olympic were wars, sometimes as violent as the maximum security offenders next door. It was common knowledge that Sydney City training sessions under Eddie Thomson and Mick Hickman, where they had coached previously, were ferocious battles. They loved it, encouraged it. Socceroos John Kosmina, Frank Farina, David Mitchell, JP de Marigny and Steve 'Rocky' O'Connor were the major protagonists and enforcers of it. There were no prisoners taken and losing teams would always pay a price of some sort.

This system, this environment, this mindset, had now carried over to Sydney Olympic and with a good playing squad, with many us either Socceroos or New Zealand internationals, the competition for spots was intense and fierce.

Tony Spyridakos and I were the centre halves, but a young warrior, George Haniotis, was on the prowl and our spots were in his sights. We are good friends now, but for a season back then we were the greatest of enemies. One particular training session left George in hospital with a broken jaw. It had been brewing for a few weeks and I knew he was trying to nail me at some point. I knew because he's just like me. He had already twice dived-in narrowly missing me with tackles that would have left a broken tibia, fibula and ACL, all in one fell swoop. I knew the attacks would not cease and when it came next, I was ready. He lunged in for a two-footed studs-up tackle, but I had my left my elbow low and his jaw hit it at full speed. Just like that, George's night was over. Straight to hospital, he had his jaw wired-up and he would have to drink blended food via a straw for the next eight weeks.

I felt nothing and made no effort to apologise. For the next few months the lads fuelled his return, and when he did, he was massive after months in the gym, doing karate and boxing, the whole lot, and it wasn't fluff either.

He would seek revenge, he was a warrior, a tough man, a top athlete and loved a rumble in the jungle. The moment came soon and as the ball dropped between us, like two lions jumping at each other, we threw everything into it. It was no UFC level, but we threw hard and fast, stopping only when Mick Hickman jumped between us and said, "It's done, finished. Any more of that you'll deal with me." From that day, George and I were cool, neither of us wanted a war with Hicky!

On top of the wars, we didn't get paid until the season started and even then that wouldn't go far, so with all day to spare, as training was in the evenings, I needed an additional, more stable and reliable income. I scoured the local newspapers for opportunities and noted a job available at Westpac Banking Corporation as a trainee clerk. I applied and was fortunate enough to be successful, in what was a rapid interview process.

On the first day I was up early and excited as I had never had a normal job before! Early morning, on a hot and humid summer day, I found myself on a crowded bus from Randwick to George Street in the City. It was standing room only on the bus and by the end of the 30-minute commute, the only thing that stopped me quitting before I had even started was the cool breeze emanating from Westpac's air conditioning as I entered the building.

At the bank I was met by a young lad, clever but geeky looking who led me to a room with no view, my mind wandering to our training ground where the prisoners were less confined and had better views. How did this happen? One minute I was playing at the Santiago Bernabéu in Madrid, the next, I was dying a slow death filing papers in a Westpac Bank. It was so mind numbing that at the mid-morning break, I wandered over to Martin Place, grabbed a coffee and a focaccia and never returned. How incredible that my brain was just seemingly incapable of doing such a simple, yet tedious task for more than a few hours.

Mentally, I struggled during the first season back in the NSL, sometimes hoping my current situation would all be just a bad dream and that I would wake up at Portman Road. The professionalism I had encountered abroad was non-existent in Australia at the time and the nightmare was compounded when Match of the Day would show many of my ex-teammates at Ipswich and Forest, strutting their stuff on the box.

In the end I would not watch. I lost interest and a little of my love for the game. Many nights I would sit at home thinking of giving up and having a trial with the Sydney Roosters or the South Sydney Rabbitohs, professional organisations in a competition that was the pinnacle of rugby league globally. The only reason I did not was because my knee was already shot, and the big gang tackles in rugby league those days would have smashed it to pieces in no time.

So, with a career in banking dead and buried after only one morning at Westpac, I found myself still seeking my first real job as I had plenty of spare time.

One day, completely out of the blue, I decided it might be a good idea to become an actor, and I enrolled myself into the Dramatic Arts Institute run by Lionel Long who had starred in the iconic Australian police drama, '*Homicide*', years earlier.

It was here that I met a lovely young lady called Kathryn Hardy. A Bondi Junction girl who I would soon marry, and not long after, we would become parents to a beautiful angel whom we named Isabella Mary Bernal.

Before Isabella's birth, Kathryn and I were both invited to attend the Ron Burrus Acting School in Los Angeles, with a student honour roll that included the TV star and stuntman MacGyver and Baywatch legend David Hasselhoff. It wasn't a bad crew to study and hang out with. I enjoyed the experience, as did Kathryn, but we needed green cards to continue exploring that career, so once again, as with my football, the dreaded bureaucratic red tape denied me the chance of becoming a star on 'The Bold and the Beautiful'!

Long time Sydney football journalist John Economos would nickname me '*Hollywood*' after learning about my newfound passion and it stuck with me for the rest of my time at Olympic. What might have been with a US work visa or Green Card as it is more commonly known, we will never know, but it had all my attention for a while. Back home I made a guest appearance on '*A Country Practice*' and '*Home and Away*' and got into the final two picks for a movie called the '*Heartbreak Kid*', beaten to the post by a younger man, and now a well-respected actor, called Alex Dimitriades.

It's a weird feeling the world of part-time football, and confusing at times. While I still sought football perfection and success, I was not fully satisfied as the achievements were not in the world's premier leagues, so the perceived achievement was kind of false in a way. While the desire for football greatness was still somewhere inside me, I was constantly being pulled in different directions chasing something new, in this case, an acting career which I attacked with the same vigour and exuberance I showed for football.

However, my dedication to my acting career was not always popular with my football manager, with one instance coming to a head before an away game to Melbourne Knights. It was not just any game, it was a semi-final, two games away from the NSL grand final. You wouldn't read about it, I would have to miss a midweek training session to appear in a theatre production having been cast as Stanley Kowalski in '*A Streetcar Named Desire*,' a play made famous on Broadway and later in Hollywood by the legendary Marlon Brando.

I called Thommo and he was fuming, his last words of the conversation in his Scottish accent were, "Stanley F***ing Kowalski, get tae f***."

I would have been fuming too if I were him, but my mind was all over the place chasing everything but football. I was dropped to the bench with no pay that week, and he only calmed down after I went on as replacement goalkeeper and kept us in the hunt for the grand final. Clint Gosling, our regular 'keeper, was stretchered off injured. In those days we didn't have a reserve 'keeper on the bench so I put my hand up to take his spot between the sticks. This was one of those moments in time where you are either the hero or the zero. "Thommo, I got this," I said. He knew I was serious, and none of the other subs wanted a bar of it, so it was me or bust.

Suddenly I had gone from being dropped to the bench, a consequence of attending a mid-week theatrical debut, to being Thommo's most important player on the pitch. The ever-changing football dynamic had once again played its part, this time the football gods had been kind. I kept a clean sheet and was straight back into the starting line-up, but it could have all gone horribly wrong.

The reality of playing in goal in a proper match, as opposed to saving a few shots after training, suddenly dawns on you when shots and crosses start reigning in from all over the place and everything in front of you suddenly becomes one big blur. The only solution was one that I had always relied on – be brave and hope for the best. Goalkeeping and football are chalk and cheese, like two completely different sports. It's a bit like boxing and wrestling, both combat sports but are a million miles from each other.

Years later, against my old club Ipswich Town, I would once again be brave and put my hand up, only this time the football gods were not so kind, conceding four in a 5-2 loss at Portman Road after replacing Bulgarian legend goalkeeper Bobby Mikhailov, who was sent off early in the game.

Replacing a 'keeper is hard enough, add a man down and away from home and the day can become a nightmare. We were never going to win that match. I made a few saves, but the sweetener was Bobby handing me his gloves and shirt after the match, a lovely memento from the custodian who captained his country in a World Cup. My two games in between the sticks netted a win and a loss but, more importantly, going on and replacing two international goalkeepers of enormous quality in important matches, meant something.

Playing for Sydney Olympic was the experience of a lifetime, in a very special time for football in Sydney. Home matches were almost like playing for Olympiakos in Greece. The whole of Sydney's Greek community rallied behind us and supported us, while the Greek newspapers made us heroes and sometimes the villains.

The Board of the club were all of Greek heritage and included two well-known men known as Fatty and Skinny. They owned the two best strip clubs in Sydney's Kings Cross, the 'Love Machine' and 'Porky's'. Another Board member, Ulysses, owned the renowned 'Bar Iguana', the jewel in the crown of his business portfolio. This was an exclusive night venue that opened until extremely late, or early depending on how you felt. The guest list often included Michael Hutchence, Kylie Minogue, Elton John, and Guns 'n Roses to name just a few of the never-ending list of stars in attendance.

It was a sensational era in Australian football that, on one occasion, nearly cost me my life! I had travelled with the Socceroos to the Solomon Islands and Tahiti for World Cup qualifiers. Preparation included taking hydroxychloroquine tablets, which we took like candy, to combat and prevent the transmission of malaria, a mosquito-borne infectious disease. The biggest mosquitos I have ever seen came at you like Apache helicopters. At the time, my knee was swelling badly so I was also taking half-a-dozen anti-inflammatory tablets daily, not aware of the dangers of mixing the two drugs. My knee was now less inflamed but the deadly cocktail inside me was slowly preparing to haunt me a week later.

Heading back to Australia with a win under our belts was good, but health wise I was in a terrible state. I had never ever felt anything like this before, but I didn't let on to anyone.

We travelled to Melbourne to play Heidelberg United in Melbourne, at the time one of the best sides in the country, and a tough place to go. It reminded me of playing away against Wimbledon's Crazy Gang led by Vinnie Jones. Still feeling unwell, I jumped on the plane with the rest of the Sydney Olympic team not wanting to let the boys down. Suck it up they say, so I did, and led the boys out for a huge clash which was not the place for the faint-hearted. From the kick-off, half-time could not come quick enough for me. I was vomiting everywhere, and my body began to mark up, everyone and everything I made contact with produced instant bruising, all over me. Like a magic trick I was turning black, but I kept fighting my body's desire to crumble, as my breathing became increasingly more and more difficult. I had headed the ball plenty of times during the opening 45 minutes and each time my world would go black for a few seconds, then come back to a fuzzy normality. Heidelberg loved a long ball, and I loved a header, the combination unknown to me on this day, deadly.

I came off at half-time and on the flight home to Sydney, I felt like I was fighting my body from shutting down, just willing myself to hang on.

Our plane landed and I jumped straight into a cab home. Kathryn, my wife at that time, took one look at me and immediately called an ambulance. Twenty minutes later I was lying in the haematology department of the Prince of Wales Hospital in Randwick.

The Head of the Department was waiting for me and testing began, but not before I was told I probably had one of three things: AIDS, leukaemia, or a blood disorder that was killing my blood platelets.

Tests came back: HIV negative, leukaemia negative. The leukaemia test was torture, extracting bone marrow under local anaesthetic with what felt like a power drill. With the worst two options excluded, I was placed on steroid treatment and began to improve, my platelet count climbing by the day. The doctor asked why I had been taking ibuprofen with hydroxychloroquine. I explained that I always took anti-inflammatories, I could not play football without them.

He then said: "You are a lucky boy Andy, one more header and your brain would probably have exploded, and the brain haemorrhage would have caused your immediate death on that football pitch."

Home matches at Olympic were like Greek National Day, a festival of food, drink, dancing, and without fail, most of the team would end up in Kings Cross – the suburb that never slept. A myriad of pubs, nightclubs, strip clubs, restaurants, junkies and ladies of the night attracted all sorts, at all hours, a human zoo. If you survived the night, a short drive down to the navy base in Woolloomooloo, for a pie at the famous Harry's Café de Wheels, would make it a night to remember.

Away from the trappings and the vices of Kings Cross, and alongside my football and acting classes, another job opportunity jumped out at me from the classified pages of the newspaper. An advertisement from the Woollahra Council for a ranger/dog catcher caught my eye. It definitely appealed to me, impacted by watching the television programmes '*Skippy*' and '*Flipper*' as a kid, and thinking what a cool job.

With the Council headquarters surrounded by Sydney's most beautiful and wealthiest suburbs, I thought why not, there are a lot worse jobs out there. The area can be described as a perfect mix of Beverly Hills, Venice Beach, and Malibu Beach, with a touch of San Francisco thrown in for good measure. If I got the job, I would be part of the Council's 'Law Enforcement Team', in an area that encompassed a number of not just Sydney's, but Australia's most beautiful suburbs. This area is home to the Packers, Lowys, Kidmans, and my great friend Harry Michaels, the film and television producer and also my former Sydney Olympic FC President.

In all fairness, I blagged my way into the job, my access to Socceroo tickets the most important part of the interview. The job required becoming a Special Constable with the NSW Police Force for which we were sent to the Police Academy in Goulburn for training. New recruits everywhere, all with freshly cut short hair and fully focused on their initial training requirements. Then there was me, rolling around the place looking like Lenny Kravitz like dreadlocks so deep undercover that nobody was even fazed.

A few months later I was issued with a NSW Special Constable police badge and off I went. It had all the perks, like free travel on trains, buses, harbour ferries, harbour bridge tolls, the lot, but the best one was free McDonald's, so that was lunch sorted every day. I even organised a birthday party for Isabella and her school friends at McDonalds bringing in Ronald McDonald himself for a show stopping happy birthday rendition! A beautiful day, and all on the house, as we left, the staff who all thought I was an undercover cop, said "Stay safe, officer."

The role itself involved all ranger duties but for the first six months I would double-up as a local dog catcher. My first mission was a call out to Robertson Park, Watsons Bay, the message originating from the Council offices, and transmitted over their two-way radio system. Once the 'pooch code' hit the airwaves, every other Council vehicle, ranging from engineers to the garbage trucks, began emanating barking and howling noises onto the open frequency. The piss-take had begun, a quick reminder that I was the new kid on the block.

As I pulled up in the pooch van I could see that the park was awash with dogs, 101 Dalmatians and more all off their leads, all shitting and pissing everywhere and not one resident adhering to the rules! Driving into the middle of the park, residents and dogs began quickly to disperse and within minutes only one man with two big dogs remained. The rest had narrowly missed out on fines ranging from unregistered dogs, dogs off leads, dogs defecating in a park or street, dogs on the beach, the list went on and on.

Most offences were impossible to enforce or win in a court battle. One example of this occurred early one morning in Double Bay. After seeing a dog shit in the park, both dog and owner walked away. I approached with a ticket in hand. The guy said "Prove it's my dog's shit". I said, "I just watched it, come out of its ass", and again he said "Prove it"! With no video evidence, it was game over.

Back to Watsons Bay, the gentleman turned out to be a big sports fan, had seen me play for the Socceroos and was one of the owners of the famous Doyles Restaurant. He cut to the chase, "Whenever your parents come to watch you play, lunch is on me and they'll have the best table in the house." That seemed like a great deal to me, so we shook hands, and his dogs were sweet from that day on.

I had deal-making in the blood, and in 2001 off the back of that Doyles' dog deal done 10 years earlier, I would take Manchester United and England legend Sir Bobby Charlton to the same restaurant where they gave us the best table in the house, the same one my parents were given on the sand with an uninterrupted view of the Sydney Harbour Bridge.

Charlton was in Australia to take part in an advertisement for a Japanese beer ahead of the 2002 FIFA World Cup. I picked him up at Sydney Airport unsure of calling him Sir Bobby or just Bobby. So I went with "Hi, Sir Bobby, how was the trip?" and he responded, "Hi Andy, trip was great. Just call me Bobby." That answer said it all and reaffirmed what a gentleman and superstar he was.

Appearing from his supplied film motor home, Sir Bobby had been made up to look like a very old man, way older than he actually was. Like Del Boy's Uncle Albert in '*Only Fools and Horses*', a walking stick and a flat English gentleman's cap. Make up and wardrobe had not failed, this was a Hollywood level makeover. The best part was to come, with the script reading '*Old man watching some amateurs play a game of football, when a player gets injured, the old man is asked if he would like to play and even up the numbers.*'

Next minute, Sir Bobby looking like a 100-year-old grandfather, and wearing a pair of dodgy old brown work shoes with no grip at all, ripped up the Domain in a performance reminiscent of days gone by at Old Trafford, or when winning the World Cup at Wembley.

It was time for dinner and what better place than Doyles at the best seat in the house. But first I had to lose the agent who had brought him out to Australia. I left him in his five-star hotel room in the city with a supply of 'candy' and other goodies, and that was him done for a few days.

So Bobby and I went to Watsons Bay and as the sun set over the Harbour Bridge, I reminded myself I was having dinner with a Knight. Who would have foreseen, that in a few years' time I would make it two Knights, Sir Bobby Charlton and Sir David Beckham?

Sir Bobby told me some great stories and gave me some valuable life advice that night, a lot of which is coming into play now, and I feel so honoured and grateful to have spent time with him. As for the London agent, he left the Sydney office to pick up the tab on all his activities including the hotel bill!

Back to the ranger duties, and this time dealing with the local ice cream vans. This was a constant cat and mouse chase that ironically would set me up nicely for the Beckham paparazzi wars later in life. I'd read about the ice cream wars in the UK, so I wasn't messing about with this Italian ice cream family. Mr Whippy would take the occasional fine and I would take the occasional chocolate nut sundae. We all played the game, the van's iconic music played loud and the children and adults flocked in droves.

Despite the fun and games, we were very protective of the area and the role of the ranger was vitally important, especially with the enforcing of the Environmental Protection Act, which stopped the illegal dumping and pouring of waste and chemicals into the beautiful Sydney Harbour.

Wednesday was always touch footy days against neighbouring Council teams, and we reigned supreme. My main touch footy partner was Colin De Costa, who is now the Head of Ranger Services.

A good man, Colin loved surfing, had done it all his childhood, convincing me one time to go with him. The location would be the famous Maroubra beach in the middle of 'Bra Boy' territory. I was absolute crap, struggling to even sit on the board and look half cool while waiting for a set to come in! It was way harder than I thought it would be, made even more difficult with my mind more focused and preoccupied with Tiger and Hammerhead sharks that frequented the area! Watching 'Jaws' the movie as a young kid had destroyed any chance of becoming a pro surfer, my fear of man-eating sharks had left me scarred for life. A floating speed bump was my best offering, my friendship with Colin, and his friendship with the locals saved me from becoming another 'Bra Boy statistic that day!

Outside of football, this was undoubtedly the best job I have ever had. We had the most magnificent Council chambers backing onto Sydney Harbour, with endless picturesque private beaches that were to die for.

The TV show '*Bondi Rescue*' was developed and modelled on procedures that were part of our initial framework for the Council's lifeguard and ranger department. These TV lifeguards are good but we were next level, as I am yet to see them rescue two Penthouse Pets heading for trouble in deep water outside the safety of the flags. On top of that, we allowed them both 'all access' parking at Camp Cove beach for the summer, which as most Sydney-siders know, is next to impossible.

In between club and Socceroo commitments, I would hang out on film and TV production sets around Sydney, scoring one role that was interesting to say the least. I would be playing an armed robber on '*Australia's Most Wanted*'. The robbery was to be filmed at the Hurlstone Park Bowling Club, the premises that Sydney Olympic had purchased, operating as their licensed social club and function centre. Award nights and end-of-season events were very weird for me, knowing that I had held the place up once upon a time!

The assortment of second jobs amongst players, many Socceroos included, was fascinating to say the least. In the end we were just trying to bring in a few more dollars to supplement what were pretty ordinary football wages.

All the lads thought my ranger job was cool, while other jobs included bank clerks, laundromat owners, builders, accountants, fish mongers and sex shop owners. Yes, you read that correctly, sex shop owners. One particular player, a Melbourne based Socceroo, had two such shops employing his teammates, a few of them also Socceroos, as sales assistants. A little bizarre but fans flocked to the porn king and business was good.

At Olympic you quickly understood to expect the unexpected and that the abnormal was, on many occasions, simply normal.

One such occasion was an away game to Adelaide City, a fantastic team back then boasting many Socceroos. I was met by two club officials at half-time in the tunnel. Pulling me aside they said "When the manager finishes his team talk, go around to all the players one by one and discreetly tell them, '*if we win today the finest prostitutes in the city will be delivered to the hotel that evening!*'" Well, wouldn't you know it, we won it, and I scored the winner. This lot wouldn't stop in their endeavours to make Sydney Olympic great.

Back in Sydney the same officials would treat the lads to the very finest girls in the country for Man of the Match performances, and I often wonder if that would constitute a salary cap breach these days?

The second major incident was also an away game, this time against Wollongong City (later renamed as Wollongong Wolves). I led the boys out for the warm-up, initially just a slow jog across the pitch heading towards the hill end at Brandon Park. As we got closer to that side, five lads in their mid-20s approached the fence, all dressed up like hardcore English football hooligans. They had all the clobber, the boots, the shirts, the braces, the lot.

The abuse began, much of it racially aimed at me. After enduring it for a couple of minutes, I was over the fence just as the great Eric Cantona did in 1995 at Crystal Palace. Dad always said go for the biggest one, so I locked in on him and did not miss. Nothing came back, so I stopped. He deserved more, and so did the low life pea heart cowards that moonlighted as his crew. All mouth, no heart, they were all dressed up with nowhere to go.

Unknown to them, my mate's grandfather lived in Green Street, and in 1987 we had many Sunday roasts across from the iconic Upton Park, a ground I played at during my time at Ipswich Town and Reading FC. On top of that, West Ham legend Billy Bonds would become my friend and also my coach for a stint during my time at the Royals so I was well aware of just how the Green Street crew could operate. This lot needed to go back to the drawing board and hooligan school.

Back over the fence and onto the pitch I returned to the dressing room for last-minute preparations. 'I won't hear anymore from that lot,' I thought to myself.

With Mick Hickman giving his final message, suddenly four NSW police officers burst through the door to be greeted by a Hicky death stare, not something I would highly recommend. He was an intense man who knew his football, playing up front for Blackburn Rovers earlier in his career. A lovely bloke but hard as nails, and not 30 seconds after telling us that no prisoners were to be taken, his captain was now taken prisoner by the NSW police.

The incident delayed the kick-off, of course, and we now had the comical sight of the match officials, four police officers, and me in cuffs. As fans continued streaming through the turnstiles, their focus was now on the entertainment outside the stadium. My excuse, "I was born here and play for our national team, representing all Australians including these idiots, so I don't need to be racially abused with my family present, who themselves don't need any more of that shit." The police seemed to be happy with my reasoning and I was let go with the words "have a good game," ringing in my ears. I put the armband on, we drew, and I had a great game.

I was lucky enough to play under two fantastic presidents at Sydney Olympic, George Pashalis and Harry Michaels. Two characters who were worlds apart, but both shared the same love for Olympic and wanted the ultimate success for the club.

We managed to give George an NSL title which he would later tell me was second only to marrying his true love Marika. I would often visit his law office in Taylor Square, located upstairs from a Greek cake shop. At the time, Sydney Olympic CEO Stefan Kamasz would work out of this law office, somehow trying to balance the books. Stefan was an amazing CEO, more like a magician at times. One minute the club had no money, the next it was raining cash. More than that though, he is a football man, it's in his blood. I learnt a lot from him, his business acumen and marketing ideas, worthy of a placement in much higher leagues. John O'Neill, Ben Buckley and David Gallop, all non-football men, became CEOs of Football Federation Australia (FFA) and, in my opinion, they could not lace his boots. Stefan was appointed to the FFA Board towards the end of 2020; better late than never I suppose but what a waste of many years in the football wilderness.

George, who passed away in 2020 one week after his lovely wife Marika died, was one of the good guys; as was the incredible, amazing, and flamboyant film, sport and TV producer Harry Michaels who became the president towards the end of my Olympic career.

It was Harry who unselfishly let me go to Reading FC, albeit for a small fee. Harry was never going to stand in the way of my football dream. We were great mates, we still are, and have shared many fantastic experiences together. Harry was always the ultimate professional, starting his career as an actor then moving onto TV production, where he would beam world class football matches onto televisions worldwide. At the same time, he would receive global acclaim for producing the fitness sensation 'Aerobics Oz Style.' It was on this show that he would give Australian rugby league star Benny Elias and myself a gig riding stationary bikes behind five or six of the hottest ladies on the planet in skimpy leotards, doing aerobics into cameras that beamed the show around the world.

Harry, at my request, kindly organised a night out on Sydney Harbour for Manchester United stars, Dwight Yorke and Mark Bosnich, and there was no better way to see the Harbour than on Harry's luxury cruiser. Harry was the man, I told the boys and "you will never forget a night out on Harry's boat."

Their pick-up point was a pier under the Harbour Bridge in the early evening. I rolled up to Rose Bay mid-afternoon, where this beauty was docked. Harry was already on board, dressed in all white crisp Armani linen and Gucci loafers, looking like Julio Iglesias. I was wearing the same, he had taught me well. Cruiser cleaned for the occasion, it looked simply stunning, a 5-star hotel on the water that had everything you can imagine.

We set towards the Harbour Bridge, and as the darkness set in, I could see two red dots in the distance where I had told the lads to wait. As we got closer, it turned out to be Bozza and Yorkie puffing on giant Cuban cigars and already in party mode. They were not disappointed, the party was epic, and Harry, as always, was the King of Kings.

I was at a point in my life where I had pretty much ruled out a return to Europe and was fairly settled into a life with what I considered the perfect job and, at age 28, an exceedingly difficult proposition. My left knee was now devoid of all meniscus, and now past bone-on-bone. My knee surgeon would often tell me I needed a knee replacement ten years ago. Before I eventually headed back to England, he gave it one final cleanout and scrape, his final words "Good luck in England Andy, how you do what you do on the field is beyond me, and medical science. I cannot begin to imagine your daily pain."

I replied, "I've known nothing else since birth Doc, it's been sore every day of my life, and on my mind every single day".

The chance to head back to England came out of the blue and was totally unexpected after running into Mick Hickman at the Iguana Bar in the Cross, in the early hours of the morning when he was home in between UK seasons. He had returned to England himself a year earlier as assistant to Mark McGhee, the manager of Reading FC. They were in the market for a right back, not my preferred position, but I wouldn't look a gift-horse in the mouth.

I told Mick if Mark was prepared to send me a contract, I would sign it. No trial, it was a contract or nothing at all. Mick seemed to think that this would be no problem, and on his recommendation, I was headed back to the big show. Knowing Mick was a part of the coaching staff was a big factor in going back, and I was determined not to let him down.

One minute I was chasing dogs at Watsons Bay, and nine months later, I was running out to a packed house on the hallowed turf of the famous Wembley Stadium. As many would say, impossible!

Dad on the left in the Spanish Army, 1954

Dad in Far North Queensland, 1963

Mum and Dad's wedding, 1965

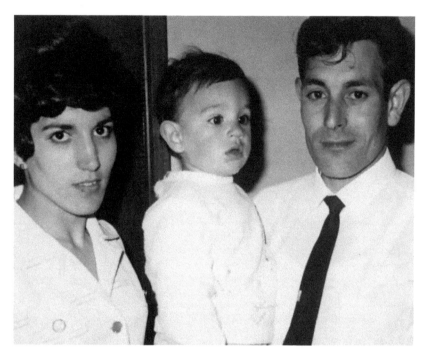

With Mum and Dad,
1967

Getting ready to
ride shotgun
from a young age!

Mum and Dad with Raquel and me, Canberra, 1978

Mum and Dad visiting Isabella in Auckland

Beautiful Isabella off to school in Reading

Both now gone - my father-in-law David and my dad Andres

Isabella, 2016

Jaynie, Isabella and me, 2017

Proud dad at Isabella's wedding, 2016

Me with my granddaughter Zoe, 2019

Isabella, Zoe and my son-in-law, Daniel, 2020

Jaynie, Zoe and me
to see Zoe's dad, Dan,
at the UFC, 2019

With Jaynie and her mum Eileen,
2020

With Jaynie and mum, 2020

The cover image of this book was based on this photograph taken at Tom Rogic's wedding

A 2021 selfie with Jaynie

CHAPTER 6

LIVING THE DREAM

A few weeks later, I was heading back to a new reality, a familiar one, but one that brought with it a feeling of trepidation. I was anxious, and even a little scared. I should have been fully focused on football, but I was landing at Heathrow Airport in London, five years after my deportation by UK Customs. The last time I was at this airport I was unceremoniously escorted onto a Qantas flight home. How ironic that my Spanish passport, that once forced me to leave Spain chased by military police, was now enabling me to re-enter the UK under European Union law.

Whilst the UK immigration computer system may have read, 'refuse entry to Australian passport holder Andrew Bernal', it welcomed a Spanish passport holder called Andres Bernal. How sweet it felt walking through the European Union gate and showing my Spanish passport to a smiling and welcoming Customs official, who just waved me through.

I had enjoyed five decent seasons with Sydney Olympic and during that time, overseas football coverage had been improving rapidly by the day. Sporadically I would watch UK football on TV, watching players that I had kept out of teams playing important league and cup matches, knowing that is where I should have been, and where I always wanted to be. It was the cause of much heartache and sadness for me. I wasn't jealous of their success, far from it, I was over the moon for them, I simply resented the system and the laws and regulations that had, up until the point of my return, denied me of all that. Out of the blue, when I least expected it, a second opportunity presented itself. This time, I was determined nothing was going to get in my way achieving my ultimate goals and dreams. Just playing in England again for five or six seasons would have sent me to my grave happy. What actually lay ahead was simply unimaginable.

I had watched FA Cup Finals, play-off finals, international football matches and international rugby league matches at Wembley, including the touring Kangaroos. As a kid growing up I wished to play for them. Wembley was the ultimate dream, the thought of playing at one of the most famous and iconic football landmarks in world football, had not even crossed my mind, not even a second thought, simply impossible, especially at a small first division club like Reading FC.

Impossible is nothing, so once again the craziness of my life would lead me to a special football fantasia. A place where twin towers overlook perfectly manicured grass, beautiful green grass, meticulously prepared like the greens and fairways at Augusta National during US Masters week. Wembley Stadium, English football's biggest stage was everything I dreamt it would be.

From the airport I travelled to meet Dr Williams, a lovely man from Wales, for a quick medical at his surgery. He took my blood pressure and my heart rate, then tapped both my knees with a little rubber hammer and pronounced I was a perfect specimen!

I had the left knee of a 70-year-old and had probably spent enough money on anti-inflammatory tablets to own a good stake in the companies that make them. No way in today's game would I have even got close to passing that medical. Today's MRI scanners would have processed deep knee images that looked more like the surface of the moon, than that of a first class footballer.

After that it was straight to Elm Park, then the home of Reading FC before we made the move to the wonderful Madejski Stadium years later. The girls in the front office were lovely and friendly. The Chairman, Sir John Madejski, who had sanctioned the £30,000 transfer fee, upon meeting me asked if I was an 'Indigenous Antipodean.' My dreadlocks and skin colour had sent him down the Aboriginal path. Surprised, he then chuckled when I replied, "No I'm a Spanish Antipodean!"

We were worlds apart but I liked John and he liked me as well. We would often have dinner in mutual company at the Bina Tandoori Restaurant, and he genuinely took on board any football advice I sometimes gave him. I would really like to have worked for him after my football career had ended. On a football level, he trusted my opinion and together I believe we would have hit the EPL and stayed there, forging and building on my connections with the likes of Real Madrid and Barcelona, but it never happened. For me, it was maybe the one thing that would have kept me on the straight and narrow!

When I joined Reading, the club had just been promoted from Division 2 to Division 1, what is now known as the Championship, arguably the toughest league in European football. For those who may be unfamiliar with the English league structure, this is the league immediately below the Premier League and most of the teams are very evenly matched. They all have one single overriding ambition and objective, that being, promotion to the big time, either by finishing in the top two, which was automatic promotion, or via the play-off final, held at Wembley Stadium, known as the richest match in football.

The winner of this cut-throat, one-off, winner takes all showdown at the end of a long and gruelling campaign would earn the promoted club around £170m of riches that comes from the massive TV deal in top level EPL football. To just reach the final takes 46 league games, from which you need enough points to finish between third and sixth, and a heart-stopping two leg, home and away semi-final.

Mark McGhee was the Reading manager when I arrived, a Scotsman who had played for Aberdeen and Celtic in his homeland as well as Newcastle United, and Hamburg in Germany. He had also been capped by Scotland and had won the European Cup Winners' Cup as part of the Aberdeen side that defeated Real Madrid under Alex Ferguson in 1983. McGhee was assisted by Mick Hickman and after clinching the Division 2 title in 1994, McGhee had brought in four new players to strengthen the squad for the rigours of a Division 1 championship campaign.

Simon Osborn was procured from Crystal Palace, Paul Holsgrove came in from Millwall, Polish international Dariusz Wdowczyk came from Celtic, and I came from Sydney Olympic. The total outlay was miniscule in comparison to most other clubs in the division, and at the start of that season nobody could have imagined the impact the new acquisitions, mixed with existing promotion-winning players, would have on the entire competition.

My first game for Reading would be away to Wolverhampton Wanderers, in their magnificent Molineux Stadium. Wolves were captained by their legendary striker Steve Bull, a prolific goalscorer over many years. They were a massive club, they still are, one whose supporters demand and expect success. They stem from a rich history, former League Champions in the 1950s having featured many outstanding players over the years.

The ground was packed to the rafters for the first match of the season, the atmosphere mind blowing, maybe intimidating for some but not me. I felt comfortable in the uncomfortable, excited I was in heaven playing my first official game in England since the deportation fiasco. The cape was on and I was flying like Superman, until a head clash late in the match, brought me back to earth, leaving me dazed, and receiving stitches courtesy of the Wolves doctor.

We put in a tremendous display that afternoon losing by a goal, and unlike most losses, we left the ground feeling upbeat by the performance, realising we had nothing to fear for the season ahead.

As per usual, my knee was killing me after the match, so I packed it in ice to reduce swelling on the bus trip back south. Nothing new here, it was my normality, but I did question how long it could hold up in the rigours and tough demands of football at this level. My head did not feel great either and a headache ensued for days, but I said nothing. There was no way a bit of concussion would derail me. Within the confines of the team bus there was something brewing, and it had the smell and taste of success. That winning feeling, a cocky, but not arrogant confidence flowed through the air, a feeling of invincibility in the aftermath of a loss is a rare thing. Sports psychologists call it 'The Zone'.

I had lived it back in my Sydney Olympic days when we won the National Soccer League and it had arisen again, that looming sense of positive inevitability that we were onto something special circulated through my body, living with me but on a whole new level, at the home of football and in the eyes of not only Britain but the rest of the world.

There are strong arguments made to this day amongst the Reading fan base that the squad I was lucky enough to be a part of during the 1994/95 campaign was the most entertaining in the club's history. You ask any Reading supporter, and they could reel off that squad from the top of their heads: Hislop, Bernal, McPherson, Williams, Wdowczyk, Gilkes, Gooding, Parkinson, Osborn, Taylor, Nogan, Lovell, Quinn, Kerr, Hopkins, Holsgrove, Jones, Lambert, and Shepperd a special team with special individuals, both on a football, and a human level.

Mark McGhee was one of the most empowering managers who I have ever played under. His pre-match team talks were inspirational, his delivery of them akin to Russell Crowe in the Roman Colosseum. The chairman, Sir John Madejski, had given him the job on the advice and endorsement from Sir Alex Ferguson and it didn't matter who we played, when you left the dressing room for the tunnel you felt invincible, we all did, and it showed in our performances on the pitch. We feared nobody home or away, big clubs with big history's, big stadiums, big names in line-ups, all held absolutely no fear for us.

We began to win a lot of matches, interspersed with the odd draw here or there, the rarity of an occasional defeat erased the very next match. It all seemed so easy, we purred along with a consistent excellence, like one of the Chairman's vintage Ferrari's or Jaguar's! Everyone was on the same wave length, appearing to have a sixth sense that enabled us to know what each other was going to do, to anticipate moves ahead of time and training was simple and fun. We worked hard, every player knew exactly what their job was, and we did it well.

But even a perfect season can bring you a few trying days or weeks, moments when injuries derail your run in the team or sometimes you just had a poor game, paying the price by losing your position in the side. There was zero room for mediocrity in this squad and if you did fall foul to the axe, the amazing thing about McGhee dropping you, was his ability to convince you that his decision was justified, that it was the correct one, and of course that you were still one of his best players.

This happened to me once for an away match at Watford. A piss-take really, but that's football and down the track I returned the favour with interest at Filbert Street. On the positive, I watched the Watford match in Elton John's private box courtesy of the greatest Olympic decathlete ever, Daley Thompson, who was training with us at the time.

Shortly after I returned to the starting line-up, I could still make no sense of being left out, but I just rolled with it though, as I was over the moon to be back in this superb team. Normal service was resumed and the team, whoever played in it, continued to rack up the points.

That season I got to play in some amazing stadiums against some absolute legends of the game. Middlesbrough away was a great day out, managed and coached by two former England internationals and Manchester United stars, Bryan Robson and Viv Anderson. I had to do a quick double take, I was playing on the same pitch against Robson, the scorer of the fastest goal in the 1982 World Cup Finals after 27 seconds!

Then there was Millwall at the Den! The New Den produced tidal waves of love and hate, and trust me it was not a pleasant outing if it was you receiving the hate. What an experience though, greeted as you travelled down the Old Kent Road with shouts of "f*** off you wankers!" and that was just the kids! Their dads took it to the next level, nasty and vicious and if you're unsure of what I mean, watch the movie 'The Football Factory' which gives you a fantastic insight into a day out at Millwall. An intimidating, and scary kind of place, not for the faint hearted, my kind of place. They liked Aussies at Millwall, at one point I was close to joining them. Now that would have been a ride.

Years later, in my agent role and looking after Millwall's young superstar Tim Cahill, I returned to watch Millwall against my old club Reading. Watching from a box, with four non-playing Reading players and Tim's brother Chris, who at one point went into Mike Tyson mode unleashing on the Reading lads, after one shouted abuse at Tim not realising Chris was the younger brother. I called him off, not easy, as he's a pit bull, but he listened and, boy, did the Reading four cop a break! They left the box quick smart leaving just Chris and me to enjoy the service undisturbed. A couple of right geezers, London types, from the box next door, stuck their heads in and said, "You alright lads?" We said yes, but I think the answer they wanted was no, keen on some extra fun.

There were also visits to Maine Road, Manchester City's former Stadium in Moss Side. You want the hood? You want gun and knife crime where all buildings around you are boarded up with razor wire resembling a war zone, then Moss Side is for you. Young lads controlling the corners, not the football pitch type, fiends buying crack, pimps selling bitches, and amongst all this, a magnificent and old colosseum full of the maddest, loyal supporters singing 'Blue Moon' to their hearts content. Just an insanely beautiful experience in my life.

I always loved baseball as a kid, so one away match was of prime importance to me, but did not come around until my second season. Derby County played at the famous Baseball Ground and one of my goals during my whole career was to play at grounds that resonated deeply with me. Grounds and stadiums that I had seen and read about from the other side of the world as a kid. The explorer genes would always fuel my fire and I had pencilled this encounter into the calendar. However, with eight weeks to go, I ruptured my adductor tendon at home against West Bromwich Albion, ripping it completely off the pelvic bone, the tendon rolling itself down my inner thigh, nestling by my knee like a tennis ball under my skin.

A few days later it was stapled back onto my pelvis, splitting in two like a snake tongue. While they had me in theatre though, they also repaired a long overdue hernia. The surgeon estimated three to four months before I could play again but nothing would stop me. With the Baseball Ground in my head, two months later with our side hit by injuries, Jim and Mick asked me if I was good to go. Without hesitation I said yes, the good news was the surgeon had told me the tendon was set in place, and wouldn't rip from the bone again. So, with stitches still dissolving and two staples in my pelvis, I played, and ticked off the Baseball Ground. On the way home, having just played against Derby County, strangely my thoughts were on how cool it would be to play for the New York Yankees. Must be a baseball thing!

Along with our success came attention from elsewhere, and McGhee was hot property. Unfortunately, he was lured away from us midway through the season by Leicester City, in search of what the gaffer called 'a bigger club.' On a professional level you could see his point, but the fans were not impressed. They went nuts, they saw it as a betrayal of the highest order, labelling him 'Judas'. His departure was considered a crime and abandonment and would never be forgotten or forgiven.

Mick Hickman had given me the heads-up that the coaching group would be leaving with McGhee. It's a funny feeling when things like this happen, realising you are losing a selection security blanket and a coach who trusts you completely, despite his occasional crazy decision. Your first thought is of the new guy coming in; are you his type of player, will he want to bring in new faces, players he trusts or rates more highly than you. In this case it was a little different as our team was in perfect motion and we needed nothing new, the current management were not leaving due to poor results they were simply moving for a lot more cash.

On a playing level we were one of the top 30 clubs in the UK and were playing a brand of football rarely ever seen before at Reading. We had a consistent eleven, sprinkled with internationals and three or four quality substitutes. After that we had zero depth, but a new manager from outside would have been a dumb decision. The job was to basically keep the lads ticking over and motivated, so the chairman promoted Jimmy Quinn and Mick Gooding as co-player/managers. You can never keep every player happy, but in general, 90% of the players liked the appointment, and in my case, they were teammates I respected. The only thing that had changed was that I now needed to show more respect, manager type respect. So I just did more of the same, and eventually the pair would hand me the captain's armband, a great honour to captain such a great club.

Quinny was a lethal striker, up there with the best finishers I have ever seen globally. He was born for that role, a natural, and because of him I saw Belfast, his city of birth, during a pre-season tour he had organised for us. The beauty of football allows you to see places you have only ever seen on TV, and not always for the right reason. I loved exploring and discovering new lands and cities. It was in our family blood and in Belfast I found another beauty. My first try of Guinness was in Belfast, like a beautiful milkshake, nothing outside of Ireland has ever quite matched it.

We worked hard and played some tough matches in a city, unreservedly divided by religion. Rows of houses with either British or Irish flags lined the streets, while street art liberally sprayed on the walls of terraced houses clearly represented the allegiance of either IRA or British sympathisers. Even with a peace treaty in place, it was blatantly obvious you were in a war zone with an oppressive feel about it. A city ready to explode at any minute, despite all this, it had a beautiful Irish attraction about it. It is something almost indescribable that makes you want to go back for more.

Mick Gooding, the other half of the new management team, was a fantastic midfielder. He covered every blade of grass, was technically competent and consistently good. There was rarely, if at all, a deviation in his performance and he reminded me a lot of the great Leeds United legend, Billy Bremner.

By season's end we had reached Wembley, but we had been effectively robbed of an automatic promotion place. In 1994/95 for the first time in modern English football history, only one side was guaranteed promotion! Are you kidding me! We ended the season in second place, three points behind Middlesbrough, who won automatic promotion after winning the league. This ruling was due to the Premier League reducing their number of teams from 22 to 20, which hurt us badly. The side that ended fifth could effectively go up instead of us. We all felt a real sense of injustice that after a superb season, losing only 13 of 46 league matches, earning 79 points, could all be in vain. Yes, we all knew the rules and the changed but it seemed so unfair. After finishing second, we could not afford to lose the play-off final. It was simply a nightmare thought!

We got there by beating Tranmere Rovers who were spearheaded by the ex-Liverpool striker John Aldridge. We nullified that threat well and played some beautiful football, beating them 3-1 at Prenton Park. Fellow Aussie Stuart Lovell scored twice, Welshman Lee Nogan bagged the other, and we comfortably saw them off back at Elm Park in a subdued 0-0 draw.

The other semi-final saw Bolton Wanderers ending any chance of a reunion with Steve Bull as Wolves were defeated 3-2 on aggregate after extra-time. We certainly weren't scared of Bolton, they'd beaten us 1-0 at Burnden Park in the regular season whilst we had won 2-1 at home, so we knew they would be a challenge, but one that we felt that we were more than adequate to match and one that I was certainly going to relish.

Wembley Stadium is an evocative name for any young footballer and I, like so many others, had grown up dreaming about playing on that hallowed turf. Watching FA Cup Finals on TV as a young kid was a special occasion, even more so when my friend Craig Johnston became the first Australian to ever score in one, when he netted a goal against Everton in the 1986 FA Cup Final for Liverpool.

For young Australian kids, Wembley is a big dream and now I too would savour one of the grandest theatres in world football. The build-up to Wembley was different for us. The management team organised a special 10-day camp in Lanzarote, Spain. The complex had a football pitch and a running track used sometimes by the British Olympic team but it was more like an overseas holiday destination for Brits. The perfect holiday destination for the lads on an end of season trip!

We trained every day, just ticking over, with a few nights out early in the week. Lee Nogan and I would both pick up slight leg strains whilst sprinting on the athletics track, a surface we hadn't been on all season but we were determined that nothing was going to stop us playing at Wembley. Ironically, together, we would create one of Wembley's greatest goals of all time - well I just passed it to him, and the Welsh wizard did the rest!

We returned to Reading about a week before the match, and before you knew it, we were back on the bus headed Wembley way, with the match only a few days out. Our hotel, not too far from the Stadium, was nice and tranquil, and we all enjoyed a relaxing dinner the night before the big game.

When I returned to my room, I looked at my Wembley suit hanging up, ready for game day. I felt happy and relaxed about the whole process, but how strange that playing at Wembley felt normal, just another day at the office, while most kids back home saw it as an amazing dream. I know I once did.

If I was feeling good, it wasn't half as good as my roommate, Shaka Hislop, our goalkeeper. Shaka was amazingly cool. He had that West Indian strut going on and was a great bloke to spend time with. Cricket was always a big part of our conversations as he had grown up in Trinidad and Tobago with the legend Brian Lara.

We both slept soundly, unusual for me, but not for the big man, he could sleep anywhere, anytime. Tomorrow we would wake up and head off to the field of dreams. Hopefully, it would be one of the best days of our lives. Win or lose I would savour the occasion and as always, my song of choice as

I arrived for a game was 'Thunderstruck' by Aussie legends ACDC.

The bus trip to the stadium was special as crowds dressed in the colours of both teams lined the streets along Wembley Way, and for both sets of fans this was their dream too. Walking out to inspect the pitch in our tailored suits pre-match, we could see thousands of fans making their way into the stands. There was a buzz about the place, like I had never felt before. My slight nervous tension mixed with excitement, left me in no doubt that this was the real deal !

Leaving the dressing rooms for the warm-up, you hit the tunnel which was awash with noise, that becomes louder and louder as you near the exit. Suddenly, like magic, you are on the pitch. It is the most amazing theatre of dreams you can ever imagine, or in my case had imagined. It keeps getting better as you are welcomed by a spine chilling crowd roar, so loud it's like being at a Metallica or Guns n Roses concert. The sun is out, there is no wind, not even a breeze. So far it is one perfect day!

For a quick moment, I drifted back to my parent's lounge room across the world in Canberra, where as a kid I would watch all the big Wembley occasions in the early hours of the morning. I was now living, exactly what I had seen on TV, as one of the players. It is an indescribable feeling, just so surreal.

I began my warm-up with a slow jog, stopping for a second, to pick a blade of grass, the most pristine grass I had ever seen. I rubbed it between my fingers and flicked it into the air, double-checking that I really was at the home of football! The faces of my mum and dad were in the forefront of my mind, their lifelong sacrifices very much appreciated. This day was for them too, riding shotgun with their boy. I knew they were proud; this day was for them, I was here because of them.

The mood in the squad was as confident as it had been all season. The message from Quinn and Gooding was to keep it tight at the back and let our magical football do the rest. We could not have asked for a better start to the game, four minutes into the match I broke down the right flank and played a 30- yard low pass into Lee Nogan's feet. His sublime control was only matched by the exquisite turn that gave him that crucial yard of space, he turned that yard into two and with a little tuck inside, he drilled a left foot shot right into the back of the net in what was a world class finish.

Eight minutes later it was all becoming too easy, routine business that had won us our place at Wembley in the first place. Simon Osborne took a quick free-kick which caught the Bolton defence standing still and Adrian Williams, another Welshman, nipped in to poke the ball home. 2-0 inside a quarter of an hour and we were flying! Amazingly we kept going on auto pilot when Michael Gilkes was upended in the area and we were awarded a penalty. A moment in time, where everybody on the planet was thinking, 3-0 and its game over, however, the football gods had other ideas and Stuart Lovell's spot-kick was saved by the Bolton goalkeeper. 'Archie' was gutted. He had been excellent for us all season, a natural goalscorer whose many goals had helped get us here. Nine times out of ten he would have buried that penalty without even blinking. It hardly seemed to matter, as we went into the changing rooms at half-time full of confidence and exhilaration, and 2-0 to the good.

I can't recall which one of our coaching staff said it, but there was a chat about 2-0 being the worst possible score in football and that we needed a third. So that's what we did, flew at them at the start of the second half, and to their credit, they flew at us. It was end-to-end stuff and both Nogan and I succumbed to our Lanzarote niggles and had to be substituted. I had played 67 minutes and was replaced by former Welsh international Jeff Hopkins, who is now coaching women's football in Australia.

I was devastated to come off. Once more, an injury had played its cruel card on me and I was forced to watch the rest of the match from the bench praying that the boys could hold on.

Owen Coyle headed a goal for Bolton with a quarter of an hour to go, with four minutes to play they broke quickly, finding their striker Fabian de Freitas who rode a tackle to slide home an improbable equaliser and send the match into extra-time. It was a sucker punch we couldn't recover from. They scored again, then added a fourth. Jimmy Quinn pulled one back in the last minute of extra time but it was too late, our dream was shattered.

I felt then, and to this day still do, that if Lee and myself had been able to stay on, we would have won that match. I say that with no disrespect whatsoever to the boys who replaced us, the goals we conceded were not their fault, but the forced substitutions upset the team's rhythm and dynamic, losing all our momentum.

The fallout and aftermath haunted me for a long time. I still think back to those days, about certain actions and moments that could have changed the course of that game, the outcome of that game and effectively, the history of both clubs. Could we have prepared better? Should we have stayed in England rather than head to the Spanish sunshine? Did the change of training routine, recovery and the extra travel take its toll on our performance in the latter stages of normal time and then in extra-time? If 'Archie' Lovell had scored the penalty, it was game over, or maybe not? Years later, the questions have never had any answers, and they never will.

The coach ride back was quiet, a sombre place in which I just sat in silence, tears running down my face, non-stop, all the way back to Reading. My thoughts were with the distraught fans who could not stop their tears flowing either. The bittersweet feeling of losing at Wembley, the place I had dreamed of playing at while juggling balls, smashing windows, and destroying Dad's vegetable garden, had hit me hard. If you're not first you're last, and never were words more accurate and pain inducing than on that occasion.

There was a feeling in the whole club that this was a missed opportunity and, up until I retired in 2000, it was never quite the same again. That team was something special and with special comes attention and interest. Welsh international Adi Williams would join Wolves, as would Michael Gilkes and Simon Osborne. Scotty Taylor went to Leicester City and Kevin Keegan made Shaka Hislop his goalkeeper at Newcastle United. Stuart Lovell left for Scotland, along with Dylan Kerr, and so, the dream team was now history. New managers with grand ideas and visions would come and go, but the manner of that Wembley defeat left a mark on us all for a long-time.

Luckily, the Reading Rock Festival would come around once a year, one of Europe's major music events and with VIP access to Eminem, Metallica and many more, it would provide some relief from the mental torture and pressures of trying to recapture the magical flow we once had.

Not long after the first season, my first wife Kathryn and I would separate and she would take Isabella, who was five at the time, back to Australia. This itself became the most impacting life event that I ever lived through.

With years remaining on my contract at Reading, I was torn between my football dream and heading home, to who knows what? My marriage was over, but if I went home to Australia, I would be closer to Izzy. But what job would I return to, if any? My UK football wages would help Isabella go to a nice school and live in a nice area with far greater opportunities in life. All this was up against my own mental torture having been denied the best years of my football life, away from Spain and England, robbed from me by antiquated laws, regulations and a myriad of bureaucratic red tape.

I made the decision to stay and see my contract out, comforted in the knowledge that Kathryn was a fantastic mum and she herself would be much happier back home studying at university and fulfilling her own life goals. Isabella would be in great hands and showered with love by my parents, along with her maternal grandparents, Maldon and Jan.

However, that was all easier said than done. Missing a child so much breaks your heart and impacts your soul in a way that you are never the same again. Time heals the guilt of separation you suffer, but not completely. It's with you all the time, hidden away for life and I am not sure if it can ever be eradicated. To conquer the time away from her, I would always try to make our limited moments together memorable ones. I would constantly be in touch and twice a year we would spend limited but quality time together.

My parents would bring her over to the UK for Christmas and I would see her for a month at the end of the football season back in Sydney. In between I would lose myself in football and wish the season would fly by, so that I could be with her again. Ninety minutes of my football dream every week, darkened and overshadowed by days and nights without my little princess.

But one Reading manager, a special man, made one memorable visit, simply unforgettable.

Terry Bullivant, aware that my mum and daughter were over for a month at Christmas, had organised with the girls in the front office for the three of us to go to Paris for a week at Euro Disney. We flew to the French capital in the middle of winter, and there we were, ice skating with Mickey and Minnie Mouse. Izzy loved that trip.

It is a week I will never forget, and I will forever owe Terry for making it happen and allowing me to go. It's the mark of a man, he knew my love for Izzy and my mum, and we often spoke about family after training. He cared about his players and their outside lives, a fine gentleman, top drawer, who I have much love and respect for, the type of manager I played my heart out for.

Unfortunately, his time at Reading, didn't set the world on fire. Injuries took a heavy toll on the squad and the results were not favourable, a difficult situation for a manager who from day one was far from a fan favourite.

Terry had also worked as a London cabbie before he got into management. He had the 'knowledge', London's taxi licence requirement akin to a human GPS, and our supporters just would not let that part of his life go, particularly when results were going the wrong way. They questioned how a man earning extra money driving a taxi, to provide for his family when out of a football job, could also manage a professional football club.

Let me tell you I have been around top managers and coaches all my life and he was a fantastic coach, one of the best, maybe even better than as a manager.

His training sessions were always well-planned and well-executed, but football is a bitch at times, unfair in many ways, that's the beast we contend with. He would move onto Crystal Palace as a coach, and upon my recommendation to him, they would sign Socceroo Tony Popovic who was playing in Japan at the time.

My parents were a godsend while I finished my football career at Reading, suddenly becoming parents again on top of their role as grandparents. Despite all my failings, my daughter was gifted with all that I had been also: a beautiful, warm and loving Spanish family.

Adapting and adjusting to a new football club can be a tricky process. You must have the ability to make new friends and integrate into the workings and mechanisms of the city you are now living in. I was extremely lucky at Reading that one of the first people I met was Michael Gilkes. Michael was an absolute champion, loved by the whole town and a firm crowd favourite at Elm Park. He was arguably the quickest footballer I have ever met or seen in action, he had a wand of a left foot and a stunning body swerve when in full flight. On his day he was unplayable. If he had been born in Australia, he would easily have won 100 international caps.

There were plenty of good people who helped me settle in: Tony Herbert, Darren Cummings, Danny Stubbs, Dave Park, Paul 'The Jewel' Ranson and Sue Roberts. As far as teammates, I was close to Gilko, Parky, Hamo, Barry Hunter and Carl Asaba.

I will never forget the night Barry was involved in a car crash at 1:00am, in Reading. He jumped into the passenger seat post-crash, awaiting the police who were on their way. When the Old Bill arrived and asked him who was driving the car, Barry, in his thick northern Irish accent replied, "the invisible man!" I thought that was hilarious but unfortunately the Judge did not and the big man was forced to hire himself a driver for a few years!

Not long after I separated from Kathryn, I began seeing a quite attractive woman, blonde, and married. A teammate who knew her introduced us. He told me she was getting divorced, and with only eyes for me, she was not going to let up until she met me!

Looking back now, I should have walked the other way the first time I ever laid eyes on her. Red flags were everywhere but like Lewis Hamilton, all I could see were chequered flags. Toxic and unhealthy, but when you're in it, you don't see it, can't see it, or maybe you're just stuck on stupid. After her visits to Madrid, while I was there with Beckham she quite fancied living in Spain with me. Of course she did! Eminem nailed it with 'Spend Some Time', written for women just like her.

Back to the football, Tommy Burns, the Celtic legend, was handed the reigns after Alan Pardew had been caretaker for a week. Burns arrived with a bus load of new players, mostly from Scotland and procured mostly through his own agent. Within a day he had sent Phil Parkinson and myself down to the reserves where we would be marooned for about six months. The message could not be clearer, there was a new sheriff in town and his first move would be banishing the club's captain and vice-captain to the stiffs in an attempt to make sure the rest of the monkeys toed the line.

After this, he called me in for a meeting and basically said, "you won't play under me Andy, I am really concerned about your knee, you're a good guy and I don't want you to end up a cripple." Translated into football language, that meant, "take a little lump sum, and off you go," freeing up a few hundred thousand pounds for new signings.

I flatly refused and expressed how much I wanted to play in the club's first game at the new Madejski Stadium. I like firsts I told him, and off he went fuming, steam coming from his head. For many months he continued to make life at the club uncomfortable for not only me, but also Parky and whiz kid James Lambert. It's standard procedure at all clubs when they want shot of a player, so it wasn't that Tommy was any better or worse than other managers, it was just the game, a horrible business at times.

What Burns didn't realise was that taking Parky and me out of the side would mean he would lose the team's heart and soul, similar to that of taking Sergio Ramos out of the Real Madrid side. It was more than just football and he should have known better after many years at Celtic, a team that pride themselves on that.

Parky and I played for the badge, the club, the fans, and they all rode shotgun. Seven months later Tommy was headed for the exit door. He had spent millions on mediocre players and staff, his pals, so surprisingly, he gave me the captain's armband for an away match at Bradford City in the League Cup. From the stiffs to a League Cup tie.

We won on aggregate, the night made even sweeter when I caught up with Socceroo Mark Schwarzer, who had just signed for Bradford, after another recommendation from me. Nobody was stopping the Royals that night although even in victory, Tommy Burns' fate had already been decided by the Board. The following day, the Chairman invited Phil Parkinson and myself to dinner at the Bina, the team's favourite restaurant. Tommy was going to be fired and as the senior professionals at the club, they wanted to let us know. What a funny old game, Tommy was on his way, but not before I played the first official game ever, at the Madejski Stadium under the manager who told me it would never happen!

There were many candidates for the soon to be vacant position mentioned that evening and I remember the Chairman telling us that they were thinking about Alan Pardew. Parky and I had been playing under Pardew in the reserves and the Chairman asked us if we approved of the appointment. Just like that Alan Pardew became the manager of Reading FC.

Pardew made me skipper of the side until I couldn't physically play anymore and retired from football. I can't speak highly enough of him as a manager and as a person whilst we were together at Reading. I followed his career from Australia as he went on to manage West Ham United, Charlton Athletic, Southampton, Newcastle United and Crystal Palace. For a while he was the next big thing, but it blew up for him as football tends to do for all of us somewhere, sometime. Who knows? Maybe an EPL resurrection awaits? Alan Pardew wasn't the first that this happened to, and he won't be the last, as a similar fate befell Mark McGhee.

Some great characters came and went in my time with the Royals. Four stand out: Allan Harris, Bobby Mikhailov, Mass Sarr, and the famous psychic Uri Geller. These men all became good friends and they all have their own wonderful life stories.

Allan was Bullivant's number 2 and the brother of legendary Chelsea enforcer Ron 'Chopper' Harris. He would turn up to training every day with a gold whistle, pure solid gold, a going away gift from the Barcelona players where he coached for a while as assistant to Terry Venables. He would tell us tales of his time in Spain with El Tel; fascinating stories that I loved as they took me back to my playing days in that country.

On one occasion, Allan and Terry went to visit the great Diego Maradona at his house in the hills of Barcelona where, as Allan recalls, "he had a chandelier hanging in the entrance hall, that was bigger than my entire house!" Upon entering the house, he saw Diego straight away, then another Diego, then another, loads of them, all Maradona clones, all wearing the same club tracksuit, all living off the king and racking up astronomical bills around the city. This was one of several reasons the great man transferred to Napoli.

Allan was regularly sent a box of Cuban cigars from Joan Gaspart the former President of Barcelona. Away at Leeds United in the Cup one year, after getting through to the next round with a win at Elland Road, the cigars were pulled out on the bus home. Allan called one of the apprentices over and pulled out a big box of Cuban cigars from his bag and said, "Give the boys one each. It's not often you come to Elland Road, a big club, with a big history and get a win. Enjoy the cigars lads, and thank you to Joan Gaspart, tonight will be a great story to tell the grandchildren."

In 1995 we signed Borislav 'Bobby' Mikhailov, a Bulgarian international goalkeeper with over a century of caps for his country. As part of the deal the club threw in an amazing house near the River Thames, not far from Uri Geller's place. Bobby was a great lad and on the few occasions we were injured together, he would tell the physio Paul Turner he was going home, taking me with him and we would do rehab there. This was a total piss-take of course. On arrival we would be greeted by his father Biser, also a Bulgarian international, and we would sit in a big lounge area where we would exchange stories. They had just bought the most expensive coffee machine on the European market that produced the finest coffee of choice. Bobby's dad would be on coffee duty while Bobby handed out the finest Cuban cigars along with a shot of the best Russian vodka.

Curious about his World Cup exploits, I once asked Bobby how his national team had prepared for their famous Quarter Final win against Germany at USA '94. He told me about how he, Hristo Stoichkov, Emil Kostadinov and Yordan Letchkov, three of Bulgaria's superstar key players at the time, went out to a nightclub the night before the match. Standing outside the hotel in New York waiting for a taxi at 10pm, they could see Head Coach, Dimitar Penev, heading straight for them.

"What did he say?" I asked. Bobby replied, "tell the taxi driver to wait, I'll get out of my tracksuit, I'm coming with you!" I think they got home about 4am, had some sleep, and the next day pulled off one of the greatest World Cup victories ever.

Bobby had a great attitude. If he played, he was happy. If he didn't, he would go to London and buy himself a £4,000 mink coat and come back even happier. Bobby went onto become President of the Bulgarian football association.

Mass Sarr, the Liberian international was a sensational player, a black Maradona, whom we had signed from Hajduk Split in Croatia. For some reason, after signing a lucrative deal he rarely showed up, just the occasional flash of brilliance. I am not sure he was happy living in Reading having grown up in Staten Island, New York surrounded by childhood friends, the rappers Wu-Tang Clan, and Liberian football legend George Weah, a winner of both the African and World Footballer of the Year awards.

I would spend many evenings with Mass in his apartment on the River Thames listening to all his New York gangster stories. He was a funny guy who drove Tommy Burns nuts. He had an answer for everything.

Two of his finest came in response to Tommy questioning him with regard to his high wages and poor work rate. Cool and calm, he first told Tommy that he was the dumbass that had rubber stamped the exorbitant wage he was picking up, and then he asked the Celtic legend if he had received the fax from Hajduk Split. Tommy, already angry and furious, said, "What fax are you talking about?" Mass replied, "The fax from the Split doctor telling you that I have small lungs so I cannot run too much". Tommy was left lost for words.

Over time, I became good friends with the psychic Uri Geller. He had an amazing house at Sonning-on-Thames, modelled on the White House in Washington DC. In his garage he kept a Rolls Royce, covered in bent spoons that he had twisted with his mind for the global superstars and celebrities who had come to visit. As well as the spoons there were watches that had stopped and other amazing artifacts that Uri had distorted, stopped, started or bent – all with his mind. He was good to me and made sure when my mum and Isabella were in England his house was their "casa" too, just like extended family. He had something special about him for sure, a charismatic and empowering man.

On one occasion he placed freezing crystals in Isabella's hand, and around 30 seconds later, almost in a panic, she released them unable to withstand their newfound heat. The crystals lay on the floor while Uri's eyes focused on them, creating an energy in the room that I can't put into words, but somehow empowered us all. He looked up at Izzy and said, "Darling, this event will bring you great luck and fortune in the future." He's on the money so far!

The King of Pop, Michael Jackson, would often be at Uri's. I even sat in his favourite chair on my visits. We always missed each other, and not by much, and Uri would be so upset. Maybe destiny had me down to write my own thriller!

By the end of my Reading days I was a physical wreck, the lifelong knee problem had impacted every other body part, and my only consolation was that I had played against all the teams I had watched on TV and read about in '*Shoot*' magazine growing up in Canberra, including Manchester United, Manchester City, Chelsea, Arsenal, Leeds United, Sunderland, Wolves, the list goes on.

Two memorable battles I will always remember, due to the quality of the opponent I was up against and the silly things players say in the heat of the battle.

Playing against Manchester United I had been given the task of marking Andy Cole, at the time one of England's most feared strikers. I had annoyed him so much that walking to the dressing rooms at half-time, he turned to me and said, "I'll have you shot!" Well, my dad was a military sniper, and I grew up shooting whatever moved, so I replied, "Let's have a gun fight," quickly adding, "Oh, that's right, you'll be getting someone else to do the shooting." Cole wasn't backing down and repeated his earlier threat before we both reached the dressing rooms. There was nothing in it, just football banter, we were both fired up, and that's the game I suppose. He was top-drawer, and it was an honour to have played against him.

Matt Le Tissier, the Southampton playmaker, was a genius, a talented player who I got the better of after being given the job of man-marking him in an FA Cup Round 3 tie played on a freezing cold night in Reading. In the build-up to the match, Jimmy Quinn informed me that he had a special job for me, man-marking Le Tissier. If I stopped Le Tissier playing, we would stop Southampton playing. I was excited, my mind went back to my debut for Albacete FC in Spain and Pachin's words ran through my head. "Stop the opposition ten and we are in the money," he told me. "I don't care how, and I don't want any excuses, full stop."

I had grown up playing a bit of schoolboy AFL where man-on-man assignments were key roles that would entertain punching, wrestling and anything else you could get away with. It was brilliant to watch and all part of the show, so that evening at Elm Park I introduced Matt Le Tissier to the game of AFL! He did nothing, and Southampton were out of the Cup.

Socceroo Robbie Slater was out of the match also. With little time left on the clock, he was sent off for foul and abusive language, frustrated after also having a quiet game. We really did wind them up, to the point that they were even complaining about the hardness of the pitch!

The legendary Saints Manager, ex-Liverpool legend and hard man Graeme Souness, was also sent off at the end, directing something my way that sounded very much like, "you dirty bastard," to which I replied, "I learned it all watching you, my man." Again, football banter in the heat of the moment. Souness was a fantastic player in his day and someone I modelled my game on.

A goal in a 4-2 FA Cup win over Yeovil Town in October 1999, put me in a special category and in a small group of Australians to have scored in a FA Cup tie.

There was also a memorable goal against my former club Ipswich Town, when I netted the winner at Portman Road. It is always special to score the winning goal against your old club, in front of your old fans.

My fourth goal was a winner as well, a strike that saw us knock Leyton Orient out of the Football League Trophy, but it is my first goal for Reading that gave me, and every Reading FC supporter on the planet, immeasurable joy. It was away to Leicester City, the club Mark McGhee had left us for, the man dubbed 'Judas' by the Reading faithful. He could never have imagined that the lad he dropped for the Watford away match months ago, had come back to spoil his party and would haunt him with a cracker goal. Mick Gooding played me a diagonal forward ball, with Zidane like precision which I met in full stride, hitting it sweetly with the outside of my foot, reminiscent of a Roberto Carlos special, the ball swerving from outside to inside beating the outstretched keeper and nestling in the bottom corner. Without even thinking I ran towards McGhee and made him fully aware, that karma was a bitch! My goals, as infrequent as they were, all mattered and as the saying goes, quality over quantity.

The lack of goals was counter-balanced with the constant accumulation and collection of cards, a compilation the local Reading casino would have been proud of. I'm sure my record still stands, a total of seven reds and 25 yellow cards in six seasons, making me the most heavily disciplined Royal ever!

And just like that it all came to an end. Away to Luton Town at Kenilworth Road, another ground I had dreamed of playing on as a kid, I picked up another injury and knew in my heart that I was done. The love was gone, it had gone a few years back to be fair, but you keep at it, earning more money and avoiding the unknown of the outside world that awaits you.

I asked to see Alan Pardew in his office on our day off to tell him I was going to retire. He said "let's meet in the middle of the pitch at Madejski." I am not sure why he said that, but I think maybe he knew too. My usual spark had disappeared, training and games had become a chore and a very painful one at that.

I cried out in the middle, let it all out. It felt spiritual, like being in an empty church, with only the football gods looking down on us. I didn't want to spend the rest of my life potentially crippled in a wheelchair with extreme pain tormenting me every minute of the day; I would settle for normal pain, that I had become very used to. I had achieved my childhood dreams and I was one step closer to returning to Australia and to Izzy.

Uncertain as to what the future would hold for me, a few friends had suggested that I might make a good player agent. I quite fancied the sound of that, so before I knew it, I was on board a train bound for London. I had a meeting with a gentleman by the name of Tony Stephens, who represented some of the biggest names in world football.

I had no idea how insane my life was about to become.

CHAPTER 7

SHOW ME THE MONEY

Arriving in Mayfair for my meeting at SFX, the names Michael Jordan, Kobe Bryant and David Beckham shone brightly as their global superstar clients. The swanky Grosvenor Street address reaffirmed their status in no uncertain terms. A friend of mine from Reading, Susan Roberts who was a bigwig at Fosters UK and who knew Tony Stephens well, had organised the meeting for me. I remember her telling me that he was a remarkably busy man, and I would get about five minutes to impress him and maybe have a shot at getting taken on to learn the trade, so I had better be prepared. So I prepared to be offered a job!

I had never had an agent myself. I wasn't a lawyer or a business and marketing expert, but I understood the most important thing you needed was world class elite clients and SFX had this in bundles. This talent created leverage when negotiating football contracts and brought in all the big corporates wanting to align themselves with superstar athletes. It's not rocket science.

Starting from the very bottom in sports management as I was, the most important quality one needed, was an eye to identify the best new talent. I was confident in my scouting ability and I knew a player when I saw one, as I had played with and against many of the best ever. All the necessary requirements I was looking for were familiar to me, they were part of my DNA. Spotting top level elite players when they are young and unknown is a special talent, an art form, which I believe you either have or you don't. Easy recruitment comes in the form of a first-choice draft pick out of college, or a David Beckham upon his graduation from the reserves to Manchester United first team, that's easy pickings!

First impressions were going to be crucial in this meeting, so I spruced up properly. I put on my best suit, making sure that I looked absolutely mint, stopping around the corner at Thomas Pink for a fresh tie to nail the look. I knew that I had to have some sort of hook to impress such an extremely successful business operator on a global scale, so I decided to go relatively simple and print out a map of the world. I put a name in every country that I could connect with, either directly or within a phone call or two. These names would assist me regarding the identification and recruitment of the best new talent available in that country.

I started with Diego Maradona in Argentina, Carlos Valderrama in Colombia, Julen Lopetegui in Spain, Bobby Mikhailov in Bulgaria, Darius Wdowczyk in Poland and Christian Vieri, the Australian-born Italian international in Italy, just to name a few. It was a list that would possibly raise questions in Tony's mind, like can he really connect with these legends? After all they were the biggest of the big, so how could I know them, he must have thought.

Strangely, he never did test me, like Cloughie never tested me. I was the real deal, and the scope and sheer quality of my network even more real.

At the bottom of the map, I had written the languages that I spoke fluently or had more than a good understanding of, including English, Spanish, Portuguese and Italian. Tony looked at it for a short while, looked up at me, and asked if I would like a coffee. "Flat white, no sugar," I replied.

I got an hour with Tony before he called the meeting to an end. When I told Susan later, she was stunned and suggested that I must have done something right. Damn right I had! I knew once I was in Tony's presence he would not let me go.

As I was leaving the office, I commented on a picture of the England star David Platt that was hanging on Tony's wall behind him. "Nice picture of Platty," I said.

He then began a mini monologue on how he had signed David, his first ever client when the midfielder was at Aston Villa, which led to Platt also playing for Juventus, Bari and Arsenal, at one time holding the world record for the largest amount of accumulated transfer fees. Tony asked me if I knew him and when I replied with a confident yep, I could see his brain ticking over, trying to place me on a football pitch with the former England skipper.

He would never have guessed, so I put him out of his misery. We had met in Jakarta, Indonesia, at the time Platt was captain of England and playing for his Italian club side Sampdoria. The Italians were playing a friendly against an Asian X1 that had been selected by Indonesian President Suharto. It was a powerhouse Italian line-up, featuring Platt and Roberto Mancini, the future Manchester City manager up front, in direct battle with yours truly, in front of a packed stadium of close to 100,000 spectators. After the match we had a few beers together at the Jakarta Hyatt. "So that's how I met your first client Mr Stephens," I told him.

At this point, I knew I would soon be learning the agent business under his astute and remarkably successful guidance. Soon after that meeting, Tony spoke with the Australian office and agreed on creating a football department out of Sydney.

A week later, back in Mayfair, Tony handed me my first mission. He had a few young agents under him but they couldn't recruit anyone of note as most of the talent they represented were hand-me-downs from either Tony himself or Jon Holmes. They had been trying to recruit a young Australian boy playing at Millwall who had been making a lot of noise. Before he could say another word, I told him I would get Tim Cahill for him. Stunned, he asked me how I knew he had meant Cahill, as his name hadn't been mentioned. I replied, "When you know you know, Tony."

The first time I saw Tim Cahill play was when I was playing for Reading FC and he was in the early stages of his Millwall career. He was on fire, an unstoppable force. He could run all day, blessed with incredible stamina like Beckham, Claude Makélélé, N'Golo Kanté and Roy Keane in that respect. He had good speed, not Ronaldo speed, but still fast, and his movement off the ball and unselfish running were incredible. A warrior of the highest order, with a fighting spirit akin to world champion boxers and UFC stars. He had the movement and balance of a black panther, ability to shoot off either foot, and was a supreme header of the ball with impeccable timing, power and precision. Comfortable high in the sky, like Michael Jordan, his hang time and 'no fear' DNA, created the deadliest header of a football on the planet.

The English lower divisions are tough to play in and tough to get out of, with every game a war between exceptionally good teams either looking for promotion to the EPL, or battling against the unthinkable, relegation. In this unforgiving environment, you either sink or swim, I know that myself.

Every ground you play at is a cauldron of fire, not for the faint hearted, and the playing surfaces can vary widely so you need world class focus. Tim thrived in this environment, bossing more seasoned midfielders, dominating games, and scoring goals – plenty of them. He had this God given ability, and a sixth sense, to get on the end of anything that was put in the box. It looked easy, because he made it look easy. For every goal, there were hundreds of unselfish runs, many of which came to nothing, something rarely picked up on TV but admired from the coaching dugout.

Tony Stephens was suitably impressed and brought up another name, another young Millwall player, Lucas Neill, but the company focus was firmly on Tim.

As I left, he said, "Let's aim to sign Tim within three months." I replied "perfect" and 24 hours later, I returned with both Tim and Lucas to the surprise of the whole Mayfair office.

Shortly after that, Tim Cahill would sign for SFX officially becoming my first client, but not before getting the blessing from his parents.

Tony would later ask how I managed to get Tim across the line. Easy. I spent a day at their family home. Tim's dad knew me from my days as skipper of Sydney Olympic, but importantly, we had mutual friends in Sydney who put us together. Tim's dad was great from the outset, with him it's black or white, no bullshit accepted, he reminds me so much of my dad. He didn't give a shit about all the SFX marketing spiel from London, he just said, "Andy, look after my boy" and we shook on it.

Not long after at Tim's 21st birthday party in Sydney, we rubber stamped the relationship Samoan style, with a huge pig cooked deep in a pit, while the drinks flowed all night long. It was a lovely evening, drinks flowing all night, the music too, amongst some of the most beautiful people I have ever met. For me, it was the icing on the cake after obtaining Tim's signature, and more importantly to me, the family's trust and faith.

Tim's star began to get bigger and bigger day by day. I told him that David Moyes, the manager of Everton, was keen on him and they were tracking him big time. "Keep doing what you're doing, make noise young man," I told him, and he made so much noise that Everton became a reality and the rest as they say is history.

Once Tim had signed for SFX the focus was to make him eligible to play for Australia as he had previously played for Samoa when he was a kid.

My specific job was bringing him to the attention of the Socceroo manager Frank Farina. I called Frank, as I had promised Tim. We had been teammates and good friends at the AIS, so the conversation was easy and as simple as, "I've just signed a kid called Tim Cahill. The Republic of Ireland are keen on him, so you need to put a Socceroo cap on him quick smart."

Frank didn't know much about Tim at this point, although he knew of him and asked me for more information. I said, "He's like your old Bari teammate David Platt, he's like Roy Keane, he's like 'Air' Jordan, he's all three rolled into one. A goal scoring machine who has the most amazing ability to get on the end of anything put into the box."

The last thing I said on that call to Frank was, "If you were going to war, would you take me?" Frank said, "Yes," so I told him, "Well, if I was going to war, I would take Tim Cahill."

It took a while because Frank and others in Australia had to deal with FIFA regulations due to Tim having played for Samoa as a 14-year-old, but Tim became a Socceroo in 2004 and the legend was born.

My second assignment for SFX was my first introduction into the murky, snake pit world of sports management. My orders were to try to steal Harry Kewell and Mark Viduka from their agent Bernie Mandic who, at the time, was the football agent for IMG.

Mandic was Australia's premier agent in those days and it was his deal that took Kewell from Leeds United to Liverpool, a transfer that caused much debate and left Leeds United globally embarrassed and short a few million quid.

The thing I respected most about Bernie was that he never once tried to steal or even tap up a player who I managed whilst they were under contract to me. If they had left me, or were free at the time, then it was open slather for all, and I reciprocated in the same way. I knew Harry was happy, so didn't even go near him. Viduka, however, had left Mandic and IMG after his transfer from Celtic to Leeds and had no agent, so why not give it a shot?

I drove to Leeds, met Mark for a pub lunch in the city and gave him the SFX Global Marketing spiel and our list of amazing clients. The big man listened, but I could tell he was not really interested, so the conversation went more towards talking about old football stories. I reminded him of a time in Brisbane on Socceroos duty when he was an 18-year-old kid, and how I told him he would one day play for one of the best clubs on the planet. He remembered and smiled.

The bottom line, he had left one giant marketing company and didn't want to jump into bed with another global giant. I respected his honesty and have a lot of time for Mark, a sensational player and a gentleman.

The London office came with many perks including daily free pasta meals at a local Italian, whose owner would never be short of tickets to Chelsea, Arsenal, or any match he wanted. Park Lane was up the road, the area graced by the finest shops, restaurants and exclusive bars in London.

When you walked into the SFX reception, you were immediately hit with glamour, the receptionists. You would then head upstairs to the football department where three young football agents would be working alongside roving global tennis agents, one of whom asked me to help him sign a 17-year-old Rafael Nadal. He offered me nada so he got nada.

I loved the area, the young agents not so much. They were everything I wasn't, and everything I didn't want to be. Football wannabes aiming to make themselves famous by their association with the footballers they represented. Without their clients they were nobodies, fan boys, and fake friendly. Always immaculately dressed and well spoken, their expensive flashy suits hiding the morals and ethics of humans that would sell their mother if it sealed a deal. The rules they lived by were:

1. We are here to f*** over clubs and make tons of money for us and the client.

2. Keep a straight face when a club signs a cheque for millions of pounds or whatever you've asked for as an agency fee, having done very little to earn it.

3. F*** the clubs, and not the mum's of the young guns that play for them!

4. No drugs.

The rules were regularly broken.

Unfortunately, for the young Jerry Maguires, the thing that they really wanted, was to be the athletes they represented, something that all the money in the world could not buy them.

An early introduction to the workings of the London team was a regular agency meeting held by Tony Stephens. One particular meeting he focused on David Platt and how, through making a scrapbook about him, he was able to create a platform to earn vast commercial sums for him. This scrapbook was old but in great condition. He treasured it, his prized possession and I have only ever seen two other scrapbooks of that level in my life: my mum's for me and my wife Jaynie's for her father, Australian motorsport legend, David Wignall.

The sheer volume of the material on David Platt was phenomenal, Tony's writing was neat and tidy, and everything glued in with perfect symmetry. You could tell it had been put together with love, he held it like a new born baby!

For the next hour, we heard about global partnerships, synergies, and alliances. If you were not into marketing, business administration and high-level corporate dealing, you'd either be totally dumbfounded, or you'd believe these guys were geniuses. Elitist, private school old boy university stuff, that I wasn't buying, but I made them believe I bought. I spent most of the meeting bored shitless, knowing that if you manage Michael Jordan or David Beckham everything comes to you and this lot were talking like they were putting men on the moon!

Despite the torturous meetings, the occasional story grabbed my attention, especially the one where Tony was explaining the fundamentals of negotiation techniques, bringing up an encounter with Sir Alex Ferguson at his home as a lesson in how to remain cool and calm under pressure. He was pretty happy with himself, telling the story with a cheeky smile, in the safety of the Mayfair office. I would have loved to have been with him that morning at Fergie's, but I'll recount the story as best I can.

It was early morning and Tony had a breakfast meeting locked in at Ferguson's house to let him know that he was now David's agent. It was not the best or the smartest thing you would want to be telling the Scotsman, as it reduced his control over the player. Ferguson wasn't a fan of agents, the one exception being one of his son's, and he was also prone to being combustible at times – Beckham's boot incident a prime example.

Ferguson's wife Cathy poured both Fergie and Tony a cup of tea, as Tony delivered the news. According to Tony, Fergie exploded. Seeing red he picked up his hot cup of tea and threw it directly at Tony's head, across the table only a few metres away, missing by millimetres and crashing thunderously into the wall behind him sending shards of teacup flying everywhere.

Tony told us he went pale, more than a little unnerved. He sat shaking but said nothing, just stared at the pot of tea in the middle of the table, the ensuing minutes an unbearable torturous silence which seemed like an eternity. Cathy meanwhile began picking up shattered pieces off the floor, with nobody saying boo, and Fergie's head looking more and more like the angry emoji.

Then, as if nothing had happened, Ferguson said to Cathy, "Well, we better pour Tony a fresh cup of tea."

Tony loved that story, stating he could easily have walked out, but by remaining calm and assured, he made certain that his relationship with Ferguson remained intact. His was a perfect example of how to react in difficult circumstances. I'm not sure I would have done the same. Fergie definitely deserved a return shot!

Part of my education was attending marketing events and the first one I was assigned to was to a Pepsi event in London, where my job for the day was to look after Dwight Yorke. Also at the event that day, was David Beckham and his wife Victoria. Our conversation was easy, and it felt like we were already connected somehow.

Teaming up with David Beckham now seems like it was written in the stars. So many parallels, so many mutual acquaintances and occurrences that led us both to Real Madrid. Of course, the fact that I had played in Spain many years before and spoke the language fluently was important and made everything fall into place, but our link was already in play upstairs somewhere, and it came in the form of the greatest selling football boot of all time.

I had previously read Gary Neville's column with '*Sports Mail*' in 2013 in which he recalled Beckham's love affair with Adidas. Neville revealed that shortly after he made his Manchester United debut at the age of 19, he received a pair of Predator boots to test alongside David Beckham, Keith Gillespie and Gary's brother Phil while in the United States. They were a new design that had ridges for extra grip on the leather and after David asked if he could try them out, Gary Neville never saw them again! On the trip David would spend every minute he could practicing with the boots, whipping those famous free kicks under the crossbar and into the top corners. He wanted the boots' new technology benefits to enhance precision ball delivery in his performance and soon after, he signed up for Adidas, because they were the company that made the boots. Over the years, alongside Zidane, both have played a key role in the promotion of the greatest football boot in the history of the game.

The boot Beckham fell in love with in 1994 was first tested a decade earlier in 1984, by a kid called Andy Bernal, at the time captain of the Young Socceroos and the Australian Institute of Sport football team. Craig Johnston, the Liverpool legend, was training in Canberra with us, and wanted a few of the boys to test his invention. A boot with fins and grooves, that gave the ball a spin, slice, draw and power that had never been seen before. His idea was formulated while playing table tennis and seeing how the rubber on those bats created special movement and effects on the ball. He took it to Adidas and the rest is history. An incredible coincidence of fate.

Back to the Pepsi marketing event and my job for the day looking after Yorkie. I had already partied with him on Harry Michaels' boat in Sydney Harbour so we had a laugh reminiscing. In between the filming, I chatted to Becks for a while, just casual stuff about mutual friends we had in the game. When both the boys were out doing their stuff for the camera, I sat with Victoria and talked about the Spice Girls. It was important; you never know when you might run into Baby Spice, so a man needed to be prepared!

Not long after this, I travelled to Spain and caught up with Emilio Butragueño and Jorge Valdano at Real Madrid and gave them the names of Beckham, Michael Owen, and Jonathan Woodgate. All three were on the SFX roster and all three ended up in the white of Real Madrid. Beckham was the most successful Blanco of the trio on and off the pitch, Owen was a fantastic finisher with speed to burn, and Woodgate was top notch too, but the latter two were not Galácticos, not the elite of the elite like Ronaldo Nazario and Ramos in their respective positions. Owen and Woodgate never quite won over the fans in Madrid. Unfortunately for Woodgate, he was not helped by injury, but both never really integrated properly into the Spanish lifestyle and culture, something that I helped Beckham with, ending in a special lifelong friendship with Ronaldo and Roberto Carlos for him.

As part of my Australian mandate, one fantastic role was to build relationships with clubs in Italy and Spain. My great mate and rugby league agent Darryl Mather, who at the time was also one of my Australian bosses, organised a trip for both of us around two of the most beautiful countries you could ever see. First Italy, landing in Milan and from there travelling by car with a plan to meet up with the Directors of Football of all the major clubs in whichever city we ended up in. What a trip – seeing amazing places like Lago di Como, Milan, Costa Amalfi, Ravello, Positano, all the way to Naples, and trying not to get mugged or robbed in Diego's city, and ending up in Rome.

Leaving Positano for Naples, Darryl asked the concierge how long it would take us to drive to Naples. "It depends what macina you drive? Fiat or Ferrari?" Clever answer. Darryl cracked up and followed with another, this time about the great Diego Maradona as we were headed to Naples. "What does Diego signify to the people of Naples, of Argentina, to most of the football world?" Without even thinking or batting an eyelid the young man turned around, pointed to a painting of Jesus Christ on the wall, then standing on a chair, he pointed above the Jesus painting and said "That's where Diego sits, "he is God." Daryl smiled, I knew it had touched him. Later in the car, with less restraint, we couldn't stop laughing wondering where his rugby league guns would sit on that wall!

We turned off the main road at a sign that said Assisi. I was a bit slow on the uptake and didn't make the connection until we approached a mountain with a town built into its side. The mountain was in the middle of a flatter plain that seemed to go on forever. As we climbed the road to the top, all I could see were monks everywhere, like ants going in and out of mountain holes and tunnels. It suddenly dawned on me that I was at the birthplace of St Francis of Assisi.

An amazing place that boasted a monastery where Franciscan monks are educated. At the top was a beautiful church surrounded by an amazing silence, interrupted only by the noise of birds chirping. It was incredible, the most peaceful place I have ever set foot on and so spiritually enlightening. The world of sport takes you to the most beautiful spots on the planet. How can you not be involved?

From Rome we went to Spain and more beauty lay ahead. Landing in Madrid we first visited Atlético Madrid then headed north-west towards the Spanish/ Portuguese border and a beautiful fishing village called O Grove for a night before heading to the stunning province of Galicia, where I was able to show Darryl two stadiums that I had played in, Riazor, the home of Deportivo de La Coruña and Balaídos, Celta Vigo's stadium. We moved to Gijón, the club I first signed for in Spain and then dropped into Real Sociedad's training headquarters, in the beautiful city of San Sebastian, the hometown of my friend, Julen Lopetegui.

While travelling around Spain, the Beckham transfer out of Manchester United was in motion, and I would receive regular updates from Tony Stephens. He called me in San Sebastian knowing that the following day, I would be arriving in Barcelona for a meeting with Carlos Rexach the Director of Football of Barcelona at the Camp Nou.

In Barcelona, and with instructions from Tony noted, Darryl and I headed for Camp Nou, with Beckham obviously a key discussion point. After exchanging pleasantries and a few mutual Ipswich Town stories, Carlos was straight to the point, asking if we had agreed a deal for David to join Real. Without hesitation I replied no, despite knowing that David had set his heart on joining 'Los Blancos'. However, at this point in time there was no official deal between the two clubs.

This piqued Carlos' interest of course and he took us out through a concealed door into the Presidential Box overlooking the magnificent stadium. "The fans would love David here at Barcelona," he said.

The words barely registered, I was so captivated by the playing surface that had been graced by my all-time favourite Diego Maradona. What I did know, was that Carlos would immediately be on the phone to Joan Laporta when we left.

Laporta had based his Presidential campaign on signing the superstar Beckham, and not long after my conversation with Rexach that day, Barcelona agreed to pay 35 million Euros to United for the acquisition of the England captain, Unfortunately for Barcelona, David was only interested in becoming a Galactico at Real Madrid, which soon after became a reality. Barcelona immediately fired back, signing a Brazilian freak called Ronaldinho !

Darryl and I continued our journey to Valencia, Sevilla, then into Portugal where we ended up staying for one week at a beautiful resort called Playa da Luz – now, sadly, forever linked to the disappearance of Madeleine McCann.

And that was that. We returned to Australia. Darryl had rugby league business to attend to, but I would soon be heading back to Spain for the most insane ride of my life.

CHAPTER 8

RIDING SHOTGUN

It is difficult to express exactly what the next three-to-four months of my life were like. The most amazing, unbelievable, incredible ride I have ever been on, riding shotgun with the biggest superstar on the planet.

With an ever changing dynamic, I quickly learnt to expect the unexpected at any given time, improvisation skills a must, with fearless but calculated professionalism, under some of the most extreme pressure situations life can throw at a human. All this, while overseeing two of the finest commando and intelligence units in the world, and hanging out with the greatest footballers on the planet, including Brazilian superstars, Ronaldo and Roberto Carlos. The sort of lifestyle you only see in movies: fast cars, glamorous women, A-list celebrities and Europe's biggest mob bosses.

During all of this, I was caught in the middle of a power struggle between two entertainment giants, SFX and Simon Fuller's 19 Entertainment, all while watching Real Madrid play live, sitting touchline watching them train, and soaking in the everyday operation of a football goliath, FIFA's club of the century. Topping it all off, the dangerous and sometimes near deadly, daily adventures with the paparazzi.

In all this initial Madrid madness, I found solace watching Real's training sessions, ingesting top level football knowledge with Brooklyn 'Buster' Beckham by my side, watching the best five-a-sides you could possibly imagine with the greatest players on the planet making it look so easy. I was after all a footballer turned agent, who had been thrown the keys to the £300 million Beckham empire. My comfort zone and happy place was right here with the lads.

After the presentation of David to the world at the media conference, we settled into the beautiful and exquisite Santo Mauro boutique hotel, in the middle of Madrid for the first three months. Maria Luisa was the Hotel Manager, and from day one was magnificent with us all.

I got on well with her, constantly touching base, either early morning or late in the evening, making sure we all were on the same page regarding the upcoming daily schedule. The ultimate professional, she was always caring and attentive, and did her best to ensure that David and Victoria were happy and adjusting to their new life in Madrid.

On the rare occasion I was not at the hotel, she would let me know everything going on. Nothing got past her and if she thought it was not right, she was straight onto me. She even hooked me up with a date, a lovely young lady who just happened to be the daughter of the former Mexican President, Vicente Fox.

Our suites were top drawer, reserved for the likes of Al Pacino and Robert De Niro when they were in town. Such was the prestige of this hotel, the week before we arrived it was home to Carlos Slim the world's richest man at the time. I scored the Pacino suite and the De Niro suite, a little larger, was the perfect fit for David, Victoria, and the two boys.

Logistically it was both good and bad as we were close to the Bernabéu, ten minutes to the current training ground, and only half an hour to the new training complex, but its city centre location also encaged us, making us easy targets for the hunting paparazzi. With everything that we required within a short distance, life should and could have been a series of easy trips, but to our horror, it was the exact opposite.

Every trip, every outing was much harder than it may have appeared from the outside, as even the simple task of driving to La Ciudad Deportiva, the club's training venue, was a Herculean operation. On top of this and worryingly for all, we would receive information from the British foreign intelligence service MI6 that the Beckham boys, Brooklyn and Romeo, were potential kidnap targets by the same group that had kidnapped my friend 'Quini' the Sporting Gijón, Barcelona and Spanish national team goal machine.

The first day of training at a new club is always a nerve-wracking experience even for the most expensive football transfer in the world at the time. The night before I had ordered coffee, toast and a fruit platter for breakfast in David's room before heading to training.

I had already made the journey once that morning with two commandos on a test run and all was good to go. I walked into David's room, and he and Victoria were still in bed. "Wakey wakey," I said followed by "I need to borrow your husband for the morning."

As we finished breakfast, Victoria appeared and gave David a good luck kiss and we were off down the fire escape exit where Merrick was already waiting for us and in game mode. This was serious business now like a 'Seal Team 6' mission he was mentally and physically locked in, which transferred to the rest of us. Vehicle inspections had been done, ranging from the basic mechanical checks through to car bomb checks. Emergency escape routes noted, and Spanish tactical response group direct numbers loaded onto our phones.

David liked driving most of the time, so I rode shotgun giving instructions and directions much like a co-driver in a rally car. Behind us a security vehicle and later, when necessary, in front as well. The route was complicated as central Madrid is a myriad of narrow one-way streets. Add traffic congestion and paparazzi and it left no room for navigational or driver error.

It was like a military operation and it would continue every day with no let up. Everybody in our security detail knew their place and their role; the goal was always to arrive at our destination with the safety of the family the number one priority, while trying to be as invisible as possible.

Engine purring, we got the green light, and we were off, heading for Beckham's first training session with Real Madrid. The paparazzi had been lying in wait all night, like snipers at the ready only with cameras instead of guns. A picture of David could fetch from as little as 1,000 euros to 100,000 Euros depending on the importance of the occasion. A deadly car crash picture, well that was a 'name your price' shot, and from their radio chatter we listened into, you sometimes got the feeling it was something they almost lusted for.

The car park at the Santo Mauro was underneath the hotel. A steep incline and a sharp left turn onto a busy one-way narrow street in Madrid was the only entry and exit point. Up the ramp you went at speed, as the hotel security blocked oncoming traffic. Because we knew the hotel staff would block the road, we never looked right upon exiting the ramp, our focus was exiting with speed in order to get some yards on the chasing pack, something that would later come back to haunt us with a bang!

Like two nervous kids on their first day off to a new school, we sped up the ramp getting good exit speed, turning left sharply, the rear wheels of the Porsche drifting a little before straightening up, only to be welcomed to the Madrid jungle by hundreds of paparazzi. Like a James Bond movie, it was lights, cameras and plenty of action as we attempted to lose the unlosable. If you lost one paparazzi, more would appear, like playing Fortnite! You could see in their faces, in their eyes, that they enjoyed this theatre, a high stakes, adrenaline fuelled game of cat and mouse, and we were the mouse! Exciting stuff for sure, but I was also experiencing first-hand how close superstardom was to post mortem.

We arrived at the training ground gate, went through security and immediately David pulled over, opened his door and vomited. I am not sure why, maybe a product of first day nerves, the car chase or both. What I can tell you is once we parked and got out of the car, I felt like I had been on the most insane roller coaster ride at Disney World. Surely it would not be like this every day?

Becks was a genuine superstar, but he was about to meet his new teammates who were also world superstars, and he couldn't speak any Spanish, Portuguese or French, which can be difficult, uncomfortable and even a little scary outside of football, let alone inside the Real Madrid dressing room.

He had 'Hola' in his vocabulary but not much else, but I reassured him. "You're the England captain," I said. "You are a Galactico too and belong in there with them." It wasn't much, but it helped and made him feel more at ease. "You need anything, and I'm just outside the dressing room," I told him.

He smiled and through the door he went. He had nothing to worry about as I had caught up for dinner the evening before with Julen Lopetegui at the restaurant he co-owned with former Real President Lorenzo Sanz. Julen had already made sure that Real's big guns – Raul, Iker Casillas, Zinedine Zidane, Figo and the boys from Brazil – would make David feel at home.

After training, I prepared the car for the return leg to the hotel and again, the paparazzi lay in wait, strategically placed around the Ciudad Deportiva, only now they had grown in number. I had a suspicion this fast and furious business was not going away anytime soon.

Before starting the car and exiting into the real world David mentioned that he had struck up an instant connection with Ronaldo, which he was happy about. He showed me a text he had sent his close friend and former Manchester United teammate Gary Neville, telling him about his five-a-side team that included himself, Ronaldo, Zidane, Raul, and Roberto Carlos. Minutes later Neville replied with words to the effect of "raining and miserable in Manchester." We had a little chuckle, as the sun shone brightly through a blue sky on a beautiful summer day in the Spanish capital. As far as football went, it was a good first day and he was chuffed that the dressing room had warmed to him.

One of the great things about football is the dressing room banter, and even the super professionals enjoy a joke or two. Former Liverpool star Steve McManaman, who was on his way out of Real Madrid, but always a prize joker, decided to have a laugh at Beckham's expense and had me in on it.

Real Madrid were off on a pre-season tour and would be leaving for the airport from training, which would be David's first bus trip with the team. On our way to the Ciudad Deportiva, we discussed where he was going to sit on the bus, it's a football thing, and the last thing you want to do is sit in the seat of an established player let alone a superstar seat.

At Manchester United he had his seat, earned over the years, and nobody sat in it, but this was a new club, a new bus, a new hierarchy, and a new seat, but which one would he sit in was the million dollar question? He was the new boy and I told him that he would probably end up at the back, next to the toilet – the worst seat in the bus!

We got there early and as usual I made sure all his boots and travel items were safely with the kit man. As always, a pair of new boots for every game. Macca was there early as well, he was looking forward to this little party trick. David got on the bus and sat down in one of the empty seats closer to the front, with Macca immediately in his dry Scouse accent saying "That's Zidane's seat!" Becks moved, but now he was in Ronaldo's seat. Okay, moved again, nope, that's where Roberto Carlos sits, that's Luis Figo's, that's Raul's, Macca continuing the torture until Real Madrid's new superstar signing found an empty seat next to the toilet! Beckham called me from the bus and said, "You were right," I said, "Yep I can see you from the car". It was a funny moment, and it was good to see that not even the world's most famous sports star was safe from the team bus equaliser!

While he was away, Victoria and the boys would head back to England. It was a good opportunity to bolster security. We needed more soldiers, special ones, as away from the sanctuary of the hotel and Real Madrid facilities, it was like a war zone, not pleasant at all for David and the family. The unscrupulous ones amongst the paparazzi had no ethics, adhered to no laws and nobody, not even the children, were out of bounds. We would find this out first-hand after a terrifying car chase with Brooklyn in the car, just days before the team's departure to Asia.

Heading to an afternoon training session at the Ciudad Deportiva, we were immediately followed with motorbikes coming from everywhere, their excitement heightened by a smaller figure in the backseat of the Porsche. The darkened windows made it difficult to see exactly who it was which only served to excite them more. With big dollars and lives at stake, Merrick in the vehicle behind us was doing his best to slow the motorbikes down, but to no avail. If you looked to the right, motorbikes, same on the left, and so close to our car that at times that their camera lenses would strike the windows, all this at speeds anywhere from close to 150km to 200km per hour on a busy motorway. This lot were so out of order, with possible death one mistake away. The extremes of danger they would go to was incomprehensible, scary stuff for adults, let alone a child. The poor kid was terrified.

Arriving at the training ground, Brooklyn was inconsolable asking why they were chasing us. David was upset too, it impacted him like never before. He was angry, because they were now messing with his boy! Tough for a dad, what do you say? He said it pretty good, nailed it actually: "It's okay Buster, daddy's here, and you're safe, they're chasing us because they want a picture of you, beautiful boy."

We parked and David reluctantly went to training, while I figured out how to erase the horror of the last 20 minutes imprinted in Brooklyn's head. I quickly grabbed a ball from the kitman and before you knew it Brooklyn and I were having a kick about behind the goal where the Galácticos were doing set pieces. Not sure if it was me or the kid, but one stray pass landed in the middle of their session, with Carlos Queiroz looking over unimpressed. Roberto Carlos diffused the situation sending the ball back from 30 metres straight onto my chest, at the speed of light with Brazilian swerve and I didn't have to move an inch! At this point, the car chase was a distant memory.

Madrid was full of stars everywhere you went, everywhere you looked, especially if you were in the right crowd.

By chance one evening, I ran into the actress Ana Obregón, a genuine Spanish movie superstar. I had seen plenty of her movies and read about her in magazines at home in Australia. After meeting her, the first thing I did was call my mum on my phone, but with Ana speaking! Mum loves Ana, so you can imagine her surprise when Ana called her, and then months later met her at her house, after the superstar graciously invited mum, dad, Isabella and myself to dinner. Can you believe, Spain's most loved celebrity was now my bestie?

Ana is a beautiful woman, who grew up next door to Julio Iglesias, babysat young Enrique Iglesias, and was best friends with Antonio Banderas. Her family owned a big share of the hotel we were in and she said, "Andy, if you need any help, you know where to find me."

Chill time for me while DB was on tour, and I was able to let my hair down a little and enjoy a semblance of some normality. Lovely dinners with two close mates, Julen Lopetegui and my friend Moli, a football agent and horse racing identity, became a frequent event at the restaurant Julen owned with former Real president Lorenzo Sanz.

It was after one of these dinners that Moli took me to a bar where I was introduced as Beckham's manager to all, including three Presidents of La Liga clubs. This place, not far from Real's Stadium was a top drawer gentleman's club. Part nightclub, strip club, as good as you would find in Las Vegas and full of unbelievably attractive women. Russians, Czechs, Polish and Swedish beauties were everywhere with a sprinkling from Spain, Colombia and who knows where else. This was glamour city full of hot tamales, all wearing next to nothing, while taking turns dancing on strategically placed poles.

The drinks were on the house. Why? Beckham! Too easy, so I opened the innings with my favourite Jack Daniels and Coke, then sat quietly observing how this zoo operated. Next to me, Moli and the Presidents discussed possible transfers of great international players between the biggest La Liga clubs, while drinking their whiskey straight and puffing on Cuban cigars. Unsurprisingly, once the ladies found out I was Beckham's man, it was game over and we were still in the warm-up phase. Many of these beautiful ladies not only danced but doubled up as porn stars, and in their quest to meet the Real players, well, let's just say they would do anything to make it happen.

I left the club that evening just after midnight, which is an early night in Spain. It had been a good night for me, I had won over three La Liga Presidents, made some new friends and was handed a few new phone numbers, which later that evening would produce a memorable private party.

When Merrick returned from England just prior to David coming back from Asia, he mentioned that the new security additions needed to be top-quality and, preferably Spanish or Spanish speaking. They must know all the streets in Madrid, the whole city, powers-that-be from the very top to the dark alleyways and bars. I had been busy entertaining some of my new friends, but not to the extent that I had forgotten the gesture made by Ana Obregón, so I told Merrick that I might just have the man he was looking for. I was going to a bullfight with Ana and the Obregón family's most trusted security guard the following day, so I would check him out.

Enter Delfín Fernández, aka Agent Otto, a former spy who spent 15 years working for Cuban counter-intelligence. He defected from Cuba and moved to

Spain in 1999 becoming one of Europe's most successful bodyguards. As well as Ana Obregón, among his clients were the actors Antonio Banderas and his then wife Melanie Griffith, Esther Cañadas, Spice Girl Emma Bunton, and bullfighter Francisco Rivera Ordóñez. As part of Fidel and Raúl Castro's inner circle, Fernández created dossiers of foreign politicians, businessmen and celebrities. He would show me his methods, fascinating they were, his speciality was disarming hotel security and video surveillance systems.

The day of the bullfight, I was picked up in a black Mercedes limousine, the latest model with Delfin riding shotgun, and his sergeant of arms, Arsenio, driving. Ana sat in the back, looking glamorous and amazing as always. I jumped in next to her to an awaiting glass of champagne. Happy days! I was doing Spain in style and there was a real buzz of excitement in the car as we were off to watch her friend, the matador, Francisco Rivera Ordóñez.

I had watched this spectacle as a kid in Australia on a video, but I had never been to a live bullfight. There I was, sitting in the front row, as Francisco put on a show. His father, the legend Paquirri, had years earlier been killed by a bull in the ring, and it resonated with me a lot. Big balls were needed; this was a deadly game reinforced by the knowledge that it was certain death for the bull and sometimes for the matador.

Front row at the Plaza de Toros, the best seats in the house with Ana and Delfin. I was excited and intrigued by both the bullfight and Delfin's stories of the Cuban Revolution. His father had been one of Fidel's generals alongside, Raul Castro, and Che Guevara. It was a memorable day that I will never forget, and even better after meeting up with Francisco for a few drinks together.

Delfin felt like the right man for the job, he knew all the right people and had two trained killers, also from Cuba, with him. Arsenio was his right hand man and then there was also Leif, a young Cuban American Marine who had escaped Cuba landing in Miami with the promise of US citizenship. It came with a price, he would have to serve and did so with distinction, his tank division one of the first to enter Baghdad in the first Gulf War.

Our Spanish intelligence was supposed to come from Real Madrid's own security team, but that only came for club specific business, not everyday life, so we relied heavily on UK intelligence and underground information. The Cubans would be great help, but unknown to all, my cousin who lives in Madrid was a senior undercover operative in Spain's elite anti-terrorist squad so he was a more than handy contact to have.

Matchdays at the Bernabéu were special. We sat in a fantastic box with the finest of everything Spain had to offer, the jamon and a wine selection to die for. I was familiar with the surroundings and the working mechanisms of the stadium, as years earlier I had played here, and a year before arriving with Beckham I had watched 'El Clásico', Real Madrid vs Barcelona, as a guest of Vicente Del Bosque. On top of that, Valdano and I would chat football and life on many occasions while walking around this imperious theatre, in a way it felt like home.

One minute at the football and the next in a nightclub, surrounded by girls, girls and more girls. It was the power of football superstardom, but you had to be very careful of who you allowed into the inner circle. Some girls, such as models and porn stars, know the deal. Some girls just want a picture, say hello and maybe get a kiss, while others want more, the whole nine yards and a box of chocolates too. But the most dangerous is the one looking for a bit of personal fame, chasing some big dollars on the side for selling a story or blackmailing a player.

When Delfin Fernandez came on board, he quickly taught me the art of strip-searching women and confiscating their mobile phones so they could not film or record any type of interlude. The first time I did this was for a famous movie star client of Delfin's. He said it was my practical exam! The young lady, a superstar model, came into a prepared room, and began undressing, beginning with her shoes, working upwards, until fully naked and standing right in front of me. She then handed me her phone and bag and said, "you like what you see?". "Very much," I replied but remained as professional as could be. I knew that she knew I was with Beckham and she was clearly already working on me, with a little of that 'impress to progress' shit.

One free evening, Delfin took me to his house to meet his wife, and while there, showed me his small arsenal of weapons, including Uzi machine guns and a nice selection of Glocks. Choosing a few, he placed them in a sports bag, adding ammunition, then handed it to me, and off we went to a friend's property to shoot anything that moved. It reminded me of my childhood and times with dad. He dropped me off at the hotel late that night, smelling of gunpowder and I couldn't wait to do it again.

To add to the cache of weapons, he also had police trackers, police sirens and flashing lights that he would use leaving the Bernabéu stadium after matches.

He would put the light on top of the car roof, just outside his driver's window. Blue light flashing, sometimes with the siren on, and 80,000 spectators leaving the stadium would part, like Moses parting the Red Sea. He wasn't a gym guy, and on the occasions he would see me headed that way he'd say, "Andy, you got it all wrong." He would then open up his suit jacket and show me a weapon "Andy, that's my gym."

The influx of international visitors and friends was building and along with this came partying and guests requesting a little more than just alcohol. Who to call? Delfin, of course, and before you knew it, there was more green and white than you would ever see at Celtic Park for an Old Firm derby. So off we headed to a palatial home outside of Madrid. On arrival, we were greeted at the gates by armed guards, one of whom patted me down. Once deemed safe, I was embraced and hugged by the head of a drug cartel, who said "Welcome to the family". Once inside the house, a maid brought out a sports bag, which contained the finest purple haze and pure blow that money could buy. I was cashed-up but they would not allow me to buy.

I dropped off the consignment, but not before grabbing an O for a rainy day when this Beckham lunacy was over.

The connection via Delfin would expand and before long I was having dinner with all the European crime families based in Spain. It didn't take long before we all became friends and anything I wanted, anything I needed, they were there for me. Once you are in with this crew, then its proper in, like family, so when my parents were visiting with Isabella, we ended up at Planet Hollywood attending a birthday bash for one of the children of the Russian boss. We had a few introductory drinks at the bar and by the time we hit the table for dinner, dad had already won them over, recounting to all the group his sugar cane, crocodile hunting and street fighting stories. They were fascinated but I was not surprised as my dad told a great story, sang a great song and in Planet Hollywood Madrid that day, he had Europe's top cartel and mafia bosses eating out of the palm of his hand.

On the other extreme, we would have important dignitaries visit Real Madrid, and of course the club's marketing team had the Galácticos meet and greet them.

After one match, President Florez introduced me to the Sultan of Brunei's nephew and nieces who wanted to meet David Beckham after already meeting Luis Figo. We invited them back to our hotel and as was standard procedure

I went upstairs to grab a marker pen and five Beckham shirts, and low and behold within ten minutes we had a Royal Brunei 5-a-side team all decked out in Real Madrid white 23s.

Before the Sultan's family returned to Brunei, David wanted them to leave with a gift, so Delfin and I took him to a jeweller where he picked out a couple of watches. I can't exactly remember the price, but it was around 200,000 Euros. The owner asked me what I wanted, and after looking at most of the prices I told him I was okay. He said, "I want to give you a gift for bringing David." He asked what brand I liked, and I told him I had seen a few Breitling's that I quite fancied. He pointed me to the Breitling display where my eyes locked onto an absolute beauty. I asked if I could try it on, and he delicately put it on my wrist. It was heavy and the price even heavier, but he knew I loved it, gave me a hug and said, "It's yours. Enjoy it."

My mother-in-law, Eileen, recently took it in for a service and came back shocked at the price of the service and more so the watch. I told her to triple or quadruple that price as it came as part of a Beckham Royal Brunei deal. I think she's still coming to grips with all these stories, and thinks I'm mad!

Trips to the military airbase were exciting and plentiful with my VIP Real Madrid pass giving me access to Spain's' most important Air Force military installation, just another example of the daily insanity I was now living. This was where the private jets came and went, with its very own small airport and Customs facility. On a regular basis it was my job to assist with the arrival documentation and the pick-up of the Beckham family and many of their close circle, including world famous designers, rock stars, actors and film producers.

One time, and not part of my SFX mandate, I was asked a favour by another footballer to do the same thing for an international flight carrying a small group of American porn stars. So there I was standing at the bottom of the stairs waiting to greet a selection of Pornhub's finest, the top ranked ones at that. I was quite sure that this never featured in my job description!

I will never forget the day David and I were on the tarmac awaiting a private jet from England, with Victoria on it, a day after nightclub images appeared in the tabloids, images that cleverly cut me out and left only two people in the photos! Kind of funny now, but not at the time. There we were in the front seats of the Range Rover as the jet taxied to a final halt. The jet door opened and Victoria began walking down the stairs. Oh boy, if looks could kill, and as she placed her first high heel shoe on the tarmac, that was my cue to jump out and head for safety in the commandos' vehicle not far away. My parting words to David were "All the best son."

David loves his cars and the arrival from England of an immaculate, powerful Aston Martin DB5, that looked straight out of a James Bond movie, got us both excited. It was a stunning convertible, and we agreed its first run would be to Real's new training ground the next day. Nursing it into the official car park, it caught the attention of all the lads. The engine noise was sexy but dulled a little by the steam whistle from under the bonnet which was not so sexy. I was looking forward to watching training that day, but now it appeared as if I would be getting this car fixed. Not the job you give to someone who knows absolutely nothing about car engines!

But hey, fake it until you make it, so I popped the bonnet confidently and pretended that I knew what I was looking for. Sensing my uselessness, Raul's security guard sauntered over and took over, relaying that the radiator hose had a slit in it. "Great," I said. "Where in Spain can I get a hose on a Sunday for a 1960s English car?" He laughed and said, "don't worry, we can fix it," and off he went returning with the Real Madrid physio carrying his bag of tricks, the same one he would use on weekends, when a player went down at the Bernabéu. Pulling out his best roll of ankle tape, he strapped the hose with the same precision and care given to a Galactico's ankle. A quick fix that allowed us to limp the car back down the highway, to a Jaguar dealership who did the rest. What a commercial that would make!

On reflection, we were never far from death, and on one family outing I was not far off from the angels taking me upstairs. Romeo's birthday at the Hard Rock Café ended up with only family and friends inside, and every window boarded up with cardboard so photographers couldn't see inside the place. The trouble it took to get there was ridiculous and life impacting for me. The kid's birthday had generated a global media frenzy, so we hatched a plan of escape from the hotel. I would drive the lead car, wearing a blonde wig to make me look like David, with Victoria's sister Louise Adams playing the role of Posh Spice! We had done it before and the paparazzi had fallen for it, following us and allowing the rest of the convoy to head off in peace to their destination.

We used our normal daily exit procedure, up the ramp, hotel security blocking the oncoming traffic, and out speedily to the left, again drifting onto the busy main thoroughfare. It had become such a habit that we would simply turn left without looking, knowing that the paparazzi would be right behind us.

As fate would have it, that evening hotel security were so focused on the motorcade coming up the ramp and carrying the birthday boy, Romeo, that they failed to block the road at the garage exit point. I drove the Porsche out like I was leaving the pits at Daytona, sliding the back out, then and sudden BANG, a loud reverberating noise like a roadside bomb stopped the world for a moment in time. Panic and shock ensued, disaster had struck almost as if the wishes of some of the paparazzi had come true. We had been hit at high speed, on the passenger side, crushing the car's front panels and bonnet. All I recall was my head rebounding onto the window near my temple, and then my world went black. I am not sure of the exact timing, but I came to not long after, the car covered in humans. I opened my eyes to the paparazzi and the flashing lights from their cameras. I later wondered if these same flashes were the last thing Princess Diana saw.

I looked to my right and Louise was saying nothing. She looked dazed and scared, and to be honest, I was too. The car was still running but it had humans all over it, their lenses flashing constantly, hoping to capture something horrific that would bring them big money. I felt sick, like vomiting, but my survival instinct put the car in reverse, and I managed to half drive and half slide it back towards the garage we had come out of. From this point, we were pulled out of the car and dragged to safety by the commandos.

An hour later, I dusted myself off and went back to making sure Romeo's birthday went ahead as planned, aided by Merrick's words, "You'll be right, mate, it's just a scratch." I had to keep rolling despite a headache that wasn't going away anytime soon. Back at the hotel that evening, I couldn't sleep trying to process what I had just lived through. I did chuckle to myself as I recalled that shortly after being dragged to safety, the attending Civil Guards asked to see my driver's license, looking very perplexed when I handed them an expired Australian one! Before they said anything else, I said, "It's Beckham's car." A couple of signed shirts later and I was no longer required. As for the car, well I called Porsche Madrid, and they told me to come grab another one in the morning!

Even out of Madrid, making sure family and friends were always looked after, sometimes with little notice, was another operation in itself. One such trip away to Valencia, I had a last minute request from a friend of the family who was on holiday and would love to watch the match. For this request my go-to guy was my friend Chendo, the former Real and Spain fullback, who was now the team travel manager and ambassador. With tickets almost impossible to get, I would need to call in a special favour, so I met Chendo for a coffee early morning at a beach café opposite Real's hotel, just off the Formula 1 track in the beautiful Mediterranean city.

I cut straight to the chase, and told him that he couldn't say no. I knew Chendo always kept a couple up his sleeve just for occasions like this, and when he asked who they were for, I told him "Emma Bunton, Baby Spice". Without hesitation, he reached for his pocket and like magic, two of hottest tickets in Spain lay next to my cappuccino. On my way to deliver the tickets, for some strange reason, the rapper 'Vanilla Ice' came into my head, only this time instead of Ice, Ice Baby the lyrics read Spice, Spice Baby!

After the game, another important job awaited before returning to Madrid. I had to head to Valencia airport from where the team would fly back to Madrid, except for Becks and a few others, who were heading for international duty with their respective countries. I was required to transport Beckham from the national domestic terminal to the private airport, where an English FA jet bound for London was awaiting the England captain.

I parked at a specially designated departure area, with the Real bus pulling up directly behind me. My phone beeped. It was a text from Becks saying that one of the lads would be jumping in with us as their private jet was also ready to fly. No problem my end.

I popped the boot, the lads threw their bags in and jumped in the car. Becks was riding shotgun and it all happened so quickly that I missed who jumped in the back. When I looked in the rear view mirror it was the maestro himself, one of football's greatest ever, Zinedine Zidane, Real's midfield magician looking right at me. We had a quick chat in Spanish and I dropped both of them at their jets, Becks heading to London and Zidane to Paris. That's how we rolled I suppose.

For me, it was a four-hour drive back to Madrid and I couldn't help thinking, 'what if I had crashed the car with those two in it?' There was at least £100 million pounds worth of talent under my charge, and I didn't even have a valid drivers' license! Who was liable in case of injury or death? I didn't even know if the cars were properly registered or not. It was just crazy, given cars whenever we wanted, and just drove away, no questions asked.

The vehicle situation had its fringe benefits also. When the Beckham family were out of town, I would take one of these amazing high performance vehicles at our disposal and use them to visit my family and friends around Spain. Porsches, Audis and Aston Martins,, more race cars than family cars, would clock up thousands of kilometres along the Mediterranean coast line, inland motorways and the winding mountain roads of northern Spain.

The week prior to David leaving SFX, he asked if I would stay with him under a new management company. Of course, I said yes, but I immediately knew something big was going down.

Already in new contract discussions with SFX lawyers that would keep me by David's side for the next four years, it was becoming strange. One of those moments where you begin to think a lot, but are unable to actually put your finger on any specific truth, and the murky waters of the agent game were now flooding the Spanish capital. The day before '19' moved in, Tony Stephens my UK boss flew to Madrid, met with David, not with me, and left. I did not even know he was there and only found out when David asked me how my meeting with Tony went! I never saw the 'scrapbook king' again, he disappeared into the English countryside and into retirement.

Then suddenly, overnight the world changed and it turned upside down for real.

David Beckham left SFX and joined his wife at 19 Entertainment, the agency owned and run by the music mogul Simon Fuller who was also Victoria's manager.

Fuller now had all the power and instructed that all SFX staff be made persona non grata except for me of course. I had the key to Beckham's safe in my possession, an upcoming meeting with '19' with a view to joining them and, most importantly, I had David's green light to see him whenever I wanted.

The meeting with '19' was strange and not what I was expecting. It was more like an interrogation of a captured military general rather than a discussion on my potential role with David under his new representatives. It was apparent to me that Rebecca Loos had stained everybody at SFX, so for me remaining with David would be impossible after I was painted by her as his 'protector'. She had gone missing but we now know she was selling her so-called story to the tabloids. A few years later she would masturbate a pig live on a celebrity TV show which probably says something about her motivation in life at the time.

Her proximity to David was the big mistake; a significant error made by experienced sports management professionals in the Mayfair office in London. A decision that allowed for a story to be written and repeated ad nauseam, even though untrue.

I had advised David and Victoria she was not trustworthy, and time would prove me right. She used my name in the papers to enhance and promote her story but I haven't read one truth in anything she has ever claimed to have happened or occurred. To get to David and score a home run, she needed to get past me and she never got past me.

I said farewell to David at the Santo Mauro Hotel as he was having dinner with a '19' marketing guy. I had gone to hand him the safe key personally and thanked him for the ride. He asked me how the interview went, and I replied with "It was more an interrogation to be honest, but I'll let them fill you in." He then asked me to join him for dinner, which I respectfully declined. I gave him the key to the safe, we shook hands and that was it. A strange ending after all we had been through. We felt a mutual sadness and parted ways, which was something beyond our control.

I then went to see his mum Sandra, who was a lovely lady. The early months in Madrid had been stressful and had taken a big toll on all of us, especially on her. We spoke often and she would invite me to her room for a cup of tea and a chat. There was something she always mentioned every time she saw me, and it meant the world to me. She would ask me about Isabella, wanted to know about her and she genuinely cared and I loved that she cared. She gave me a hug and a gift as she always did. Her final words to me were "Thank you for looking after my boy."

I walked out of the hotel, and nodded to the security guards. The English showed no emotion, the Special Forces were now under a new command. The Cubans had tears in their eyes, but unknown to them their fate was sealed, they would soon be gone too.

Heading to my villa, feeling betrayed and let down by many and wondering where to next, I decided to see what all the white fuss was about.

Stopping outside a lit-up Santiago Bernabéu Stadium, the home of Real Madrid, the greatest most successful club in the history of the game, I decided this was the place to christen the finest Blanco at the home of the team affectionately known as Los Blancos.

Chopping it up on a Jay Z CD cover, it hit my brain, seconds later sending me into narco heaven, my nervous system twitching like I was listening to the CD itself. The rocket man had begun his flight into space, and sadly, it would be almost like going back in time to my favourite show as a child. I would be 'Lost in Space' for years to come.

CHAPTER 9

THE GALÁCTICOS

I was extremely fortunate to have worked for David Beckham, it was an absolute honour and privilege. As a bonus I would end up watching, socialising and befriending arguably – along with Pelé, Maradona, Messi and Cristiano Ronaldo – some of the of the greatest footballers to have ever played the game. Global superstars, the elite of the elite, the mortals they called Galácticos.

It was an out of this world experience, being deeply entrenched in the inner workings and mechanisms of the most successful football club in the history of the game. I had a phenomenal role, assisting the world's most famous sports star to integrate not only into a football team, but into a new country and a new culture.

Working for Beckham came with the added pressure and workload of also looking after a Spice Girl, in her own right a global star.

Free time was hard to come by, but these hard to come by free minutes, if not taken up by wild parties, were a source of further education for me. A football education at Real Madrid is akin to a university education from Oxford or Harvard, so I made time to watch all first team training sessions in an attempt to better understand the club's historical philosophy and culture, from the current coaching staff through to legends of the game who were now employed in a multitude of roles throughout the club. What was it about Real Madrid that stood them above the rest?

The unwavering and super confident belief that this was the best place in the world was the first message.

There was no middle ground. They were either the best or the worst. For the players, this meant a constant demand to deliver the very highest quality of football in a theatre where winning is the only outcome. On top of winning, the fans demand beautiful football, *jogo bonito*, made famous by the great Brazilians. Entertaining and exciting, with the spectacular the very minimum, but all this only relevant if the team wins.

From the stadium to those that inhabit it – fans, media, officials, club directors and players – once you arrived on match day there was a special feeling, an aura, that you were part of history, a part of the nation, a team loved by plenty but also hated by many, a product of the nation's history including the Spanish Civil War. It's something that transcends football but any hate is worn as a badge of honour, spurring and creating a greater desire for more success.

The Real fans believe they are the greatest, that it's not even a topic for argument. They have a self-appointed aristocratic belief, an energy that flows throughout the stadium to all its corners. Hollywood stars, celebrities and royalty from all the corners of the world, want to be associated with this white diamond, a beacon of the refined upper echelons of not only Spanish society, but of global society. An elitist mob with a mindset that in some cases, dated back to the days of the dictator, Franco. Real Madrid were 'his' team, the team of the nation. There are sections of the stadium for the more hardcore fans, who bring the mad passion of Atlético, of Boca, or River, but not the whole stadium, as many Real Madrid fans for the most part are seated in luxurious private boxes that have a royal reverence about them.

The players are treated like gods and must have felt godlike at times, but the reality is they are quite normal in many ways.

This also applies at management level and was confirmed by Ronaldo when I asked him about Del Bosque and his coaching style. R9 said "El Mister" would say very little, he was a beautiful man, a kind and caring soul they all respected first and foremost as a gentleman. His football pedigree as a player for Real and Spain could not be questioned and because of this, they all played their hearts out for him. In most cases simple messages were enough: "If we win more individual battles than the opposition then we win the game ... If we match their work rate and desire our talent will do the rest" ... and most importantly, "It's not rocket science, you tell and show these players the system you want played and they do the rest."

Successful managers at Madrid must win the boys over quickly, especially the big guns in the side. It's a delicate process, psychology the key and not negotiable. If you don't get it right, you won›t last long.

I played at a high level, but these Galácticos were another level completely. Apex predators like tigers and lions all born with special world class genetics that contained the best speed, endurance, balance and football brains of the highest calibre, in other words genetically blessed. All these world class assets blending together shaping footballers built specifically for a defined position. Their actions and thoughts are instinctive, refined over the years but having been learned many years ago, like a baby cub watching its mother hunt for the first time.

Nature and natural selection quickly embed themselves in the club and so it was with these Galácticos. Their body positioning, special awareness, angles, how to move cleverly, and like predators they quickly scanned their opponents, immediately working out weakness, then preying upon them. Their brains put everything together quickly, under maximum pressure, and they all knew what was required from them. They knew their strengths and weaknesses and did not deviate from the tried and trusted formula.

They were not jealous of each other and to a man they knew their position and status within the club framework. In training and in games, their work ethic was always world class, it never wavered. Be fearless in attack and even more so when winning the ball back was the message. Appreciate and value the ball, do not give it away cheaply because no-one can rock the world without the ball.

Simple things we've all heard before, mastering the basics I call it. These lads had incredibly special buttons, so a manager able to press the right ones would win silverware, league titles and European titles as frequently as clockwork, but press the wrong ones and you would become a managerial statistic.

Beckham once told me his mindset was to do the basics with perfection time and time again, creating a consistent excellence, after which it was all icing on the cake.

They were all brave and confident footballers playing to their strengths and almost impossible to beat if their minds were on it..

Courage is not always big tackles and putting your head in the way of danger. Sometimes it comes in the form of wanting the ball, when you are 3-0 down and the whole stadium is booing you, wanting your head. Galácticos showed when most would hide.

It is not a fluke either that they all work on their gifts to make them important assets. Zidane and Beckham would play a form of golf, choosing a different club then pinging the ball to each other with both feet mimicking that chip or drive for hours after training.

Free kick practice was interesting and educational. Zidane and Figo had a similar technique, Roberto Carlos had power and swerve and Beckham had power, swerve, and top spin like Rafa Nadal on a tennis court. Unlike the others, after striking the ball Beckham would nearly always land on the foot that had struck the ball, but slightly ahead of where the ball had initially lay.

On one occasion Roberto Carlos, so frustrated that his power and swerve were not working this day, decided to kill the wall, made up of five individual metallic players which, when hit, would be knocked over then automatically, rebound back up into their original position. Carlos hit a rocket that struck the wall at head height and that player never rebounded back up such was the power generated. The lads could not believe what they had seen, the man was a Ninja turtle.

These practice sessions would transfer to the pitch as with Carlos's swerving goal vs France, and Beckham's last-minute winner against Greece, when he had a whole nation's expectations on his shoulders. That showed exceptional bravery, with a World Cup Finals place at stake.

If you miss, you are vilified for a long time; but with no margin for error he puts it in the top corner. It was a complete piss-take of the highest order. Magical in many ways, but for him it was work, the culmination of a process that was perfected in so many training sessions, so much so that it became the norm.

Dealing with the pressure? Well, I believe that is more inherent, something players are born with, and that is why there are many incredibly special players but only a few that are the chosen ones, god's favourites.

This was all a fantastic learning experience and one that I wouldn't mind putting into action one day.

I am often asked if I stay in touch with the boys from the Madrid. Not really, as everybody is on their own journey. However, if for whatever reason, we met again I guarantee you that there would be mutual warmth and respect. They know that I am a stand-up guy, and in the football world that goes a long way especially at this level.

In 2010 I caught up with the Real President at the Bernabéu and handed him David's book 'My Side' that was still in my possession. It was signed with a personal message and put a big smile on Perez's face when I handed it to him. It felt good to be back, and I was welcomed with open arms.

Early in the piece, not long after arriving in Madrid, on a boys' night out – or 'team bonding' as it's referred to – Roberto Carlos pulled out his party trick, keeping up a football in the middle of a packed nightclub to the amazement of all present. This was one of the best things that I have ever seen, so good that every punter had now focused on the Brazilian left back, who was pulling out every football trick in the playbook. Everything you have seen Maradona or Ronaldinho do with a ball, he did, only Roberto did it with an imaginary ball! His body movement was so realistic, it looked like he was juggling a real ball, so with around five minutes of magic the greatest left back to ever play the game had welcomed us to Madrid.

Roberto had a lot more in the locker than just his club party trick. He was an incredible athlete, genetically blessed, rapid with an engine that could take him from box-to-box, all day long. Strong and powerful, his left foot was like a heat seeking missile. Like R9, he loved to party, but at show time and on all the big stages, he shone brighter than bright.

One evening, whilst partying at his house, we chatted about how he managed to stay up so late, party hard, but still produce the goods when it mattered the most. He said it was cultural and the way that Brazilians were taught to live.

"We love to dance, laugh and have fun, and that transfers to the pitch," he said. "If your life has no joy, no fun, no beauty, then there is no beautiful game."

He was a fantastic host as well, not quite R9 level but world class nevertheless.

I only spoke to Luis Figo on a few occasions. He was always cordial, respectful and a magnificent professional. He didn't party like the Brazilians, he led a quieter more homely life as low key as possible. He was the first Galactico signed by Real Madrid, transferred from their arch rivals Barcelona whose fans never forgave him, sending many death threats his way and on one occasion going as far as throwing a pigs head onto the pitch close to where he was about to take a corner kick!

For a winger he was not as fast as Cristiano Ronaldo, but still fast and with impeccable ability. His skills and football intelligence allowed him to dominate opponents with ease, he had a great motor, always wanted the ball, and could play 7, 11 or 10 equally well. He was simply world class, a great ambassador and captain for his nation. His achievements speak for themselves, FIFA Footballer of the Year in 2001 and Ballon d'Or winner in 2002.

The maestro with the nickname Zizou, captain of France, Zinedine Zidane was a privilege to watch in action. He was just incredible, with a sublime touch and a beautiful elegance about him. A tall man, with perfect balance, complemented with pace, strength and the mind of a genius,. A clever ability to always have his body between the opponent and the ball, so it became almost impossible to tackle him without fouling him. Everything he did he made look so easy and effortless like a stroll in the park. A leader of men, captaining his country to the 2006 FIFA World Cup Final, and scoring twice in the 1998 showdown helping France to a majestic 3-0 win over Brazil in Paris. He was softly spoken, always respectful and always said hello.

The Spanish Galácticos were the striker Raul Gonzalez and the goalkeeper Iker Casillas. Both Spanish football legends, loved by the supporters of their club side and those of the national team.

Raul was a genuine superstar, who came through the ranks as a homegrown player and ended up with over 300 goals in all competitions for Madrid. We would say hello to each other at the training ground and he was always pleasant. He was fast, not lightning, but very sharp over 20-30 metres and could run all day. For a front man, he was always the first line of defence when the ball was lost, something many never saw in him, but a special quality that he was exceptionally good at. In attack he possessed an unbelievable ability to get in between lines, drop into false nine positions, or maintain a high traditional number nine role. A natural born finisher with every finishing skill in the book, from headers, lobs, ice-cold and clinical in one-on-ones, he had whole lot, the icing on the cake was his super football intelligence.

Funnily, the most time I spent with him was at a physiotherapy session when David was getting treatment at the same time. Raul had one of his children with him, sporting a new BMX bike so I rearranged some furniture to build him a ramp instructing him to jump over me. I then lay on the floor, and just like that, the lad was flying over me like Evil Knievel, the legendary American stuntman. The physio was a little stressed, but the kid was top drawer like his dad, cool, calm and collected!

Sir Alex Ferguson once said that Raul was the best player in the world. Figo said Raul was from a different planet. Zidane simply said Raul is numero uno, number one, so I would say that's probably sufficient to quantify his abilities!

I did not have so much interaction with Iker Casillas but when I did he was always pleasant and a gentleman. He was an understated character, drove a modest car and dressed like a university student, well, like a Harvard law student to be more precise. If it wasn't for his fame and position, you could probably have seen him in the street and he would never strike you as a Real Madrid goalkeeper. It is well known that he was pulled out of a class to make his debut for Real Madrid, and over the years, he has won everything there is to win at club and international level. A FIFA World Cup and European Championship with Spain, multiple Champions Leagues and FIFA Intercontinental titles are just the tip of the iceberg in his incredible collection of accumulated awards.

He wasn't particularly tall for a goalkeeper, but possessed brilliant footwork, creating phenomenal ball distribution. He was world world class in the facets of shot stopping and closing angles he possessed the reflexes of a jungle cat and a power ratio in his legs equal to Olympic sprinters. In the training drills I watched, Casillas would go first out of all the keepers, leading the way and setting a standard that was world class even in the simplest of warm up exercises. His record is simply amazing, but if he had been born in the UK he probably wouldn't have got anywhere. The UK Academy system always appears to call for big, tall, monster keepers and Iker would possibly never have got through.

If I were asked what were the two key attributes that made Casillas stand out above all others, I would say firstly, it was his communication on the pitch despite being quiet off it. Once between the posts, he became the general, marshalling the troops and making sure everybody in front of him was doing their job.

The second was his ability to stay alert and focused every second of the game. Playing for great sides like Real Madrid and Spain, there are many occasions where you are just watching ten great outfield players dominate matches. You may be called upon once or twice in a whole game, and you must be ready. Iker was always ready.

Ronaldo Nazario, aka '*El Fenomeno*', aka R9, was simply a beautiful man and a football freak. Both he and Roberto Carlos were the two main guys in the dressing room who embraced David with the most love and care from day one.

The Brazilians spoke no English, and David spoke no Spanish or Portuguese, so I immediately became an important cog in the chain. On football trips Real Madrid would always have several English speak representatives easing David's language hurdles somewhat, two in particular Jose Angel Sanchez and Emilio Butragueño, spoke perfect English.

Away from that controlled environment, I was required in person or via text to interpret everything, something that I did not take lightly and something that came with a responsibility of supreme confidentiality. This required trust, implicit trust from all parties in our conversation group that included David, R9, Roberto Carlos and me. It was never spoken of or mentioned by any of us, a code that exists and would never be broken by any of us. I could write another book based on these messages that would be a global best seller. Normal stuff, childish pranks daily, fun times, that I was blessed to share with these guys, and they are certainly memories to treasure.

Ronnie was a magnificent physiological specimen, genetically blessed at birth, he is the fastest footballer I have ever seen with my own eyes. Like an Olympic 100m sprinter, he was strong, powerful and rapid when combined with his beautiful balance, sublime touch, and Maradona or Messi like skillset, then you had an exceptional and special footballer who many believe is the greatest ever.

At training he could be the best; or sometimes put in minimal effort bordering on zero. Very few can get away with this but in his case, he had the perfect answers. Game time came, then showtime came and boy, did he show up, shining bright on the biggest stages. He was also a great laugh off the pitch and without a doubt hosted the greatest parties the world has ever seen.

One of David's first outings with the team would be for Ronaldo's 28th birthday bash at the compound where he lived in La Moraleja. This joint was like the Playboy mansion and then some! The Spanish media had labelled this occasion as the party of the century, and my first observation on leaving our hotel was that paparazzi numbers had doubled. That told its own story. David and I arrived a little late after spending an hour in front of the mirror at the hotel, like two old tarts, trying to nail something cool to wear. After we exchanged the obligatory "You look the bollocks in that" we headed for La Moraleja.

On arrival our own security convoy was met by R9 security. Armed guards surrounded the compound, carrying way more than just simple Glocks. The guards in the tower at the front entrance looked down at us, rifles in hand and extremely excited to see their boss's new friend. There was no delay as the immense steel gates opened, and flanked by security cars in front and behind, we drove into a new world. Once inside the compound, Ronnie's security team took charge of all operations. It felt like Brazil within the nation of Spain. The Carnival had come to Madrid and we were now both centre stage and if I had thought that rolling with Becks up to this point had been out of this world, we had just gone to a whole new level.

Amazingly, Ronnie would greet every single party guest with his amazing smile and a hug, making everyone immediately feel at home. It may have only been early evening, but the place was lit up like Rio De Janeiro and its famous Copacabana Beach. Looking around, most of the ladies were dressed for that iconic venue.

Ronnie had flown over his mates from Brazil which included a band from Porto Alegre who were already playing warm and inviting Latin songs. They were dressed for the occasion too, all wearing Ronaldo shirts and went all night, only downing tools for the DJ to play 'It's Your Birthday' by 50 Cent via their sound system. A special moment, almost iconic in its own way, that had everybody with their hands up.

It was a sight to behold, equalled the day before at the training ground by Ronaldo's friends already in party mode.

Carlos Queiroz the new manager, had lined the team up in the middle of the pitch in a semi-circle facing him, assistants on either side of him with their laptops in hand. I sat on the sideline with the Real physios and the kit guys, while behind us in the stand Ronaldo's mates had gathered, eagerly awaiting a magical training session! Carlos began addressing the players who were also keen to get out there to train. Five minutes went by; Carlos talked and the assistants typed. Ten minutes, still talking. Fifteen minutes, still talking. At this point you could see that the players were clocking out. Ronaldo and Zidane had clocked out 10 minutes earlier but Queiroz continued his monologue which seemed to be never ending.

Ronnie's mates from Brazil had behaved up to this point, but enough was enough. Anaesthetised with boredom, having been led to believe they were going to watch a session of five-a-sides featuring R9, Roberto Carlos, Figo, Becks, Zidane and Raul, out of the blue they began making bird noises. One chirp set off more bird noises, which turned the training ground into the most magical Amazonian concert you could ever imagine.

Queiroz was cooking, and the boys were cracking up, and the sounds did not fade, they only grew louder until Queiroz was eventually forced to abandon his philosophical monologue. With a wave, he sent the team on a warm-up lap and just like that the birds disappeared!

The consensus amongst the squad was a huge respect for Carlos Queiroz with respect to his coaching, but for them, there were far too many rules, far too many curfews, too much coaching and too much control. His tenure as boss would soon end.

It was the polar opposite to Ronaldo's lifestyle and this party we had just entered, was to become legendary.

Pretty much everybody at the party came alone except Luis Figo who came with his wife. Florentino Perez, Real's President, once famously said to Ronaldo, after word got out about his constant partying out on the town, "Why don't you stay at home like Figo?" to which the Brazilian cheekily responded, "If I had

Figo's wife, I would stay at home too!"

At the party David, being the new man and a global superstar, attracted a lot of attention, pretty much all eyes were on him as we made our way out of the SUV and into party central. The only other time I had seen this level of admiration and almost godlike worship was in Sydney around 1989 when 'Beaver' Thomson, Socceroo coach Eddie Thomson's son, took me with him as VIP birthday guest for INXS frontman Michael Hutchence. Like Hutchence on that occasion, everybody now wanted to see Beckham, touch him, feel him and adore him.

The house and grounds were amazing and palatial, like something out of a movie. Lounges inside and outside, a games room, a large cinema, swimming pool, a 3-par golf hole, the whole kit and caboodle. The only thing missing was a white tiger like Mike Tyson owned, but Ronnie's blue attack dog was close enough.

The day before the party, I had organised for Ronaldo to show us his home museum, so he took us both straight upstairs to one of the floors of his amazing house. This whole floor was half art gallery, half proper museum and full of gifts, awards, medals and paintings. It was really something else. Beckham, Ronaldo, and I wandered around this impressive display by ourselves, just the three of us with no party noise and no interruption. It was certainly a beautiful moment.

Looking at the collection of silverware and plethora of awards won by *El Fenomeno*, it was almost incomprehensible. There are many levels to this game and his level was the best of the best. A collection that included two FIFA World Cup winners' medals, two Copa America winners' medals, a FIFA Confederation Cup winners medal, Golden Boots everywhere, FIFA World Player of the Year trophies, only the three if you don't mind, and even an Olympic Bronze Medal from the 1996 games. And that wasn't the half of it. How does someone win all this? It was simply mind boggling!

Beckham, eyeing off this silverware, turned to me and said, "Andy, I've won f*** all!"

I thought to myself if you've won f*** all, where does my one Australian National Soccer League title rate?!

This guy was a whole different beast, Michael Jordan level. Like Jordan, Ronnie was a killer on and off the pitch, and like Jordan, he always had the last dance!

Back downstairs and the party was in full swing. Ronnie was happy, the vibe was relaxed, and everyone was having a great time, but as always, the paparazzi loomed and were gathering in large numbers outside the property.

We chatted to Zidane, Figo, Roberto Carlos and Christian Vieri, who had flown over from Milan. David's first real conversations with them away from training, and in a more relaxed setting. The world's top models, actors, rock stars and gangsters, all enjoying the occasion, alongside Ronnie's family and friends. Every girl at the party wanted to meet David, a photo with him was a much-prized possession, but only a select few were allowed, filtered initially by Ronaldo, and then me.

At this point, I began receiving calls from around the world but mostly out of London. Victoria and SFX staff were frantically trying to connect with David who wasn't answering his phone.

You've got a pool party going, backyard 5-a-sides happening, in the middle of a carnival with everybody wanting a piece of him including new teammates Zidane and Figo, and his phone is lighting up like a Christmas tree. Like many other times, I held his phone and other personal belongings, always filtering and monitoring situations for him. He was with me, and his phone was with me, and I recall thinking to myself 'can't this man get a little peace?'. Well not really, and neither could I translating maybe a hundred conversations by night's end.

Ronnie was disappointed that we were leaving 'so early' – about 3.30 am, but he also understood the need to return the calls from London, so it was better we left while ahead. He had plans to keep going all week, and he had more busloads of supermodels rolling in.

The big problem was how were we going to get out of there. Paparazzi were now ready and lay in wait for us, but never fear Ronnie had a plan as deadly as his goalscoring ability. He took me downstairs to his study and pulled out a map. I knew he was cooking something special, that cheeky smile gave it away. He had done this before: a secret tunnel would be our escape route with the paparazzi none the wiser.

"Are you kidding me, Ronnie? This is James Bond shit."

El Fenomeno just giggled. This was all a game for him. If the backstreets of Brazil couldn't destroy him, Madrid and the paparazzi were easy street.

As I left Ronaldo's study, I noticed some top-notch golf clubs. There was something about them that wouldn't allow me to take my eyes off them. Ronnie asked if I played.

"I love golf I said," his face lighting up with the biggest smile you have ever seen.

My eyes still on the clubs Ronnie said "Tiger Woods gave them to me."

"Tiger, the real one?" I asked. He said yes as he handed me the legend's putter and a ball. Next minute we were sinking puts into creatively made holes away from the party, and for me a moment I will never forget.

Part of our Cuban team departed in the vehicle we arrived in and the paparazzi took the bait, while we escaped secretly into the dark of the night, in a vehicle provided by Ronaldo. Like always, the great one was sending people left, right and centre!

Having spent a fair bit of time at Ronaldo's house on a few other occasions, what impressed me most about the man was his generosity, his love for family and friends. All of them had played a key role in his life and he did not forget a single one. Nobody left behind, making sure to look after those who were there for him when he was nothing or no-one.

The little things mattered to him and he couldn't do enough to repay you. One time I rescued his dog, getting it to a vet while he trained, after the beast had jumped off his second floor balcony in attack mode, breaking its front legs in the process. Ronnie went overboard with appreciation and that's just him, a wonderful human and I'm forever blessed having spent time with him, in his home and with his family.

One night he very kindly organised a night out for a few Australian NRL St George rugby league players on a fact-finding mission to Real Madrid. I ran it past him, and he was excited to help. Ronaldo loved making people happy and as a bonus, he got Nathan Brown, Paul McGregor, and David Barnhill into one of Madrid's hottest night spots. The queue went for miles but not for the lads. Straight to the front and passes for them all, courtesy of Ronaldo. The place had about five floors and we partied until around 7am. Who was the last man standing? Who had the last dance? *El Fenomeno* of course.

All these Galácticos were born with a gift, all super athletes in their own way and all brilliant technicians. Masterful visionaries on the pitch, with a football intelligence that allowed them to analyse space and angles in milliseconds. They solved puzzles with supreme ease and had the innate ability to cope with the extreme pressures and expectations heaped upon them. To a man, they were all favourable towards Beckham, the English Galactico, and his quality as a footballer.

David had arguably one of the best 'motors' of any player that I have ever been around. He could run all day at high speeds and never fade. His passing ability from all ranges is unequalled and his dead ball excellence puts him amongst the greats in that category, if not the greatest. If it came to a war, he would go to war too. Ronaldo bestowed upon him the greatest accolade ever, by saying that "he could play in his Brazil team."

The other fascinating aspect about Beckham was something I didn't realise at the time but now can see clearly, having watched the Michael Jordan Netflix documentary.

His capacity and ability to fulfill the many and varied marketing commitments from autograph signings to big brand corporate promotions and events, yet still maintain the very highest performance levels was simply amazing. Add paparazzi wars, a Spice Girl wife, and the expectation from both Real Madrid and England, and it tells you a story. David was a special breed, made of special stuff, the kind that transcends football itself.

There is no greater example than when I took my sister and daughter to meet him. After a two hour wait on my sister Raquel, dolling herself up for the occasion, we eventually made our way to Beckham's house. I entered the code into his private gate, sweeping up the dirt road that led to his home in the Spanish countryside. As we arrived Becks came out to greet us, looking fresh having just showered. Shirt off, hair long and wet was his look back then and he didn't disappoint. Well, Raquel just froze, could hardly even talk! Tongue-tied and sensing this, David gave her a hug while I thought 'you idiot, I put David Beckham in front of you, and you go to pieces!'

We headed inside, got some shirts signed and back in the car for the 30-minute journey back to my place. Isabella sat in the front seat on the way back, not overly impressed. She just rolls with all this big show stuff, while my sister sat in the back in silence. Gazing out the window and lost in her own thoughts, I said, "What did you think?" I'll never forget her reply. "You are the best brother ever!" followed by, "Did you smell him?"

I've never been a fanboy, but my time in Madrid allowed me to have Galácticos and many other contacts to die for, my mobile had them all.

Players phone numbers, club Presidents, Technical Directors, Nike and Adidas bosses, cartel bosses, rock stars, porn stars, world class models and movie stars.

I can only imagine what the British tabloids would have paid me for that list but unluckily for them that phone would die a watery death, in the same way a watery death would end the Titanic's maiden voyage.

In the aftermath of my exit from team Beckham, lost in space, but body still in Madrid, my 'famous' phone fell into the toilet as I bent over to snort a line of cocaine, flying out of my shirt pocket and into the bowl below that thankfully was clean.

The moment it left my pocket was that same moment the cocaine hit my brain, and I was caught in a state of combined ecstasy and panic. Despite a momentarily frozen body, I still managed to stick out a hand, a reflex action, like Australian cricketer Steve Smith at first slip, hoping it would hit my palm and stick, but it was a fruitless attempt, I never even got my hand to it. The splash of water was a sobering message, that my phone and I were in deep shit.

The treasured phone was now resting in the toilet bowl, staring up at me, still working, still alive thank god, but in half a foot of clear water. The fluorescent blue glow of the screen, shone brightly through the water, highlighting the network carrier "MOVISTAR" and reminding me once again that I had just lived a movie.

Maybe the movie was still going, maybe it would not end for years to come, maybe my old Hollywood dreams were still alive, unlike the phone that shortly went into its final stages. Now dead and taking with it many secret messages of the rich and famous, I threw it into a bin, a stone's throw from Real Madrid's stadium. Such is life!

My first club: Belsouth in Canberra, 1974

Playing for the AIS team which won a German youth tournament in Dortmund in 1984 vs Real Madrid. This is when Julen Lopetegui and I became friends

With Australia's first Liverpool star and my good mate, Craig Johnston, the creator of the prototype for the Predator boot, at the AIS, 1984

A Sporting Gijón player at 18 years

The first team for Albacete Balompié, 1986. I am third from the left in the back row

The first team for Xerez, 1987. Again, third from the left in the back row

Playing for Xerez vs Real Madrid at Santiago Bernabéu Stadium, 1987

Playing for Sydney Olympic against Melbourne Knights, up against a young Mark Viduka, 1993

In my 'Hollywood' days in Sydney

Playing for Australia vs Croatia, 1992. I am second from the left in the back row

Playing in an 'Overseas' vs 'Locals' Socceroos team when Terry Venables first took over the role as manager in 1997. I am centred in the back row

With Shaka Hislop on my first day at Reading

A falling Roy Keane for Manchester United, 1996

Playing for Reading vs my former team Ipswich Town, Portman Road

A lofted drive playing in a celebrity fundraising match at Reading

Playing for Reading vs Manchester City, 1998

Riding shotgun with David Beckham

A paparazzi shot of David and I in the car with another paparazzi in the background

Tom Rogic with my friend, lawyer and agent,
Daniel Berman

Two of my standout clients, Tim Cahill and Tom Rogic

CHAPTER 10

AFTERMATH

No longer part of Team Beckham, I remained in Madrid for a while, partying hard before returning to the UK, with no contact from the London office for months and months.

Holmes and Stephens went silent, they had lost Beckham, and the Yanks were not happy. They were lying low and I'm sure they just wanted me to disappear back to Australia and let Darryl and George in the SFX Sydney office determine my future, whatever that would be.

Rebecca Loos was haunting them, making loads of money selling her own brand of 'snake oil' to the tabloids. Rumours began to circulate that I too would sell out after approaches from nearly every media outlet in Britain. Then, just like that, I became relevant again, when Holmes and Stephens realised they had forgotten to give me a confidentiality agreement before sending me off to Madrid.

In a panic they flew my friend and Australian boss Daryl Mather to London to persuade me to sign a document that was dated nine months after the events of Madrid.

I calmly told Jon Holmes I would sign nothing, only my resignation letter.

Not signing the confidentiality agreement would force me to leave SFX, subsequently parting ways with Tim Cahill whom I had brought into the agency. Tim was now at Everton and a Socceroo, and there was no way I could represent him on my own. The power and prestige of SFX were unmatchable, and I had promised his parents I would look after their boy, they had my word. So I walked away from a little brother, and a young man on his way to superstardom, my only reward was the satisfaction that I had kept my promise to his parents. SFX kept Tim in the dark about what had happened to me, but he is not a silly boy and years later, he would leave them too.

I got up and left the Mayfair office, hailing a cab that would take me to the train station and then on to Reading. It felt good to be out of there, but not as good as the rock of crack I was about to light up felt. In this part of London, where most gentlemen are pulling out expensive Cuban cigars, I pulled out a crack pipe, melted the rock into the wire then lit up and inhaled, seconds later blowing out a perfect cloud of white haze that filled the entire rear of the cab making me almost disappear. I had now graduated from powder cocaine to the more powerful and deadly crack cocaine and was spinning out of control.

The cabbie looking in his rear vision mirror couldn't believe his eyes. In total shock, he opened the security divider between us, and said in a London accent "what's that then?" "It's a Peruvian flake extract that does wonders for my chronic and lifelong bone degeneration," I replied with a straight face. So high that nothing in the world even seemed real.

Minutes later I was at the station, handing him a nice tip for his troubles. I knew he wasn't having the bullshit I'd run past him, so the tip was more a thank you for rolling with my madness. "Thank you," he said, followed by "Very generous of you, mind how you go son," and off he drove into the London traffic.

I should have listened to those words, "Mind how you go son", as only a few months later I would find myself in more trouble than I could have ever have imagined. Locked up in a prison cell in Reading, the same city whose football club I had served and captained for many years.

I can still recall that morning vividly, thrown into a cell, high on crack cocaine, with my body cut to shreds from barbed and razor wire. Unable to sit still, manically pacing round and round in circles, my mind constantly revisited the morning hell and madness I had just lived. Thankfully, the crack cocaine circulating in my body helped to numb the pain from my injuries, but my mouth was now so dry that I would have killed for a glass of icy cold, clean water. Time passed but the pacing continued, now with changing direction, clockwise then anti-clockwise, the repetitive process somehow relieved the noises in my head. The four walls, the toilet, the thin blue mattress and the solid steel door were my only home comforts. Anxious and distressed with my freedom denied, I was feeling like one of Joe Exotic's tigers!

How on earth did I get here you may ask? Well, the answer, as complex as it may seem, was straightforward and simple.

The aftermath of Madrid had created the beginnings of an addiction to cocaine, and by this time, mentally and emotionally unstable for many reasons that I wouldn't confront until much later. I had taken self-medicating to a new level and my drug of choice was now crack cocaine.

I had only ever played around with normal powder cocaine, but only after my football career had ended. Squeaky clean, the ultimate professional, I didn't even drink much, my Reading teammates bestowing upon me the phrase "Andy likes a Shandy"!

After retiring from football and years of discipline behind me, I succumbed to temptation and tried the devil's dust, contrary to all my beliefs and values from childhood. Not the greatest choice for someone with an excessive compulsive and highly addictive personality.

My first line of cocaine ever would be with a work colleague in Sydney who was waiting on a call from Tom Cruise, Hollywood's biggest star at the time. He called me into his office and next minute 'Maverick' was on loud speaker and I was flying high and fast, requesting fly-bys and buzzing Sydney tower like top gun himself. Unfortunately, it was a flight I wish I had never jumped on, one that would end in a 'crash and burn'.

Most people don't come back from a crack addiction. They either finish brain dead or dead, and my life was now sadly heading that way.

Once I discovered the crack cocaine houses in Reading and London, they became strangely attractive, warm, and inviting appearing quite normal to me then. Normal people who were now junkies, living in filthy sub-human conditions were commonplace, and to think I would drive past these places, many times on my way to football matches thinking, 'how the f*** can people live there?'

High on crack I would walk the dark streets of Reading and London in the early hours of the morning, from crack house to crack house, with fiends lurking in the dark shadows everywhere. I wasn't scared but I was wary at all times, walking in the middle of the road, ignoring the footpath on either side as it decreased the chance of being jumped and jacked. From the middle of the road, my brain would register a picture as if I was on a football pitch, setting my stall out, and from central midfield, I was constantly and discreetly observing all around me in a 360° circle, ready to attack or defend any potential threat. It's all about spatial awareness and once you understand that, any game is easy.

Walking through the shady streets of London and Reading didn't faze me. Years earlier I had done the same in South Central Los Angeles. I was at acting school , drug-free and chasing that Hollywood dream in a place where copious amounts of crack was readily bought and sold on every corner. That was a proper dangerous place, a war zone with daily battles for street turf when rap group

NWA beats blasted the streets and drive-by shooters blasted people dead for wearing the wrong colour. My now comfortable in the uncomfortable mindset, in part, was a product of hitting Florence and Normandie before the LA riots hit Florence and Normandie, always rolling the dice, the City of Angels had taught me well.

Inside these crack dens, I wondered to myself what had happened to these people and how on earth did they end up here? Did these street kids have families? Where were their mum and dad? Did they ever have a normal life, a normal, beautiful loving family like I did? It was an incomprehensible environment, a zoo, a circus, but I rolled with it. Inside Reading crack houses more so than in London, it was at times quite bizarre, crackheads and crackwhores would stare at me as if they had seen a ghost, confusion reigning inside their fried brains, as they tried to figure out what the hell 'Skippy' was doing here.

I ended up in a council estate once across a lake from where I lived while living in Reading. My home, a little farm, was within a lovely collection of English barn style cottages. The rear of the houses backed onto a lake that separated us from a new hood, that was created for, and populated by, people that all the other London Council estates didn't want. Police helicopters, SWAT teams and undercover detectives were all part of the daily routine, the sort of place I looked at and thought there is no way I'm ever setting foot in there.

The world works in mysterious ways as early one morning, I found myself looking out of a crack house, over the water at the bloke who had bought my house, mowing the lawn that I used to mow! I'm not sure if it's funny or sad but it was real and the lyrics 'You may ask yourself, how did I get here...' by Talking Heads, a band I liked as a kid, now made sense in a peculiar way.

After football finished, when I was in England I would usually stay with my good friend, Paul 'The Jewel'. He is a good man, solid, the type you go to war with and have a laugh with. I have never forgotten how he was there for me in my time of need. One day, he put a picture of Isabella that I had lying about in my wallet, so every time I opened it up, her angel face was the first thing I would see. He said "She is your why, and right now it's dark, but the sun will one day shine bright again my friend."

My arrest was the end product of an all-week bender. Arriving at The Jewel's house early that morning, I noticed he had not left for work yet. I didn't want him to see me in this state, although I am sure he had already suspected something wasn't right. High on crack, I came up with a plan.

I decided to drive approximately 1km to the end of the road, to a small car park which led to a walking track used by walkers, runners, and horse riders. My only intention was to continue smoking and then return to Paul's after he'd left for work.

Near the carpark were a row of houses backing onto an open field, that backed onto the golf course. It was also the beginning of a nice English country lane, that ran in front of the houses, and that I often used as a shortcut to my friend Charlie's house, or to the stables where she kept her horse.

Smoking crack is not is not like smoking a cigarette, you can't sit discreetly in the car and continue smoking for fear of attracting the attention of passers-by either walking, jogging or on horseback. So I headed for the dirt trail, smoking and walking continually, avoiding any human traffic that may have come along, until I hit the golf course, walking part of its perimeter fence, then doubling back towards my car. From the golf course, I walked through a field until I hit the row of houses, walking along their rear fence line. As I approached the last house, I thought I'd quickly skim through the back yard then through their big gate and bingo I was at my car. That shortcut of maybe a few hundred metres would prove more costly than I could ever have imagined.

It was an exceptionally large backyard, a quarter of a football pitch maybe, or it seemed like that to me. I entered the yard through a small gate, and immediately decided to have another puff, the things you do when high on crack. I continued walking towards the big front gates, which I couldn't open or climb over, so I doubled back through the garden ending up at a distant shed where I planned to exit and walk the long way around towards my car. In hindsight, that is what I should have done in the first place.

One more hit, why not? As I blew out the cloud of white haze, I heard what sounded like a gun shot, that scared the shit out of me. Then another bang as police burst through the big gates, the gates that I had initially intended exiting through. That was the moment we locked eyes on each other maybe 30 yards apart. They shouted, "Police. Stop!" I was frozen in time, standing next to the metre high fence separating the open field and the backyard. It was so like that moment when you are out shooting kangaroos, that instant, that millisecond, when hunter and prey look at each other before death or flight. Only today, I was the prey and like 'Skippy' the bush kangaroo, a nickname that the Reading fans had bestowed upon me, I was up and over the fence in a single bound and headed for the hills, or rather the river.

Adrenaline and crack cocaine are a powerful mix, my heart was pumping fast, and my legs even faster. I couldn't even feel my dodgy knee, damn it, I could have played a few more seasons if this shit was legal, but it wasn't, so continuing in flight mode I worked out an escape route, which I decided would be the River Thames.

Why was I even running? Simple, I panicked, I had never been in trouble before and I was scared the drugs on me would put me inside and ruin any future football endeavours. There was absolutely no other reason to run, which was confirmed by my lawyer later when he revealed that the lady who had contacted the police about me and simply said "He's walking around," and something to the effect that "He seems confused."

As I ran through the field, I looked back to see that I had built up a decent gap. While sprinting, I dropped the crack pipe, all my rocks and the jet lighter in the thick long grass and none the wiser, the cops ran straight past them.

So far, so good, but I knew I had to get to the river, I had to get off the field that led to the golf course on onto the trail; in fact go over it, up the little slope on the other side, and then downhill to the Holiday Inn!

At high speed, I exited the field down a 10-metre slope, flying across the walking trail and then up the other side, when I was stopped dead in my tracks, hitting the ground hard. The impact, despite being heavy, wasn't my biggest problem right now. To my horror I had hit a wire fence laden with barbs and razors, camouflaged and overrun by thick brush and blackberry bushes that I simply didn't see. Smashed like a big hit in rugby league but luckily with no head trauma, allowing me to know exactly the situation I was now in, and it was far from great.

I immediately knew that I couldn't get out, but like a trapped animal fighting for its life, I kept struggling. The more I fought, the more trapped I became, the barbs and razors digging deeper into me, cutting and slicing all my body to bits as I battled to escape.

The struggle was a hopeless one, so I decided to just lay still and await my fate. I would not have long to wait as within a minute, the four police I had left way behind, were now looking down at me. They had got lucky.

One of them, the more evil one of the lot, dragged me out of the wire fencing, in the process slicing my arms and legs even more. He then picked me up before throwing me back down and smashing my face into the track. I was now face down, not resisting, hands cuffed behind my back, the four angry police officers would now dish out their own justice in the middle of a forest and with not a soul about. I could feel two on my legs, two on my back, and with their weight all over me, I found it hard to breathe. I could do nothing.

Unable to move, my only relief from the physical pressure was the nasty one whispering in my ear "dirty Paki bastard".

Suddenly I was pulled to my feet, and walked towards the police vehicles. Waiting for me was the police dog standing by the K9 van, barking its head off and salivating like Pavlov's dog, with a chunk of 'Skippy's' ass on his mind!

A hand on my head pushed me down and into the back seat of the police car where I sat alone with two police officers in the front. At this point I wasn't thinking about anything in particular. I was just running purely on my animal instincts. I could feel my heart beating exceptionally fast, so I focused on breathing slower and lowering the beats per minute, decreasing the chance of a heart attack. On the crackly police radio, I could hear chatter, something about a helicopter returning to base.

By now, I needed water, the cuts to my body were agony, and my knee felt like a screwdriver was being drilled into the bone without anaesthetic. To top it all off, the handcuffs had been put on super tight, and were now digging into my wrists grinding into the bone and the more I tried to move, the more pain they inflicted. I asked if they could be loosened but I was told "No".

Upon arrival, I was processed and led to a holding cell into which I was unceremoniously thrown in, followed by the horrible sound of the cell door slamming shut behind me, a reminder of exactly where I was.

Funny thing is I wouldn't have been here if a few days earlier I had been arrested and taken into custody when I was stopped in the early hours of the morning on the Basingstoke Road. Having just left a friend's house, I picked up a Thames Valley police tail and shortly after, I was lit up like a Christmas tree.

With a crack pipe and cocaine rocks all over the passenger seat, I did not stop until I had hidden the pipe under my seat, the worst hiding spot in the world, and swept the rocks off the passenger seat. At this point I was nervous. I wound my window down handing the copper my license he had asked for. He stared at it, then stared at me with a confused look, asking me if I had had anything to drink. "No sir," I replied. He handed my license back and said, "Are you okay Andy?" I replied "Yes". He then asked if I would kindly sign an autograph for his son, which I did.

Looking back I wish I had said no. His parting words, "Get yourself home son, and get some sleep, I don't want to see you again tonight" only made me think I was a protected species and bulletproof, having ridden my luck again. It would be short-lived.

The police station surroundings were now hitting home and took me back a few years to the Australian Federal Police Headquarters in Sydney where I was given a VIP tour, and spent time at the indoor shooting range with two detectives, and how I had left the Goulburn Street building that evening with forms to join the force. They had said I had all the qualities needed to join SWAT or the Drug Enforcement Agency. Not filling in those forms is maybe the one big regret I have in my life.

Not long after I was led to an interview room that looked exactly like a scene out of 'The Bill', one of my favourite TV shows back in the day. I knew I was in a little bit of trouble, maybe a slap on the wrist for disobeying the police order to stop.

Two detectives, one playing good cop, one playing bad cop, entered the room for the interrogation. Bad cop kept coming up with different scenarios, but not once dealing with fact, because the fact was they had nothing on me besides my attempted flight. He continued his interrogation bringing up a few items that I had in a sports bag which contained many other items that he chose to leave out, manipulating items to create a scenario that gave the impression of something untoward.

Good cop was playing the 'I love football' card to put me at ease or relax me a little, so I would admit to whatever they threw at me.

Bad cop continued his assault with make-believe scenarios, fantasy after fantasy like Walt Disney, at one point you would have thought I was a serial killer like Ted Bundy or Richard Ramirez , aka 'the nightstalker'.

I blocked every ball they sent down, and upset at their line of questioning, I asked for a solicitor, something I had initially declined because I knew I hadn't done anything besides run from the police. The solicitor arrived and from that moment, I answered no comment to every question.

Prior to the police interview, I saw the doctor on duty and he asked me if I had taken any drugs? I replied "No". I doubt he believed me, any doctor worth his salt would have known. He then cleaned up my wounds and conducted all the usual tests, including blood, fingerprints and the rest.

Opportunity knocks, and here was a 'cry for help' moment that may have changed the course of that day, by simply saying "yes, I'm addicted to crack cocaine, can you please help me?" The detectives may have then looked at it in a very different light, ending in a warning and a slap on the wrist. But after Madrid I was angry, and with crack now fuelling the fire, my mental state was either incapable of seeing, or didn't want to see, an opportunity to begin fixing myself.

They ran the prints and came up with a big fat zero; I had never been in trouble with the police and have not been in trouble since that day.

After spending all day at the police station, they finally let me out on bail. I was picked up by my former teammate Barry Hunter, and my man Paul the Jewel, and off we went to Kevin's in Caversham for a Chinese meal, after which I hit the sack and slept for about two days.

When on bail you are supposed to stay out of trouble, but it found me again about a week later, this time in the way of a racist national front lad who rented the ground floor apartment at the Jewel's house. I'd never run into him before, had gone out to grab a takeaway curry and on return, blocking the middle of the pathway is you know who looking like Edward Norton and dressed like him in the movie *American History X*.

As I approached, he said "We don't like your sort around here." I asked him what sort did he mean and he replied, "Pakis and Niggas," and followed it with, "If you are here tonight the boys will be round and we will give you a beating you will never forget, you dirty Paki bastard."

With that I calmly placed my chicken jalfrezi on the grass, and with my right hand I delivered a straight punch to his face sending him falling backwards, his head the first part of his body that hit the brick pathway. I thought I had killed him and in a slight panic, I filled a bucket with cold water and poured it over his head as they would do in the old western movies. Still no movement, he was lights out, stiff as a plank so I called the Jewel, who was having a beer down the local with a few of our mutual friends.

One of them told me to drag the guy into the large hedge and bushes in the Jewel's backyard then cover him as best I could. "And, when you're done, get yourself down here for a pint son," he said.

So that's what I did. At the pub they all thought it was hilarious but I was in a state of panic. After all, I was on bail and this was the last thing I needed.

"What if he's dead?" I asked.

"If he's dead, we will grab him and feed him to the pigs," they replied.

Hours later when we returned, the body had disappeared but not far as we discovered. Looking through his window, we saw the Edward Norton wannabe lying on his couch snoring, his head covered with a big bag of ice and I never heard a peep out of him ever again.

My arrest would begin the worst period of my life as super excited detectives chased fame off my name, a certain promotion and a career legacy that they could pass on to the kids and grandchildren.

When you are arrested, you are taken away from the supposed crime scene, where the police now have total control. They can plant, move, and manipulate evidence to create something to suit their narrative. They are then further aided by court reporters, pressured by big news corporations who regarded anything about Beckham – preferably negative – as good for sales and profits. Some will even go to the extent of writing what they want, regardless of the truth.

In my case they manufactured a charged aided by court reporters and journalists working for the tabloid press and local newspapers who majored in creative writing. It was easy pickings taking advantage of a mentally fragile and unstable human, who three months later would be locked up in a Sydney psychiatric hospital with his folder marked 'Not Fit For Society.'

Initially, they tried to get me on a burglary charge but had nothing because I am not a burglar. Then they tried to get me on a voyeurism charge. Again, they had nothing because I am not a voyeur. Then clutching at straws, and with vivid imagination, they charged me with attempted voyeurism. That means attempting to look at someone or spy on someone but not actually doing it!

So in the middle of a crack cocaine addiction, and what would later be diagnosed as transition anxiety and PTSD, I was convinced by a team of lawyers to take a plea deal and admit to something I didn't do, on the promise it would all disappear.

The police offer a plea deal because they had nothing. They then stack evidence, get some bullshit statements from persons who were not even there and scare your legal team into submission.

I don't need to be spying on anyone. It's not my *modus operandi* and the first I knew about a lady even being in the house was at the police station. To this day I could not tell you her age, what skin colour she was, what hair colour she had, if she was fat, skinny, Chinese, Japanese, tall or short. Not a single thing about her – but somehow, I got convinced into paying a complete stranger for a stress recovery holiday. Well guess what, she owes me three thousand quid

I gave her for being complicit in this miscarriage of justice.

After being charged, I returned to Australia for a while until the case could be heard in court, but I had no contact with my lawyers in England. From day one I had always denied the manufactured charge, and upon returning to England I was adamant that I would continue with my stance.

Self-medicating had now become a normal routine to forget my painful and confusing reality. Up in space, I was the 'Rocket Man', at peace with the world, alone and on a never ending journey, hoping maybe for a slow suicide to end my mental trauma, sometimes an inner hope of just not waking up because every other method of not being here somehow didn't grab me, especially the thought of how that final moment would feel. A gun to the head? Too messy. An overdose? I'm not a chemist, how much and what do you ingest? Hanging myself? That really scared me and just my luck I would probably screw it up and be hanging there for a week, dying a slow torturous death.

Back in the UK for my trial, I had one meeting with my legal team, where I was again high on crack. Nothing new there, I was pretty much high every day. The legal team discussed the plea deal while I just sat there staring out of a window at the River Thames wondering how on earth this would ever go away.

I would do anything to make it go away and in a sane state, I would fight a murder charge to the death, even if I had done it. So where my mind was while this was going on was anybody's guess.

The whole plea deal with the police was just bizarre, and even more bizarre was that I agreed to it. I was to admit to heavy drinking, another lie, as I drink very little alcohol, if any. I saw a Harley Street psychologist who charged me £1,000 and gave me a letter confirming depression in about five minutes. Counselling sessions that addressed everything except my addiction to crack cocaine, the final piece in a jigsaw puzzle that would be part of this nightmare going away, with an admission to something I did not do.

Try making sense of all the above while smoking crack all day! Bottom line I perjured myself to the court for a slap on the wrist and a fine, after which we could then all return to our normal lives.

They forgot that I am not normal. I am a former Socceroo, Reading FC captain and David Beckham's manager in Madrid. With that CV, I will never be classed as 'normal'.

Prior to my trial, many British and global newspapers made me substantial offers – I am talking millions of dollars – to confirm the Rebecca Loos story as well as stories about several other women who they said were rumoured to have "slept with David".

In making the offer they said my "nothing case" in Reading would disappear, would not feature in world news of any sort. They added that if I did not cooperate, I needed to understand that any event big or small linked to Beckham would be magnified like no other and that, in most cases, would destroy that individual for life. They meant me.

There would also be one condition attached if I was to go on the record about Beckham. My answer would have to be exactly what they wanted me to say, whether it was true or not. It didn't matter.

Caught in a trap, you are damned if you do, and damned if you don't.

So unless you end your life, you are placed in a position where you must live it out as a tortured soul, living a lie, hoping one day the sadness, anger, and shame you carry would somehow disappear.

Then one day, as if by divine intervention, I received an email from a Scotland Yard detective. It was a game changer that saved my life.

It turns out I wasn't mad or insane after all. I had been one of the victims of the biggest media scandal in British history, and possibly world history. The scandal, which involved several UK papers, led to several high-profile resignations, including that of the London's Metropolitan Police Commissioner along with many officers serving at the time.

Police raids would later seize around 10,000 pages of handwritten notes, listing close to 4,000 celebrities, politicians, sports stars, police officials and crime victims whose phones may have been hacked to exercise improper influence, including bribery and character defamation in the pursuit of stories. Nobody was spared not even the Royal Family. Dozens of notebooks and computers containing thousands of complete or partial mobile phone numbers and PIN codes plus many tape recordings were seized.

In July 2011 it was revealed that the phones of murdered schoolgirl Milly Dowler, relatives of deceased British soldiers, and victims of the London bombings had also been hacked. On top of all this, victims worldwide also had illegal surveillance conducted on them, and had data stolen from computers.

During the three months I spent in Spain, we were all hacked and spied upon, and it continued when I returned to England.

After Madrid, my life changed forever. Even a simple visit to London to spend time with my sister and her kids would see me stalked and followed by every newspaper in the country. They would even hound my sister when I was not around, a relentless and ruthless pursuit that knew no bounds. In Reading it was even worse, 24/7 everywhere I went.

Personally, I was a mess. I had gone from 100 to 0 in employment stakes, and with the global media on my case every day of the week, I resorted more and more to excessive drug use. Strange things were happening, voicemails and messages on my phone were not as they should be, and I began to believe that my madness was real.

So with a world of baggage on my shoulders, I returned to Sydney for my life after SFX. A lost soul carrying a lot of anxiety and a crack cocaine addiction. I was unemployed and maybe even unemployable, with a state of mind that was far worse than I could ever have imagined possible.

Within a few months of returning to Sydney, which has its own significant cocaine culture that involves body builders, models, actors, police officers and sports people, I was out of control.

Soon would come a psychotic episode that would end with me being locked up in a psychiatric ward by the local detectives. My daughter Isabella was with me at the time and on my instructions, she called the police telling them that her dad thought there were men with guns surrounding our home. When you call a police station with that message, they send the Tactical Response Group and a whole lot more.

She couldn't see anything of course but she's a clever kid. I know she made that call as a cry for help, for me.

Suddenly, I could hear sirens coming from everywhere and when I looked out the window, the whole place was surrounded by troops in SWAT gear and plain clothes detectives, all with guns out ready for action. After scanning the whole place and declaring it as all clear, they then knocked on the door. I was a mess and hadn't slept for days, wearing tracksuit bottoms, no shirt and my hair was sticking up like I had been electrocuted. I kept them at the door, but they saw pictures of me on the wall playing for Reading and the Socceroos, at which point they invited me to come outside for a chat, away from Isabella. I thought I was in real deep shit, but they were both great guys and I'm grateful that in one of my worst lifetime moments, they cared enough to help me.

I was already known to local police so the detectives had my history in the area. The first time was when I had chased a burglar at 1am. The sergeant gave me a high five after I gave the would-be thief a little touch-up. "Well done Andy," he said, "keep up the good work".

On the second occasion, I was chasing an imaginary burglar with my baseball bat at 3am. I was stopped by two female police officers on patrol near Bronte Beach. They asked what I was doing walking around with a baseball bat and I said "looking for a bloke that was trying to get into my house." They took me home and sat with me for a while until I had calmed down and reassured me there was nobody about. "No burglars around Andy, go to bed and get some sleep!"

So the day the Tactical Response Group was called to my house had been coming. It was just a matter of time. Cocaine psychosis had begun working its magic. Only a few days earlier, my mind had me believing that every car on the street in Sydney was a police car and on my tail. Not one or two, but every single one. The one behind me, the one behind that, the one in front of me and all those headed my way in the opposite lane.

My mind would create a story for each and every one and I would plan the escape, heading for roundabouts and if the car behind me kept following me after going around this thing maybe ten times it was surely a cop! The madness was that if that car did not follow me round, it was working with the following one who then would follow me, and so on, and so on.

A garbage truck, an ambulance, they were all undercover cops; then suddenly, just off the Harbour Bridge, a Random Breath Test unit that frightened the life out of me but luckily, I was waved through, the joy cut short, as my mind told me they had done it on purpose because their highway patrol vehicles were waiting for me further up the road. It was insanity at its finest.

Every single thought was turned into a negative that somehow reinforced to me that I was not doing the right thing, but I kept doing it, I couldn't stop. By the time I got home the whole city was following me, the noise in my head was deafening, like feeding time at the zoo. Lions roaring, birds chirping, wolves howling, and every single monkey screaming at the top of their lungs.

I parked the car and ran inside, quickly escaping the world. What to do? What I always did: more cocaine, which somehow stopped the noises for a bit but it didn't stop the million conversations to myself, some of them working out who I would ask for help. When I did find that person, it came with a vision of their face but they never stuck around, they just disappeared as quickly as they had appeared because they were not real. In the darkest moments I would hear what I thought was my mum's voice from outside my house calling out "Andrew" to which I would immediately shout out "Mama" four or five times, but she would not reply. Still believing I had heard her call my name, I would go outside and do laps of my house in the middle of the night for hours on end looking for her. I was sure she had called my name but to my disappointment she had gone. Sadly, for me she was never there, maybe in spirit, in some angelic way looking over me.

With a gathering crowd outside my place, I pleaded with the detectives not to take me to the station. "I have to go to Colombia next week," I told them.

Their faces said it all, thinking that's the last place a cocaine addict should be travelling to. They then asked why. I told them that I was the Socceroos chief scout for the final qualifying games for the 2006 World Cup. Dumbfounded for a minute, they then moved me away from the crowd, one of them telling me, "Andy, you are too good for all this shit, I am going to help you".

And they did, taking me to hospital where the nurses were brilliant. Can you believe one of them was from Reading and she knew who I was? How embarrassing!

Yet I wasn't embarrassed because I was too high to be anything at all, and was subsequently transferred to the psychiatric ward for assessment, a scary looking place that looked more like a prison. I was given a room and medication, enough to tranquilise an elephant and I made up for plenty of lost sleep.

One of the other patients was a young Aboriginal lad, who would spend all day walking up and down the corridor talking to himself while bouncing an imaginary ball. Curious, I asked the guard what his story was. He told me that a few years back people were saying the lad was going to be a rugby league great, but he found speed and ice, and this was him now, his brain fried so much there was no coming back.

I was intrigued. He was the top boy in the ward and I was told by a guard that it took a lot to win him over, but somehow, I wanted to. I felt like I could help him. How insane was that? The guard warned me to be careful around him, as he had the ability to go off the rails quickly and had tried to stab several other patients over nothing.

On my second day, he was walking towards me on his daily routine, bouncing his imaginary ball, when out of nowhere he threw it to me! I instinctively pretended to catch it and threw it back. He caught it and smiled. It's a football thing, it brings the world together, and we were now friends through our mad genial connection.

After breakfast on the third day, I asked if I could leave and was informed that I firstly had to be psychologically assessed, and then, if all was well, I would be discharged. For now, I had been declared "not fit for society" and therefore would not be allowed to leave.

When I saw the psychologist, the first question was, "So, Andy what have you been up to the last few years?"

I replied, "I was in Madrid looking after David Beckham and his family after his move to Real Madrid from Manchester United". I cannot find words to describe her face, but I knew I'd just delivered her a Shane Warne special to Mike Gatting, back in the day! She gathered herself and smiled condescendingly then followed up with "So, you were looking after David Beckham?"

"Yes, I was organising all his football business, translating for him, coordinating British commandos and former Cuban intelligence officers as part of our security team, everything to be honest." She just hummed while looking at me with pity.

She then left, had a laugh with the nurses before returning and asking, "What about Posh Spice, did you look after her as well?"

I replied "Yeah, she's cool, we hung out." And with that off she went, probably thinking that this guy's file should say "never to be released"!

I was let out at the end of the week after passing all the tests. With Ron Smith in tow, I was off to South America to watch Colombia vs Chile, Venezuela vs Colombia, then onto Buenos Aires for the Argentina vs Colombia clash.

A mission that would be easy money for a mad man!

CHAPTER 11

PATIENTLY WAITING

After many years of what I thought was madness, I decided to sell up in Sydney and head back to Canberra, my birthplace. It was here as a child, I had formulated goals, worked hard, and ended up living my dreams.

The nation's capital is home to important landmarks such as Parliament House, the National Library, the War Memorial and is built around a man-made lake known as Lake Burley Griffin. Perfectly manicured parks, ovals, bike paths, football grounds, rivers, lakes and mountains, all interwoven making for what is an exceptionally beautiful city. Sports fans can enjoy seeing the Brumbies (rugby) and the Canberra Raiders (rugby league), but we do not have a Canberra team in the A-League. International sporting facilities including the Australian Institute of Sport, once my home, are the perfect fit for those seeking a healthy lifestyle, so with all these positives, it was time to return and be close to mum and dad again.

Walking, cycling and running tracks are everywhere and in the winter, you are only a few hour's drive from the Snowy Mountains for those who love skiing and snowboarding. I had left this place 25 years ago, returning for a few days here and there, a birthday, Christmas or a funeral. All the beautiful positives of the city remained in place and, strangely, I had now come full circle to begin a new life.

Sydney no longer held any attraction for me as Isabella was now living in Auckland with her mother who had moved there for an academic position. Looking back, that was a real blessing in disguise. Isabella completed her last two years of schooling at the beautiful Auckland Girls Grammar School, going on to university attaining a degree in Journalism and Communications.

Not long after arriving back in Canberra I got into cycling. Like Forrest Gump with his running, I would just get on my bike and ride and ride and ride amidst the lakes and mountains. It gave me a feeling of freedom inner peace, something I could no longer attain from running and something that was now not possible.

I had been away for many years, and while cycling one morning, I was struck with an unhappy return to my childhood, a haunting reminder of the racial abuse I suffered daily for years as a child.

Out around 6.30am, I was on cycling around Lake Burley Griffin in casual mode, bum on the seat, slow peddling just contemplating the assault on my own body that the return leg home would dish out, when from nowhere, like the paparazzi in the Beckham days, a monkey dressed in a Tour de France outfit, flew past me shouting, "Get off the f***ing bike path wog!"

Seriously, what did I just hear? That word had not been directed at me for a long time and said in the wrong way created anger and rage within me.

I was initially so surprised that I spent about thirty seconds trying to talk myself out of believing what I had just heard, but it would not go away, it would not leave my mind, and as with everything in life a price had to be paid. I took off in Tour de France time trial mode myself, yours truly on a mountain bike vs 'old mate' on his expensive, light as a feather, road bike. Off in hot pursuit, it was just a matter of time before I would catch up to the asshole and I was prepared to cycle for as long as it took.

The winding path on the lake edge was my ally, the kilometre he had on me was decreasing slowly, my mountain bike allowing for little shortcuts that I could take and then come back onto the main bike path and closer to him. My excitement increased as the distance between us decreased and now with him totally oblivious to me, I had the gap down to 20 metres. Licking my lips was an understatement as we hit Commonwealth Avenue Bridge where the path slightly inclined before crossing the main part of the bridge itself. The little incline slowed him but pushed me on. Once onto the bridge, the path narrowed and midway across it, I made my move. Drafting him like a NASCAR, I popped out and suddenly we were even, with me right next to him, and at the very precise moment he looked to his right, I looked to my left and said, "Remember me?"

He was in shock, as if he had seen a ghost rider. He had! My next move rammed his precision-built racing bike into the railing that saves casual lake walkers and runners from a big drop into the water. It was a good hit too, his front wheel buckled, his handlebars as well, and he was now going nowhere fast.

Both off our bikes, his few seconds of bravado soon faded as his body went into shock watching me throw his expensive baby off the bridge into the murky waters below. Looking down, the bike sat briefly on top of the water as if to taunt its owner, before slowly sinking. He was now screaming and crying, and an unimaginable happiness came over me, much more than if I had physically hurt him. To be fair, he had a result, I kind of regret not throwing him over too.

He threatened to call the police, and I encouraged him to do so advising him that the Water Police nearby were probably his best chance of recovering the bike. I doubled back past the Hyatt Hotel and the Embassies, heading to my aunt's house nearby where I chilled for a while before finishing my morning ride.

About a month after this, a similar incident happened in Sydney.

I had been looking forward to catching up with my good friend and old Council work mate Colin De Costa. We decided on a game of pool in a pub somewhere between Redfern and Surry Hills. After ordering a beer each, we started shooting some pool, shooting the breeze as they say. Mid-game three guys walked into the pool area, and as I was aiming at the pocket, the biggest of them all knocked the ball in with his hand. Yes, the ball that I was planning to pot. I let it go, making out it was funny but moments later I was again lining up my shot when the same dude repeated his earlier party trick knocking the ball in and saying "What are you going to do about it, you wog c***?"

He was a big guy, around 6ft and juiced up to maximum. He had all the tattoos as well and I was kind of perplexed as to why the supposed tough, hard guy would resort to childish bully boy tactics. I thought we as a society had left this all behind. His comment rubber-stamped his punishment. Immediately after his insult, my mind was made up, he would pay. As he approached and we were face-to-face, I delivered a headbutt with pinpoint accuracy that split him open, a two or three inch deep cut from his eyes to his mouth. He was not expecting it and didn't even see it when it was staring him in the eyes. He fell back on his ass, screaming in agony. I then smashed the pool cue over his head but it didn't break like it was supposed to. In the movies they always break, damn I must have got it wrong! It must have felt like a hammer hitting him, he was done.

His two mates just stood there looking at him on the ground, then looking at me, so I handed one of them my pool cue, and told Colin we were off. My parting words, "The table is all yours lads, have fun."

Why me again? Minding my own business, catching up with a mate over a game of pool and some tough guy had to call me a wog!

Two especially important and defining moments arose while I was back in

Canberra trying to make sense of everything that had occurred in my life up to now.

Both gave me evidence, clarity, new perspective, and immense confidence to rewrite history and state facts as they should be. It was now time, after many years, to reveal the truth as it was, not as it had been creatively written and manufactured by some British tabloids and the police.

I was always planning on it, I just needed the right cards, the right hand, like a poker player in Vegas. Life deals you plenty of shit, so I waited for that special hand, the one that changes the whole game, history and destiny itself.

The first great card was when Scotland Yard detectives confirmed that I had been a victim, along with thousands of others, of phone hacking, data theft and surveillance by the British tabloids.

I left it in the hands of my lawyer who took care of it all from London, but I couldn't take my mind away from certain specific evidence within the case, evidence that was now helping put the puzzle together, and somehow put into words what actually happened to me.

The second, and most important moment for me, the light bulb moment, for want of a better word, occurred while watching the Netflix documentary on Aaron Hernandez, a tight end who played for the New England Patriots in the NFL.

By day Hernandez, alongside Rob Gronkowski, was Tom Brady's receiver extraordinaire, an all-American College champion out of Gator country. By night, he would play gangster and it would eventually lead to an arrest for murder. For a year homicide detectives, just like the fans, would watch the New England Patriots in action culminating in a Superbowl appearance, not realising that the man they were looking for had just scored a touchdown in the biggest game in American sports.

Hernandez was convicted of murder in 2013, and a few years later he hung himself in his cell. In the hands of medical science, his brain was sliced in half and found to be rotting away slowly from the middle, an empty space similar to when the seed of a plum or an apricot is removed. During his career, head trauma had been a big factor, some of the hits he received were extremely violent and heavy, like being hit by a truck at high speed causing over a career, concussion after concussion. On top of speculation about his sexuality and drug use, the end was inevitable, a tragedy that destroyed many lives.

It got me thinking about how much trauma my head must have received over the years. Thousands of headers, including seven concussions that I know of, and of course, the car crash in Madrid. I calculated it as something more than 200,000 ball heading impacts from the age of seven.

I loved heading the ball. (How good is a goal from a diving header?) That feeling of attacking a cross at full length like Superman parallel to the pitch, with your head in amongst defenders' studs is the greatest feeling ever.

Modern balls are a lot lighter and softer than they were years ago, and now made of water-resistant material, but in earlier days they got extremely heavy when wet, the stitching would protrude, and it would take a massive toll on your head, and inside it! That was at the professional level; at an amateur level, it would be even worse. The balls were like medicine balls and sometimes you would have a headache for days and days. If you complained most coaches would say you're heading it wrong, "you've got to head through it son, attack it harder son, put your head through it," so I would go away and put my head through it for hours and hours!

Aaron Hernandez's story got me thinking even more about mental health issues in society. I began discussing the topic with my friend Todd, an Australian Special Forces Commando who had been medically discharged with PTSD after losing five mates when the vehicle they were travelling in was blown up by a roadside bomb. We became close and I revealed many feelings and emotions that I had felt during and after football including all that I had gone through.

I also began reading more and more on soldiers returning home, both ones who saw combat and those who didn't. Many of them suffered from a variety of PTSDs and anxiety disorders, one in particular, "transition anxiety", was strikingly like my own feelings and emotions, especially after my time with Beckham.

I told Todd I felt embarrassed that I was in any way trying to equate what he went through with my life. His answer was never to compare brains and journeys, as we all react differently to life's many impacting events.

I continued to investigate my state of mind over the years. After retiring injured, I had never thought that I would end up spending a part of my life living in what was a real-life version of a Hollywood blockbuster as an agent, manager and bodyguard to the most famous footballer on the planet.

If you thought '*Jerry Maguire*' the movie was good, this was a whole different level. We are talking Jerry Maguire, James Bond, 'The Wolf of Wall Street', Real Madrid, Manchester United, the Spice Girls and a bloke called Ronaldo Nazario who would ferry busloads of supermodels to his palatial home on a regular basis. It impacts your life forever and it's all bottled-up inside and there is no release. Who can you tell this to?

A return to normality is kind of weird. For example, try telling people that you looked after Beckham in Madrid, hung out at Ronaldo's mansion entertained by bus loads of super models, and chatted with Elton John on the way to training! They think either you're full of shit or you've done so much cocaine or ice that you actually think you chatted to the Rocket Man. It's insane and sometimes much easier just to fuel up and be Rocket Man yourself!

My role in Spain had developed exponentially and many of the stresses accumulated while working, would later surface. Everything that happened in Spain went through me before it got to David so, in effect, I was the gatekeeper with relatively little training or experience in many of the jobs I performed. As daunting as it may seem from the outside, I just did it, took control of the entire operation, a Beckham brand that left no room for error. Failure or incompetence, was just not acceptable.

Sometimes there are no words to explain what went down, but as always I approached it, like with my football, brave and fearless when I entered the arena, this being the only way I knew. Looking back now with a little pride it's true what they say about the 'Big Show' – it's only for a select few of us!

The departure of David Beckham from SFX was ugly. The American owners wanted answers, and their javelins were firmly locked into the London office that had lost him. With this, the London bigwigs would need scapegoats, a need that would see them use all their powerful football and media alliances in the process. They went into 'muddying the waters' mode, where character and integrity destruction became part of their plan.

They threw shade at Rebecca Loos, and deservedly so, but it was measured because it linked back to those who put her in that role.

They also threw shade at me after finding out I hadn't signed a confidentiality agreement. Why? They were scared that Beckham would sue them if I spoke, so they character assassinate you, making sure that anything you say has no validity.

The comedown was a killer. Exciting and intense pressure-filled experiences are suddenly over, and it had nothing to do with my actual performance. It left a frustrating rage, an enemy within, that slowly crushed me day-by-day. What now? What could I possibly do with the rest of my working life and where would I get the same excitement?

When you are no longer part of a team as such, you can become lost, with no mission that brings you a sense of purpose. Camaraderie built over many years, over the many adventures, both in football, and then with Team Beckham, created special bonds for me and a sense of belonging, which was now non-existent. The transition into what I guess you would call a normal world, was for me stressful, dominated by anxiety, depression, and many other behavioural issues, unfortunately leading to me trying to fix myself in all the wrong ways and places.

Identity loss, a man without a purpose, would lead to relationships with family and friends becoming conflicted and distant. Of course, they had absolutely no idea of everything I had been through, so my silence and mood swings would be countered by their anger and sadness. I missed the adrenaline highs and longed for the great moments and occasions that had passed, a surreal life that was now a distant memory and not easily relayed at a family BBQ in Canberra.

How do you even begin to convey to family or friends what you just lived? They just look at you almost with pity as if you've really gone mad. Substance abuse, a constant self-fix ends up playing a big part down that slippery slope. It's something that takes total control over you, so much so, that you know you are doing the wrong thing, hurting everybody around you, yet continue doing it.

However, in moments of calm and reflection, I began thinking of events, aside from cocaine use, that could have affected me or shaped my mindset and behaviour especially as a young boy.

My dad going next door with a loaded shotgun, with me behind him. Taking a hunting knife to high school every day. Hunting wild animals and stabbing them through the heart when I was just a kid. The cane-cutting stories that included fights with fists and machetes were all stuff I considered part of my normality.

Could all these things, added to head trauma, PTSD and anxiety disorders create mental instability? Damn right it could, and then if you added cocaine to the mix, you had a nuclear weapon, one push of a button away from disaster.

The paparazzi experience still lives with me to this day and if a motorbike comes up on my car and sits right next to me without going past, an immediate memory and sensory recall hits my brain and ignites a fuse. They leave an indelible print on a human's mind, a horrific one that never goes away. I remember their chatter wanting death, wanting fatal crash pictures that never leaves you, and brought back every time I watch something about Princess Diana, the most hunted human on the planet. Well, I can tell you David and Victoria Beckham were not far behind.

The greatest torture is sometimes an untold story and in my case, one that needed correcting. Just a pawn in a game played by higher powers, but I am not your average pawn and like Dr Dre, I'm Still "A". Time brings vindication and that time is now and after all those years of self-doubt, my friends' doubt, my family's doubt and the world's doubt, isn't it ironic that the only ones spying were the tabloid newspapers themselves!

CHAPTER 12

SOCCEROOS: PLAYER, SCOUT AND AGENT

Many people have told me that I was a pioneer, a trailblazer, someone who ventured into the unknown, leading the way for future generations. I was the first and youngest Australian footballer ever to play professionally in Spain. It is an incredibly special achievement.

How many 19-year-old Australian footballers could do it today? Sign for a top five Spanish La Liga club at the time, and play 72 matches over two seasons in the first team, out on loan to Albacete FC and Xerez CD, against all the giants of Spanish football. Zero.

Don't forget, this was 1985 before everything was put on a plate for you by agents, advisors, club scouts, doctors, sports scientists, and player welfare officers. Growing up in Canberra, at a time when there was no internet, no social media and global scouting systems were pretty much non-existent, made Europe seem so far away, it could well have been the moon.

In 1984 aged 18, I became the youngest player to captain the Australian U-23s, or what now is commonly known as the Olyroos, at the Merlion Cup tournament in Singapore. One year later, I captained the Young Socceroos to World Cup qualification for the 1985 FIFA Youth World Cup in Russia. I obtained my full Socceroo cap in 1990 but I always believed that my senior international call-up was a little late in coming, and at a time that I was an inferior player to the young man playing in Spain in the mid 1980s.

Truth be told I was playing NSL when capped, and although I gave my all when playing and training, the part time football environment meant my focus was not entirely all on football. Ranger duties at Woollahra Council, acting classes, and the Sydney beach life were not conducive to producing the best footballer I could be. I had been playing in Spain regularly every week in the starting eleven and coming up against the likes of Real Madrid, Sevilla, Valencia,

Deportivo de La Coruña, and Celta Vigo, followed by a productive spell at Ipswich Town, but had heard nothing from then Socceroo boss Frank Arok. He had his players, that's how it goes sometimes.

However, while researching for this book, I discovered that higher powers at the then Australian Soccer Federation had instructed Arok not to select me for a while as punishment for choosing to sign a professional contract with Sporting Gijón in 1985, rather than play for Australia in the World Youth Cup.

A few big wigs at the ASF believed that my loyalties were to Spain over Australia, but that was far from the truth. On a football level I was a little angry that I was being overlooked for inferior players plying their trade in the NSL, quite a few from Arok's own club side, but at the end of the day, he was the boss and my opinion counted for nothing.

When Arok finally called me into the squad at Eddie Thomson's request, we never really spoke but I gratefully accepted and enjoyed being around some of Australia's greatest ever players at the time.

Playing for Australia back then wasn't as sexy as it has become now. I used to watch the national Rugby League team the Kangaroos, touring England and fancied that way more. I remember chatting to Craig Johnston and we were both so obsessed with playing professional football in England that it seemed more important than a national call up from home.

As time passes you begin to feel differently, however, and I certainly did.

I played 21 times for the national team, my constantly recurring knee injury, and clubs not releasing me for internationals cost me many more. It is life but it hurts you, and one match in particular, that I missed through injury really impacted me for a long time both mentally and physically and still does.

It was 1991, and England were coming out to play.

I had hurt my knee again playing for Sydney Olympic the weekend before we went into camp, in what is always a huge match-up in any sport at any level for Australia. I said nothing in the hope that it would hold out for this mammoth clash. In camp, it unfortunately got worse. Smashed internally, and again I was shipped off to hospital for more drilling and cleaning and I missed a really special match I had dreamed of all my life. While I was out for over a year, my good friend Mehmet Duraković took my spot and went onto play over 60 internationals for Australia. One man's misfortune is another man's opportunity, and my spot could not have gone to a better guy who was also a fantastic footballer.

Playing for Australia did give me the opportunity to play against Argentina at the River Plate Stadium in Buenos Aires, against a team that included Gabriel Batistuta, Claudio Caniggia, Fernando Redondo, and Oscar Ruggeri. The great Diego Maradona was suspended on this occasion, so I missed out on playing against my childhood idol, but nevertheless his presence was felt. Shortly after arriving at the stadium to watch the match, the great one received the loudest and longest applause that was heard all night.

I also played against Croatia at the Sydney Football Stadium in what was another great occasion, and I earned a Man of Match recognition for my performance against Sweden in Sydney, a special memory. On my Socceroo travels I played against many nations and discovered wonderful places, none better than my final Socceroos appearance against Chile in the amazing city of Antofagasta, a fixture that was also the international debut of a young Harry Kewell.

My last Socceroo international call-up was for a match vs Saudi Arabia in 1996. I had injured my knee again playing against Wolves at Molineux on the Saturday so I called Thommo to tell him I wasn't sure about the Saudi game, what with it being midweek in the desert. He told me to get on the plane leaving London on Sunday morning, and then see how I pulled up on arrival. The worst-case scenario was that even if injured, he would put me on the bench for the game and I would pick up my match bonus, which is exactly what happened.

It was the middle of winter in England and it was too good an opportunity to pass up some sun. After the team doctor ruled me out, I just hung out with Thommo by the pool in the blazing Arabian sunshine. Thommo and I had a great time; his mind was already on a multi-million-dollar deal to coach in Japan.

My roommate on that trip was an upset young goalkeeper, Mark Schwarzer, who at the time was third choice stopper at Kaiserslautern in Germany. He wasn't too happy with where his career was at that stage and asked me if I could help him out, so I called Barry Silkman, an agent I knew in England who worked with many of my Reading teammates. Silks soon after worked his magic getting Schwarzer a move to Bradford City, from where his career skyrocketed, joining Middlesbrough and later, Chelsea.

For Tony Popovic I did the same after receiving a phone call from my former boss at Reading FC, Terry Bullivant, who was now assistant manager at Crystal Palace. Terry said we are looking at a young Australian playing in Japan, and if you say grab him, we will grab him, so I said grab him and that's how Tony Popovic became a Crystal Palace player.

Australia was a member of the Oceania Confederation until 2006, so there would be no World Cup appearances on my CV. The preparation was substandard as we were never given the support that we needed to be successful. On one World Cup preparation tour of South America and the United States we would have to endure 40-to-50-hour plane trips in economy class and then be asked to play a day later against some of the best players on the planet who at the time were dominating Italian and Spanish football leagues. Good luck son!

We were paid peanuts. The travelling administrators would give us maybe £1,000 cash for a three-week World Cup preparation tour while the briefcase they paid us out of remained laden with bundles of cash in US dollars from match fees our federation were paid by the home nation to play the games! I'm not sure where that cash went but one thing for sure, it did not go into our pockets.

For me, the football trips were like holidays and a chance to travel somewhere new, content in coming back to my job as a Ranger feeling I had the best of both worlds.

I might not have won 100 caps, but I think I got the most visits by a Socceroo to the judiciary committee! My great friend George Pashalis at one point became Legal Counsel for Soccer Australia and told me that his biggest filing cabinet was mostly taken up by two names, Andy Bernal and a young Kevin Muscat!

Staff at Soccer Australia were becoming genuinely concerned that the NSL competition was becoming too violent with our assaults on club players and fellow internationals, but we would not be stopped!

The end came when Terry Venables took over the national team just as the players to be known as the 'Golden Generation' were coming through. I was in the first Venables-led camp held in London, followed by a series of matches in Australia named the 'Travellers vs Home' stars, a version of the 'Possibles' and 'Probables' trial matches that you would play as a kid. It was set up as a promotional series but also to give 'El Tel' a good look at his best 22 players.

His assistant was Raul Blanco who I never really got on with finding him dictatorial and arrogant. It works at lower levels but at the top it wears very thin with players. I hated all that shit, like when Daniel Passarella dropped Redondo, the best number 6 on the planet at the time, because he wouldn't cut his hair, a moronic mindset from a truly great player. Please!

There was also a bit of politics from a few years back, between the AIS and the Young Socceroo coaching staff, and of course, I was always backing Jimmy Shoulder and Ron Smith in that war. Blanco did a fantastic warm up, that included all the Maradona tricks and flicks, I'll give him that much but when given the Olyroos to manage for the Olympic games in Australia, he failed miserably on home soil, his team losing every match they played.

During the home and away series, I was certainly one of the best four defenders on show, but I would never be selected for the national team again. Average squad players were seeing a lot of game time, several of them ending up at English clubs via a handful of UK agents staying in our hotel. Funnily enough, the then CEO of Soccer Australia not batting an eyelid!

I rated El Tel, great manager, you cannot argue with his football career, it just would have been nice to hear why from him, man to man.

After one match in Sydney, I was in a group of five UK based players who got back to the hotel a few minutes after the curfew, all of us greeted by a smiling Raul Blanco. The following morning, I was the only one reprimanded by Venables, so I will let you guys do the math. It brought my Socceroo career to an end despite at the time playing good football, week in and week out for Reading FC, and denied me the opportunity to maybe play in that famous match vs Iran at the Melbourne Cricket Ground in 1997.

My Socceroo career was not illustrious by any means; it was more about what could have been, rather than what was achieved. At 19, I was way ahead of some of the guys that had far greater Socceroo careers than I did but my dodgy knee meant I would never be a player to make 100 caps, despite having the ability to do so. It is what it is, and as you get older, you realise that to play once for your country is an incredibly special honour reserved only for a select few.

As a Socceroo, but more importantly as an Australian, I was a pioneer into the UK and Europe, along with Joe Marston, Craig Johnston, Tony Dorrigo, John Kosmina, Dave Mitchell, Eddie Krncevic, Frank Farina, Jimmy Patikas, Graham Arnold, Robbie Slater, Alan Davidson and Mark Bosnich. Frank became the first Australian to play in Italy on what was a record transfer fee when he joined Bari from Club Brugge in Belgium, while around the same time Lou Hristodoulou and Chris Kalantzis would sign for Panathinaikos, joining Jimmy Patikas as the first Australians to play in Greece.

It was an absolute honour to be a national team player. Jimmy Shoulder, Ron Smith, Vic Fernandez and Eddie Thomson were the best coaches within the national set up that I played under. Great football minds and top guys, all of them.

* * *

After going a little crazy in England, I returned to Australia and in 2005, and was asked to attend a meeting with Graham Arnold and Ron Smith at FFA Headquarters in Sydney. We had a good chat about all the nonsense that had happened over in the UK. They called me a dickhead for putting myself in a situation to be exploited, then placed a document in front of me which was a South American scouting plan, to create a dossier on Australia's possible World Cup qualification opponents. Australia would be pitted against the fifth-placed South American team for the final spot at the 2006 World Cup. With my ability to converse in both Spanish and Portuguese, they there was no better man for the job.

The job description was to create a tactical, technical, logistical, geographic, and a climatic dossier on all possible South American opponents, which meant we had to watch Brazil, Argentina, Colombia, Chile and Uruguay in action.

In the weeks before heading over, I made a few phone calls to the Technical Directors of South American National teams, all of whom gave me a dossier on every other country I needed, except theirs of course, so in effect, I had done most of the work before leaving. The scouting operation was a holiday watching some of the best nations on the planet fight for a World Cup spot.

Our accommodation was always top drawer and the pick of the bunch was the five-star Hyatt Hotel in Barranquilla in Colombia. This was a beautiful Spanish colonial style building, with a pretty beach, lined with palm trees and located in the north of the country on the Caribbean Sea. It was a tropical paradise, simply outstanding.

On this trip, our first stop was Bogota, the capital of Colombia. The airport was full of military and national police. It felt heavy and it was, with an invisible tension in the air that I got a thrill from. While sitting in the airport waiting for the connecting flight to Barranquilla, I was trying to decide who was moving stuff and who wasn't, picking out cartel couriers and 'sicarios' from legitimate travellers. It was the best method of killing time in between flights.

Once we had boarded the flight to Barranquilla, I set my mind to the task at hand: football and cocaine.

I was also looking forward to catching up with Carlos Valderrama, the Colombian football legend, who has an apartment in Barranquilla.

Travelling from the airport to the hotel, was an education in itself. Extreme wealth on one block and extreme poverty on the next, full of kids playing street football everywhere and anywhere.

After quickly unpacking my bags, the first thing on my mind was to get some Colombian powder. It would be very rude not to in the country that produces its finest. I made a call and within ten minutes a young lad rolled up, knocked on the door and we shook hands. He was very respectful as I had come recommended from the Madrid cartel boss and when I told him my link to Valderrama, Andy B instantly became a VIP of the highest order. The kid was not more than 16 or 17, but would put a bullet in your forehead and not even flinch.

Those signed Beckham shirts in Madrid had paid off previously and still held weight even on the other side of the world. The price was USD$10 per gram, so I asked for 20 grams. The look on his face was priceless! I had a 'loco sicario' thinking I was the mad one, but let me tell you USD$200 for 20 grams of pure white Colombian was not to be sniffed at - pardon the pun! It was quite possibly one of the greatest value for money exercises you can ever get on planet earth.

I gave him a little extra, approximately the amount needed for him to take a human life, and from that point on I was safe as houses both inside and outside the hotel.

Once the sicario left, I couldn't resist trying the product I had just purchased despite knowing I needed to be downstairs shortly for dinner with my security guard that the FFA and the Australian Embassy had organised. Frozen for a few minutes, I sat on my bed in total exhilaration, unable to move, just talking to myself and thinking how the f*** was I going to get through this dinner.

Minutes later and feeling a million bucks, I headed downstairs to a beautiful Caribbean sunset and a restaurant by the pool, the most idyllic and tranquil place you could imagine.

The bodyguard had taken the liberty of ordering me a large snapper, traditional he said, but the cocaine had left me with the driest mouth on the planet and without an appetite. Talking for fun and not hungry at all, my mouth was semi-open, like a cod fish for most of the dinner. I ate about a third of the fish and every bite had to be washed down with a glass of water. It was useless so I made a lame excuse and went straight up to the room to rack up another line that again left me frozen until the Caribbean sun and breeze reminded me that I was in paradise and I was ready to rock and roll. In party mode, I waited for the young lad who was returning soon with a plan of entertainment for the duration of my stay.

When he arrived, he asked me what kind of girls I liked. He said he could get me a 'girlfriend' for the week! A girlfriend? Why not, I was single, and it would add some fun and excitement to the trip. After another line of pure cocaine hit my system, I could hardly talk so he asked me to draw a picture of my type. I can't draw but then I remembered that I had bought a copy of 'Inside Sport' magazine when I was waiting at Sydney Airport before flying out. Quickly flicking through the pages in the magazine, I pointed and said bingo. He gave me the thumbs up and we were on.

Before leaving to get her, he said "Not a prostitute? A special girl, one that my big boss reserves for FBI, DEA and CIA agents." He was good but you can't trick a trickster!

Not long after, he returned to my villa with my new girlfriend in tow. A stunning young lady who had that JLo, Sophia Vergara thing happening. Intelligent and beautiful, but she spoke no English so we just rocked the Spanish. By the pool, by the beach, everywhere; and in between I watched a football match, Colombia vs Chile, so pretty much the perfect job in world football – after playing of course.

I woke up the next day around mid-morning and went to the pool for a tropical breakfast that included my favourite watermelon sugar high. I clocked four men swimming away, chatting together and enjoying themselves talking football. My initial thought being, isn't this nice, two male couples in love on vacation frolicking with gay abandon! That was until I clocked the three-armed SWAT policemen strategically located around the pool, weapons at the ready. They were the match officials, kept under a protective guard as the waiter informed me. Football in South America is a different beast, and Escobar in his day, allegedly bribed and killed many referees for making what Pablo considered was the wrong decision.

Referees have always infuriated me. There is something that I have never liked about match officials. To be fair, they were not huge fans of mine either!

Not long ago in the middle of writing this book, a friend of mine Michael, told me that his dad had copped a 40-year ban from Capital Football, the governing body in Canberra, for hitting a referee, his assistants and anyone else who got in the way. He then calmly got in his car after the game and drove away without batting an eyelid, had dinner and slept like a baby that night.

My face lit up. Throughout my career I had always wanted to do the same, I hated them, not all of course, but most of them. Cleverly, I never followed through on it, but to Michael's dad, well done George, you are in my Hall of Fame.

The first game I attended on this trip was Colombia vs Chile and the heat was awful, around 40 degrees. The game was played at 4pm under a Caribbean sun that penetrated your skin within minutes coupled with humidity at around 80%, it felt like sitting in a sauna. I was sweating just watching so playing in it would have been horrible, but it was all part of their plan to deplete and destroy visiting teams even before the football came into play. The stadium itself was rocking, like being in a mad zoo, the smells of humanity, animals, food, and alcohol fermenting around the ground were intoxicating.

Getting to the stadium was an event in itself, the cab navigating dodgy back street lanes that you really wouldn't want to be caught alone in after dark, but which strangely attracted me. I was buzzing in anticipation of what was to come, in fact double buzzing from a livener at the hotel prior to jumping in the cab.

On arrival at the ground itself, the home of Atlético Barranquilla, everything was loud, like watching a 'Guns 'n Roses' concert in the early 1990s. Armed police were present, some with police dogs as big as lions. They were huge, and just my luck one of them took a liking, or rather a disliking to me. I had been told that dogs can sense a more rapid heartbeat and the little livener I had before I left the hotel had my heart rate higher than normal.

The handler was dressed in full riot uniform being part of a military police presence complete with machine guns, he was hauling back on the dog's lead, my eyes now facing the growling dog's teeth about chest height. Fortunately, the dog seemed to pick up another scent and off they went, so I quickly took off for the entrance. When I turned back, in the distance I could see the same dog, ears pricked up, once again scanning and maybe looking for me again so through the gates I went into a mad South American bazaar.

FFA had provided me with two seats, one for my bodyguard and one for me but when we got to our seats they were taken by a pair of Colombians, who looked like two of Pablo's hitmen.

"Excuse me, I think that you are in our seats," I said.

"No, these are our seats," came the reply. I was about to open my mouth again when I got the look that basically meant, 'f*** off, move on and don't stop walking.'

The bodyguard grabbed my arm and aided me in this good life decision. Sometimes, in enemy territory, it's best to keep on moving and wise to pick your battles!

Most of the game we spent walking around in a stadium full of crazy Colombians screeching and screaming for their heroes, with no real place to sit or stand. While walking around, I made mental notes on formations, set pieces and everything else. Despite never finding a seat, I managed to get all the information I needed and survived game one of this three match tour. I thought it deserved another celebration, so I headed back to the sanctuary of the hotel to do just that.

When in Colombia, you must always catch-up with 'El Pibe', Carlos Valderrama, so I did, spending a lovely evening in his beautiful penthouse apartment in Barranquilla. He must have told a hundred stories of the two Escobars but when recalling the assassination of his friend Andres Escobar after his own goal in the USA '94 World Cup, it clearly made him very emotional. I was made to feel at home by the legend, both he and his wife, two beautiful souls who I feel very honoured to have spent time with. As a parting gift, he signed one of his Colombian shirts for me, a beautiful gesture that would not long after help me navigate Customs while departing Bogotá international airport.

After handing my Spanish passport to the Customs official, my preferred passport in South America, the official's elongated silence began to make me nervous. I had that 'déjà vu' feeling, my mind flicking back to that awful day when UK Customs deported me back to Australia, although this was Colombia, and the atmosphere was a lot heavier.

Believing I was a drug mule, my nightmare only ended after asking them if I could show them something out of my carry bag which was one of the reasons for my short visit to Colombia. Luckily, the official said yes, so I got on one knee and began to open the bag while over me stood three young soldiers with guns in hand. The soldiers' eyes were firmly focused on my every move, the wrong move and it was curtains for me, lying dead in a pool of blood. Slowly and nervously, I proceeded to pull out a Colombian football shirt signed 'Para Andy, con carino. El Pibe, Valderamma, #10.'

The gift from the national captain, a hero to millions, the greatest player Columbia has ever produced, a South American legend had immediately given me Colombian VIP travel status. 'El Pibe', as he always did in the middle of the park, was pulling all the strings.

We moved onto Venezuela where my dad's brother, my uncle Angel, had lived many years ago, working in the oil industry at Lake Maracaibo before returning to Spain. Angel Bernal was also a pioneer, it must be something in our DNA. At Lago Maracaibo Airport we were picked up by a member of the Venezuelan Football Federation.

Upon leaving the airport, and to our surprise, we became part of a military convoy that was escorting the Colombian national team to their hotel. Ron and I were totally blown away by everything that was happening around us, our vehicle directly behind the team bus. Four other vehicles in front and another four behind in all terrain military jeeps with open top roofs. Machine gun bearing commandos with one leg hanging outside the jeep and one leg inside, locked and loaded for war it seemed. Not long after, we arrived at a beautiful gated resort with two hotels and a casino. We were booked into the same hotel as the Colombian players' families and their fans, so for us, it was carnival all day and all night long.

South American football is a beast of its own and in a continent where the game is far greater than life or death itself, either outcome is never too far away, it's simply embedded in the cultural fabric of society.

It would not be long before I encountered a cultural experience for myself around 1am at the casino. Blackjack is the game for me so I headed to table occupied by one player. An older gentleman, Pablo Escobar looking and wearing a cowboy hat, he was in the first seat. He was betting large amounts and seemed a house regular or favourite, a VIP I sensed. After a little observation I respectfully asked if I could join the table. He obliged but told me to sit at the end of the table. There are times in life where it's smarter to do as you are told. I immediately understood it was his way of increasing his chances, of winning and my role within the hierarchy had been established.

We were soon joined by a young punk who sat himself in the middle without asking and began to upset player one. It wasn't long before player one pulled a gun and placed it up against the punk's temple, quietly asking him to grab his chips and leave. Thirty seconds later, the table was back to only two players and while putting his gun back into his trousers player one apologised for the inconvenience and asked if I would like a drink! Best make it a double I thought! With normality restored, player one proceeded to split the aces he had been . dealt seconds before the altercation.

The Venezuela match was mental, a typical South American fixture, scary, but exciting. During the game, fans were lighting flares and firing handguns into the air, it was sheer insanity. There were no issues when we got to our seats this time, as we had been seated in an executive box between the Venezuelan football president and the Colombian football president. The place looked like a Miss World and Miss Universe pageant with a football match thrown in for good measure. Silicone lips, boobs, and asses everywhere, hot tamales the national product of both these countries, and all their assets were on full display.

The game reached half-time and I was thinking to myself, 'I need to say something half professional to Ron, so he thinks I am focused on the game,' so I came out with, "Ron, I think the Venezuelans might be playing with a four…" and that was as far as I got. Ron turned to me and said, "Birch, never mind the formations son, what about all the cans," as he pretended to prop up a pair of boobs!

We were introduced to the President of the Colombian Football Federation, his wife and two daughters seated in the box next to ours. They were genuinely interested in Australia having never been before, so in typical Aussie style, I sold them the nation like Paul Hogan did in 'Crocodile Dundee' and his tourism ads. While I regaled the wife and daughters with my stories, Ron was talking football tactics with the husband.

However, once the game commenced Ronnie whispered in my ear, "Birch, I know those girls are attractive," he said, "but best you behave son or we might end up, strung upside down in a Medellin backstreet like you see in those Pablo Escobar movies!" So I behaved!

In Argentina we got to our seats and sitting on my left was Jorge Burruchaga, the man who scored the winning goal in the 1986 World Cup Final against West Germany, sliding home a finish after being set free by a magically weighted through ball, from the great Diego Maradona. We had a great chat and like Valdano, he recounted many amazing stories about Maradona. During the game a funny moment occurred as, strangely, Ron could not work out the system Argentina were playing, so he asked me. I told him I didn't have a clue either. Ron then suggested we ask Burruchaga, so I did, and he said he didn't know either. We all agreed that based on how Argentina were playing, their players didn't know either!

In the end, Ron and I created a comprehensive dossier, a blueprint to success if you like. Our ideal scenario, that we presented to the FFA upon our return, would be to play Uruguay and as we all know, that was who the Socceroos ended up playing. Our information on the Uruguayans was taken as gospel and the Socceroos claimed a memorable aggregate victory securing the final spot at the 2006 World Cup Finals in Germany, Australia's first appearance at the finals since 1974.

The one team we didn't see live and in the flesh was Uruguay, as interrupted flight schedules in South America prevented Ron and I travelling to Montevideo. Capturing the atmosphere on match days is of prime importance, especially in South American stadiums where at times it can be a complete mad house, so we needed someone we could trust and have confidence in.

Luckily for us my friend Darryl Mather, one of Australia's leading rugby league agents, was holidaying in South America at the time. Weeks earlier we had agreed to meet up in Montevideo for this match, so on this occasion he would be our saviour.

Darryl is a rugby league man at heart, his agency SFX Australia that he co-owns with George Mimis, represents former and current superstars like Darren Lockyer, Billy Slater, Ivan Cleary, Nathan Cleary, and Wayne Bennett to name a few. He understands sport, loves football, especially Tottenham Hotspur, so he was our man in Montevideo.

It's a crazy world we live in, about as crazy as the match report on Uruguay in Montevideo being done by a rugby league agent. Darryl provided great information for us that day, as I had done for him years earlier at Seiffert Oval, while watching the Australian Schoolboy rugby league titles. He told me to pick who I thought was the best player of the tournament, so I picked a kid who the Australian selectors ignored, telling Darryl he should recommend him to the Brisbane Broncos, which he did. The kid's name was Sam Thaiday.

I had a beautiful time in South America, a continent where football is life and life is football. They live and breathe it, and for me a few crazy nights were part of the process, but when it came to the professional art of gathering information, along with Ron, you won't find a better pair in my opinion. A beautiful continent that can be dangerous too, but I know Ron felt as safe as houses with me by his side. We had the best time and enjoyed so many laughs and to do it all with my great friend, and AIS Coach, Ron Smith, was a privilege and a pleasure. Maybe someone will dig up the document one day and think, who were the two geniuses that wrote that?

We placed the blueprint in Guus Hiddink's hands, the time came for the

World Cup play-off match against Uruguay, and to the victor, the spoils.

I didn't really fancy going to the stadium, I liked playing in the big show, not watching it, but my mate Elkin was keen to go. His life revolved around moving bricks and gambling on sports, any sport, even if he knew nothing about it and he was keen to have a punt on this one.

He convinced me to go and I agreed but on the condition that we travelled by car and must avoid all traffic in or out. I received my two complimentary tickets from the FFA, in the middle of the stand with all we other forgotten Socceroos. I worked out times to avoid driving to the stadium, which was most of the day, so the plan would be to get there five minutes into the match. Heading up the old Parramatta Road, my man Elkin found a TAB to get his bet on. First goalscorer odds of $9 on Marco Bresciano looked appealing, so he slapped $5,000 on telling me over and over, "I've got a good feeling, I've got a good feeling." Standard banter in gambling circles of course.

We got to the stadium five minutes late and I couldn't wait to leave five minutes early. For some reason I did not feel a part of it. I felt used after not even a thank you for my work, except for Ron of course. The beautiful game they call it, the reality is at times it's the complete opposite.

At half-time Elkin had two lines ready for us to sniff in front of 82,696 other people who were none the wiser, as they focused on the half-time entertainment. The match, as we all know, went to penalties, and with everyone in the stadium and the country fixated on the penalty shoot-out which would soon commence, we left!

Entering the city skyline as the penalties were nearing the end, with the whole nation holding its breath. John Aloisi scored the crucial spot-kick, and the nation erupted. We hit a Kings Cross bar, the Bresciano bet had paid off handsomely and we ended the night in a penthouse apartment at the casino enjoying the finer things in life.

After the 2006 World Cup, I continued scouting duties for Graham Arnold, the last two destinations being Kuwait and Jordan for Australia's first ever Asian Cup assault in 2007.

* * *

My Socceroo career could have been more illustrious, but it wasn't. Destiny would take me down a different Socceroo path, and bring me together with three of our finest.

Tim Cahill was my first ever client and for my money the greatest Socceroo ever. His international performances are nothing less than stellar.

A Ballon d'Or nominee in 2006, he would provide key contributions, goals, and assists, many of which would define his legacy. The first Australian to score in a FIFA World Cup, when he netted the first in the memorable 3-1 win over Japan in Germany in 2006. He then went on to score in three successive World Cup tournaments and ended with a total of five World Cup goals, which is an incredible feat. Tim was also the first Australian to score at an Asian Cup.

Who can forget his volley against the Netherlands in the 2014 World Cup, which should have been goal of the tournament? I rate it so highly that I think it was, in fact, one of the greatest goals in World Cup history. If he had scored that in the orange of the Dutch team, or wearing Adidas boots, he probably would have scooped that award! To cap it all, he also bagged the fastest goal in MLS history. The list is almost endless and simply staggering.

Harry Kewell and Mark Viduka were incredibly good players at club level, outstanding talents, but Tim was equally as good and his goal scoring at Millwall and Everton was consistent over many years. His record of 50 goals for his country in 108 internationals is equally comparable to the best strikers who have played the game including Alan Shearer, Cristiano Ronaldo and Lionel Messi. Don't forget also that Tim operated a lot deeper than your traditional goal-getters. As an attacking midfielder he could also play centre-forward, or off the number nine position if necessary, but if required, could also play the defensive midfield role at a Keane level, that all round ability being a priceless commodity in the eyes of world class managers.

Tim was born for this business, and the very top of it at that. Simply put, a world class footballer, who shone brightly on the biggest stages, when it mattered most. A gentleman and a friend, I call my brother.

Carl Valeri, a kid from my hometown and son of former NSL player Walter, I would take to Italian giants Inter Milan. I recall that deal vividly, a Milanese experience that I will never forget greeted by a young man, Piero Ausilio, who at the time was in charge of the Youth Academy. Waiting at Milan Airport on his Vespa wearing designer clothing of all colours, none of which matched, was my friend Piero looking a million dollars. He is now the big boss of Inter Milan.

That was a gigantic feat in itself for Carl and he would go on to have a stellar career with various clubs in Italy eventually returning home and captaining Melbourne Victory until his retirement. Good lad, and a gentleman who won 52 caps for the Socceroos.

Tom Rogic came to my attention via Ron Smith who asked me to look at a young lad who he thought was special. We were joined by the kid's father, Peter at my junior ground Hawker Oval in Canberra. My first glimpse of him told me he would require far more work than Tim or Carl.

Immediately the match started, you could see his talent, his first touch was sublime. It reminded me of Zinedine Zidane and I was hooked. However, he also looked lazy, unfit, didn't want to track back, and walked around with his hands on his hips, while now and then displaying a myriad of futsal tricks that didn't really translate to the outdoor game, but certainly got a few of his female school friends in attendance excited. In between these bouts of ineffectiveness though, was the occasional Maradona turn that excited me, the bum off seat kind of stuff. Even then, Tom had that magic ability to create an expectation that something great was about to occur and that is gold dust. On top of that he was lefty, like Maradona, like Messi, like Nadal, there is just something about lefties, that makes them seem to flow extra smooth.

Towards the end of the match, he received the ball about forty metres from goal and set off, swerving past would-be challenges and curling a long range bullet into the top corner reminiscent of his Scottish Goal of the Year effort many years later. It was an incredible moment and raised more than a few eyebrows from the watching public.

Tom had the Nike Academy trials in the UK looming on the horizon and his dad asked me to take him under my wing for three months, to work with him on the parts of his game that needed improving. I agreed and my plan was to either break him, so he quit, or turn him into the player that his talent was crying out for.

By chance, or good fortune, I was able to create the perfect training plan that fit in perfectly with my place of employment at the time. I had ventured into the combat sports business and a facility that I part owned in Canberra became home to the Olympic Games Boxing team preparing for the London Olympics. I was one of the strength and conditioning coaches, so guess who would be joining us ?

I laid down the law early and told him that if he missed one session, we were finished. In the same sentence I also told him that the day he became a world class athlete, he would play for a world-famous club somewhere on the planet.

Two sessions I gave him stood out above all else. The first of these was at a suburban AFL oval on a wintery Sunday afternoon. The Australian War Memorial was directly across the road and I would use it to inspire him before the session.

Tom arrived with boots and balls, but his first job was to put them back in the car. He would be doing only 400m and 800m runs this particular day, arguably the toughest events in all of athletics, and my plan was to push him to limits he had not been to.

Tom seemed aghast, "No ball work?" being his query.

"No you don't need ball work, you need to find fitness, grit, internal fortitude, the bottom line he needed to understand suffering. See over there?" I said, pointing towards the War Memorial. "There's a few walls over there with the names of brave men and women soldiers who have lost their lives for this country, so the pain that you will endure today, will be very insignificant in comparison."

He was silent then put in a sensational session.

The next time we met was at Mount Stromlo Running Park. It was in the middle of winter, halfway up a snow-capped mountain, with freezing sleet coming down and getting dark by the minute. It wasn't the greatest place to be on a Sunday evening and the last time I had felt this cold was Sunderland away, at a full Roker Park on a Tuesday night when we left with all three points and the flu!

The track was soft and foggy, visibility restricted, and you could only see a couple of metres ahead of you at any time. Tom had yet to arrive, but I had my assistant Jaynie with me, who was just about frozen, standing under an umbrella and holding the stopwatch. She said, "I don't think he's coming." To which I responded, "Well, he's got five minutes to get to the start or we're done."

Jaynie was sceptical and asked me whether I was serious about my threat, to which I told her, "As serious as I am going to marry you one day."

Suddenly she went from frozen to half-frozen and lit up the whole mountain with her smile.

In the distance, headlights approached and I knew it was Tom. He made the start line, visibility was poor, my only instructions were to be careful that you don't run into a 6-foot kangaroo, or a wild dog that's come down to try and eat the 6-foot kangaroo! It didn't matter, he was focused and on a mission and I knew that night that mentally, he had the goods to succeed.

Tom would eventually sign for Celtic FC and go on to win 12 trophies, scoring the winning goal that secured the famous 'Treble Treble' for the club, a goal that will go down in Celtic history. Daniel Berman, my agent partner and I, are both enormously proud to have concluded all Tom's Celtic business up to now, his last contract the greatest afforded to a foreigner in the club's history.

A career on one leg denied me many more international caps but in all my roles it was an honour and a privilege to serve the nation. They were good times.

CHAPTER 13

OWNERSHIP

They say that silence is golden. Well I can tell you first hand that it isn't. To say I have been to hell and back during my years of silence is an understatement.

I am in a better place now but it has certainly been a long time coming. A long time trying to make sense of everything good and bad that has happened in my life, and more importantly, why it happened.

Some may feel it is a redemption of some sort, which maybe so, but it's more than that, its accepting ownership of the whole journey, its highs and its lows. Understanding that yes, some people did you harm, some used you and some never repaid the loyalty I showed them, but ultimately I was also culpable in my own self-destruction. Once this was understood, I became free again, which in turn allowed me to welcome new beginnings and inner peace.

Questions and constant confusion haunted every day of my life, as my mind never ventured far from my arrest in Reading, England. Every single day this has troubled me because it was not the truth. It was fake news, is fake news and I am more than happy to take any lie detector test to prove it. I would bet my life that the police officers and prosecutors who brought the bogus charge against me would not do the same.

They got lucky after throwing a plea deal to a man who at the time was a mess, addicted to crack cocaine, and mentally unstable. That man was me, and what my legal team agreed to and advised me to accept, is simply not true.

It makes you wonder how a human brain that can achieve international football success, manage global superstars and create World Cup scouting dossiers can then go to a level where every sense of reason, normality and common sense no longer registers or exists?

There is no doubt crack cocaine is a major factor where very few, if any, comeback from that nightmare. When you add what has now been diagnosed as PTSD and transition anxiety, sprinkled with possible chronic traumatic encephalopathy (CTE) brain trauma from countless impacts and concussions over decades, it becomes the perfect recipe for abnormal and nonsensical behaviour.

Left alone without professional help, without digging deeper and understanding the possible why, your life becomes a torturous hell. Unable to control emotional variances, there is no peace, your sanity is compromised and it is why many out there choose to end their lives.

I thought about it on many occasions but never went there, the voices saying 'no' far outweighed the one saying 'yes'. I guess it wasn't God's plan at the time.

The physical trauma impacting a footballer over their career is tough to endure, but the psychological trauma that can mentally impact a human can be far more damaging and terminal.

In 1984, football took me away from my family when I was 18. Still a teenager. I was alone on the other side of the world without any of the modern communication technology that we take for granted today. No mobile phone, no laptop, no social media, no communication apps, just handwritten letters and the occasional collect call from a land line that was super expensive for my parents who couldn't really afford it. Letters that would take anywhere from a few weeks to a month to travel from Spain to Australia, and vice versa, were in effect, my only form of communication.

On arrival in Gijón, Spain, I was put in a room in the city centre owned by the club, above a bar that was no bigger than a prison cell. A black and white TV that carried only two Spanish channels which on most days provided only a fuzzy reception that I would sometimes be able to conquer by using a coat hanger as an antenna. My window looked out onto another wall, four stories up where, in the street below, junkies would shoot heroin into their veins seeking an escape from reality.

The lure of the big stages is too big a draw that overrides crushing sadness and loneliness. In solitude you begin talking to yourself, who else do you talk to? In the big leagues, you are a nobody until you become a somebody, and both coaches and players have no problems in making you fully aware of it. The machine that is the football system itself thrives on destroying souls, knowing that the few remaining will be the players kept, with the more elite ones becoming internationals.

I was the Australian U-20s captain when I signed for Sporting Gijón and it commanded zero respect, absolutely nothing. Being Australian was their fuel for more ridicule and laughter, so I quickly learnt that my best option for respect, was to play my Spanish card.

Initially you have no friends, and they don't want to be your friend. All those in your age group are after the same prize you are after, and for many of them a life out of poverty is threatened by your presence. As a young pro you might be sold or loaned out somewhere, and off you go again, on an overnight train to a city you have never heard of, or only ever seen on a paper map of the world. On arrival, you would be greeted by a few representatives of the new club and again taken to a prison-like hotel room, your only companion loneliness. Those times were the hardest and until you make a first team debut, a decent one at that, you are afforded no respect.

Arriving at a new club for the start of your loan period, a necessary evil as a young man in Europe in order to become a better footballer, you would get little sleep in anticipation of what was to come. Walking into a new change room the next morning, you would be greeted by 25 to 30 men, older professionals, some happy, some bitter, and most of them not at all pleased to see you as your presence decreased their potential ability to feed their family ,and that says it all.

When you finished training, you would head back to your small hotel room and the cycle would continue, while all the other players headed home to their families, like you once did back in Australia. By the time you had established yourself in this team and city, you were recalled by your parent club and loaned out to another club in another city, or another country and so it began again; an endless cycle. There were no agents as such, no advisors, you went where the club placed you. In essence, you were owned like a slave, your only possessions being the dream of superstardom and a little suitcase, not too dissimilar to the one your parents carried when they arrived in Australia.

Being alone on the other side of the world really hits home on special occasions such as Christmas, New Year's Eve, Mother's and Father's Day and birthdays, as most are spent apart from your family. No Messenger, no Instagram, no Zoom, nothing, just four walls and your imagination taking you home to Canberra. I see people going mad over 21st birthday celebrations; I spent mine alone. Now birthdays are insignificant to me, just another day.

Over time your brain adapts and all these special occasions become almost meaningless, you see them as just another day, a horrible day, a product of the coping mechanism you once used to erase the pain they caused you. It is soul destroying and crushes those who are mentally weak. Years and years of chasing the dream on the other side of the world, the perceived success, fame, money and whatever else the world adds into the mix, are offset by the realisation that you have spent 20 years away from family, years you cannot get back, but you are reminded of it every now and then by the little demon in your head, asking you if it was all worth it.

Life can be horrible at times, but more so when you see how quickly all those fake friends and even family disappear when you find trouble. Those same ones who happily accepted match tickets when Manchester United were in town, or when the Socceroos were playing, or when they wanted a signed David Beckham shirt, or Tim Cahill shirt. I gave them my world unconditionally, that's what I do, but many gave me nothing back and went missing when I needed them most.

The football establishments in this country of recent times are no better. You put your heart, soul and body on the line playing for the Socceroos, crippling yourself in the process and what do you get in return? Not even a simple phone call from anybody, asking "Andy, are you okay?". It would have meant the world to me.

I was their chief scout in South America and then I see a picture of the Socceroos in Germany for a pre-World Cup camp with more assistants than players. You couldn't find one spot for your scout? An ex-Socceroo who, god forbid, could whisper helpful advice in the ear of some of the players? I was good enough to do the homework in South America but not good enough to be in a team picture.

However, in a brilliant twist of fate it brought Jaynie, my wife, and I together. We watched the Socceroos play Croatia together, yes the very ones I had scouted for, some of whom, in a group of friends that included Jaynie, would frequently rip bongs and get as high as kites in the nation's capital on football scholarships, the hypocrisy of it all.

The PFA (Professional Footballers' Australia), where are you ? I know plenty of older Socceroos doing it tough, and all I hear is talk and no change when it's your role to look after player welfare.

The complete madness of it all hardens and changes your soul so much so that you have now have many fronts and protective shields, sometimes perceived as arrogance or cockiness. Confusion reigns all the time, it did back then and does now, always wondering why I kept chasing this football dream, this thing that at times brought more misery and pain, than joy and happiness. Addicted to it just like a drug, eventually wearing you down and changing you forever. These days my mum always says, "You were such a sweet little boy."

If I have learned anything from my post football troubles, it is that we as a global population are managed by media giants left and right, who like to direct our thought processes with financial and political agendas. We live in lands with governments, court systems and police forces where corruption exists. I have been a victim of their work first hand. Just so there is no confusion, I was offered millions to divulge information about David Beckham and his family. My "nothing" incident in Reading – their words – would go unreported if I complied. When I refused, blackmail tactics were used and still I refused, infuriating them so much that character-destroying missiles started coming from everywhere, to protect everybody but me.

I'm not overly big on playing the racist card. I've lived it and got on with it, but if you come at me with it as the police did in Reading, I'm coming back at you with guns blazing. Not only did you manufacture a false story that Walt Disney would be proud of, but you also took advantage of me while I was cuffed and unable to fight back. You had nothing then, and still have nothing now, only a creatively written police charge and the all-time dumbest admission of guilt, made under what has now been diagnosed as mental and physical duress.

For those who called me "Paki", "black bastard" and "curry muncher", all I can do is point to Imran Khan, one of my favourite cricketers back in the day, and say to the police that I am honoured that you thought I looked like the handsome, superstar cricketer who is now the Prime Minister of Pakistan.

Let me be clear, I have nothing against the police as an institution and have friends who are current and former police officers. In fact I nearly joined at one point in Sydney. It's unfortunate that one or two bad apples always give the majority a bad name. I know how I was treated that day and it is not unusual in England, just watch the news. I was racially and physically abused and how ironic that the only black cop on duty was the Alsatian that wanted a piece of my ass!

The world's leading sports management company threw their own missiles to protect themselves from a multi-million-dollar lawsuit from the Beckhams if I spoke out negatively. Where was their duty of care for me during and after the Spanish mission? There was none, zero, nada! They screwed up, millions and millions of future dollars lost upon losing the most famous sportsman in the world, from the greatest schoolboy error of all time.

Despite knowing and understanding everything that has come before, it's difficult to process and fix, until you fix yourself. That started with addressing a cocaine and crack cocaine addiction which most humans do not come back from. While the world provides a million methods, you are the only person who can stop it, the brain must desire it and you must find a reason why.

For me there were many, starting with wanting to be a father, a better brother and a better son, like the one they were all once very proud of. Unfortunately, with all the baggage I had accumulated and fake news that came with it, it would be difficult a fight. An everyday fight for your life, a fight for the love and respect from the ones you love the most.

The major turning point was meeting my future wife and soul mate Jaynie, who from minute one gave me unconditional and unwavering love. A beautiful caring soul who became my guardian angel. There were many nights where she would sit next to me, lay next to me, staying awake to watch me breathe, making sure my heart didn't stop after week-long benders. Sometimes she would drive around all night searching for me, just as the Chilli Peppers' band members would do for their front man Anthony Kiedis, both of us on a mission to nowhere slowly killing ourselves.

She sacrificed her life for me while she was battling her own demons after suffering a trauma of her own, held up with a gun to her head in an armed robbery at her Canberra workplace. She too has PTSD as a result of this horrendous incident and now there are so many more things about her that make sense to me.

Jaynie is a warrior of the highest order, a badass with a good heart, soft but strong, the type of woman you go to war beside and the type of woman you marry, so I did.

Her parents were great from day one too, embracing me like a son. Her father David and I always watched the big motorsport races together whether it be NASCAR, V8s or F1. The first time we met he handed me a pump action shotgun, set-up a few targets to hit in the backyard and said "If you miss you can't be a part of this family." Luckily for me, it wasn't my first rodeo.

As you get older, other life events away from your football matter more. Things like Isabella's university graduation day in Auckland, where she introduced me to a young man with his own big dream and who not long after, asked in a very gentlemanly fashion for my daughter's hand in marriage. Isabella is now the wife of UFC (Ultimate Fighting Championship) lightweight star Dan Hooker, otherwise known as The Hangman, and I now have a beautiful granddaughter, Zoe.

In 2016 Jaynie and I were married in Canberra. A few months later, Isabella and Dan tied the knot in Thailand at a simply stunning resort in the middle of paradise. Being there, surrounded by family and friends, seeing your daughter with a good man, an absolute gentleman, who will take care of your little princess for life, there is no greater feeling for a father.

Throughout your own professional sporting career you must, at times, be very selfish but I am happy to say that one of the greatest moments I have ever savoured in sport was not my own. It was watching my son-in-law Dan, fight live as co-main event at UFC in Melbourne, sitting in the front row with Isabella, Zoe and Jaynie. In front of a record crowd of 62,000 at Marvel Stadium, he defeated Al Iaquinta whilst his teammate, and our friend, Israel Adesanya, beat Robert Whittaker to become the UFC Middleweight Champion.

Football of all types is tough, but these UFC boys are the ultimate gladiators. We footballers, even the toughest ones, are not of this ilk. These guys are a whole different level and on a whole different planet. It was a great night for all involved, but so nerve wracking on the sidelines as just a spectator with the occasional shouted instruction that he probably didn't hear, or ignored, but it helped me get through the fight.

I found joy in both Dan and Izzy's success, the family success, the team success, and relished the buzz and electric feeling of being back inside a big stadium.

Still I was haunted and traumatised, my mind not right on many levels, as there is no greater pain than an untold story and living a lie.

For me it was more about the principle of it all. If you do the crime, you do the time, I'm happy with that; but in my case it never sat right because I never did the crime.

How could I change this? How could I get my version of the truth out there up against global media empires, police, management companies and private investigators, all screwing you because you won't sell out David Beckham? It's insane.

As fate would have it, in the middle of writing this book my, father died. My hero and my inspiration, an immigrant who boarded a ship in Spain and travelled across the world in search of a better life, living his own crazy adventures. Who would have guessed that years later his son would return to the country he had to leave, becoming the first Australian to play in Spain, arguably the world's top football nation? That made him immensely proud.

Visiting my dad in hospital over the last month of his life I showed him the emails and evidence I had received from Scotland Yard.

They clearly showed that my arrest was part of a grander operation that targeted not only myself, but Beckham, the Royal Family and many others. All of us were victims of Britain's greatest media scandal, all of us innocent victims.

Those emails made him happy but at the same time angry and there was nothing he or any of us could do. I know he was always proud of my achievements, but after the Beckham days, my addiction and the troubles that came with it, something changed. I knew that he still loved me to death, but I knew I had disappointed him. If he passed away without ever knowing the truth, I think I would have been destroyed forever. Scotland Yard came to the rescue, the good cops dealt me a few beautiful cards and I saw his glow again, I saw his real love for me again.

"Write the book and tell your truth, everything, the whole truth, whoever doesn't like it can go f*** themselves, I am proud of you son and maybe this Di Caprio fella I met in New York can maybe make the movie," was one of the last things he whispered to me.

That last week by his side, holding his hand almost all day had a big emotional impact. I spoke a lot and he just listened. Saying nothing, he just stared at me all the time, his eyes following me everywhere I went. At night when I left the hospice, he would say "Look after mama."

The night before he passed away, four rabbits appeared outside the glass sliding doors to his room, which looked directly out to the lake. We spent many times together hunting rabbits, ending their lives but now his life was ending, and I wondered if this occurrence was symbolic in any way. My father's time on earth was done and the next day he left us. He died in my arms, and I'm so glad I was with him at the end.

Life's natural highs are the greatest of all. After football retirement and managing David Beckham, I went looking for those same highs in all the wrong places, unable to recapture those unbelievable euphoric feelings. Lining up against Manchester United in an FA Cup match, standing in the tunnel beside Roy Keane, Eric Cantona, Ryan Giggs, and Andy Cole preparing for battle, is the ultimate high. There is no greater rush and there is no drug on the planet that can replace it.

Watching Michael Jordan's 'The Last Dance' was another light bulb moment, discovering that Chicago Bulls coach, Phil Jackson, a 13-time NBA champion as a player and manager would, on many occasions, roar like a lion while on acid trips. It shows that the craziness amongst sporting greats is more common than you think. Maybe it's different wiring, who knows? I never roared like a lion but on many occasions, I would hear them in the early hours of the morning. Despite his occasional madness, Phil would later become an NBA winning coach, and it is stories like this that give me hope, inspiration and new dreams to chase.

A football pioneer, a trailblazer representing Australia, with many historical firsts that will live until the end of time; of that I am very proud.

I have made poor choices that I thought I never would, of them, I am not proud. Embarrassed and ashamed, to be honest, but I offer no excuses and I seek no sympathy. It is what it is. I own a crack cocaine addiction. I own defeating a crack cocaine addiction.

I own a multitude of great achievements, but I will no longer own all that is not true about me.

I have lived a truly amazing life; a uniquely special one reserved for a chosen few. Regrets, I have a few, but like Frank Sinatra sang, 'too few to mention'.

They say God's favourites have a hard time and they're not kidding because this was definitely no fairy tale. As a boy, my father would tell me to shoot for the stars and achieve things that money could not buy for then you will have a rich life, happy and content when you die. So I shot for the stars and I will die happy and content.

Impossible was nothing for the 'Original Wizard of Oz'.

ACKNOWLEDGEMENTS

In the last two years I have lost my father and father-in-law RIP. Mum and Dad, thank you for your lessons, guidance, many sacrifices and unconditional love, all the reasons why I am here telling this amazing story. You are why I achieved my dreams, why I never gave up on the truth and rewrote history.

Raquel, Gabby, Alyssa, Lucas and Victor, I love you all very much, I wish New York was closer and we saw more of each other.

David and Eileen, I not only gained in-laws but two beautiful friends, who like my parents have showered me with unconditional love.

Isabella, you are my baby girl, my princess, my big WHY. In good times and bad times, I have always loved you with all my heart and will do so, until the day I die. You have grown into an amazing beautiful lady, wife and mother, who I am immensely proud of.

Daniel, you are every father's wish of a husband for their daughter. A good man, a gentleman, and a world class fighter, we are all very proud of you.

Zoe, I hope when you are older you are proud of your *Abuelo*, he is a little crazy, but cool for cats like you are. I love you to death beautiful girl. Go conquer the world with your superstar genetics.

To Kathryn, Jan and Mal thank you for making sure Isabella was safe and well in the times I was not around. It is very much appreciated; all three of you are wonderful souls.

To all my wonderful friends and family, too many to mention, the real ones know who they are, and I know who they are.

Thank you to my friend Russ Gibbs, who encouraged me to put down my memoirs, convincing me that it was a story way beyond football, of a life so amazing and unbelievable that it would impact people from all nations and from all walks of a life. Russ' forte is football commentary; a natural, born for it. Given the opportunity he will develop into a world class commentator, very capable of calling the biggest matches on the planet.

To Daniel, my friend and business partner, you are a fine gentleman, a man of honour, trust and integrity, on top of being one of the world's finest legal eagles. I'm blessed to have you by my side, and I wish I'd known you many years ago we would have kicked a few detectives' asses. Still will, if they fancy it, but they won't.

To Bonita and the team at Fair Play Publishing, before I had even written a word you said you would publish my book. That meant so much to me and I thank you for your faith and patience.

Dr Jess Nathan my friend, my doctor, thank you for listening and thank you for helping me find peace. The doctor by day is also a wildlife photographer who National Geographic need to sign up, before the rest of the world does.

Horry Money, love you my man.

Paul 'The Jewel', thank you for being YOU. There are not enough words!

Mick Hickman (Hicky), my Wembley dream came true because of you. Thank you.

Hammo and Parky, your unconditional friendship is always much appreciated.

To all the wonderful athletes I have worked with, just thank you. You all inspired me, I hope I inspired you a little too.

Many coaches have impacted my football journey. They are: Sito Gonzalez, my uncle Luis Arranz, Stuart Devlin, Jimmy Shoulder, Ron Smith, Victor Fernandez Snr, Tom Sermanni, Enrique Perez 'Pachin', Brian Clough, John Duncan, Mark McGhee, Billy Bonds, Mick Gooding, Jimmy Quinn, Terry Bullivant, Tommy Burns, Alan Pardew, Eddie Thomson and Mick Hickman. You all gave me a piece of your knowledge, expertise and magic. Thank you.

To Christopher Paul Toth your portrait of me that has become the book cover is simply amazing. The different colours representing the many feelings, emotions and happenings I have experienced in my life, but more importantly, creating a portrait, that depicts my journey, the wars, the battle scars and the amazing accomplishments.

To Janae McLister, thank you for your time and expertise. Very much appreciated, my friend.

They say the woman by your side makes you the man you are, so last, but not least, my best friend, my soul mate, my guardian angel, my wife, Jaynie. When it would have been easier to walk away, you held tighter, stayed closer and left your light on. You are a beautiful caring soul and I am enormously proud of how you continue to honour your father and take care of your Mama. I love you 'Harry' and look forward to plenty more adventures with you. The world is ours, so let's go get it.

APPENDIX

CAREER RECORDS

Name:
Andrew (Andy) Bernal
Date of Birth:
16 May 1966
Place of Birth:
Canberra, Australia
Height:
1.78m (5' 10")
Position:
Defender / Defensive Midfielder

CLUB CAREER

1985-88: Sporting Gijón

1985-86: Albacete Balompié (loan)
23 appearances

1987-88: FC Xerez (loan)
38 appearances

1987-88: Nottingham Forest

1987-88: Ipswich Town
9 appearances

1989-94: Sydney Olympic
121 appearances, 6 goals
Champion 1989/90

1994-2000: Reading FC
226 appearances, 4 goals

TITLES

**Champion National Soccer
League 1989/90**

**Champion National Youth
Soccer League 1983/84**

AUSTRALIA

Cap Number 361
21 appearances, 1989-1996

Australian Schoolboys captain

Australian U-20 Captain

Australian U-23 Captain
(youngest ever)

2006 World Cup Chief Scout

2007 Asian Cup Chief Scout

*Australian playing statistics
provided by Andrew Howe, Australian
football statistician.*

CAREER MILESTONES

1st Australian footballer
to play in Spain

1st Australian footballer
to play in both Spain and England

1st Australian to captain
an English football club (Reading FC)

1st player represented as FIFA agent:
Tim Cahill, AO

**Youngest ever Australian
U23 (Olyroos) captain**

Year	Date	Opponent	Venue	Comp	Result	Mins
1989	17/02	Malmo	Melbourne	FR	W 3-2	23
1990	03/06	Hajduk Split	Sydney	FR	W 1-0	90
	06/06	Hajduk Split	Melbourne	FR	D 2-2	90
	20/08	Malaysia U23	Jakarta	IC	W 3-0	90
	21/08	Indonesia B	Jakarta	IC	W 7-0	90
	23/08	Thailand U23	Jakarta	IC SF	W 2-0	90
	25/08	Indonesia	Jakarta	IC Final	W 3-0	90
	06/09	Korea Republic	Seoul	FR	L 0-1	90
	09/09	Korea Republic	Seoul	FR	L 0-1	90
1991	30/01	Czechoslovakia	Melbourne	FR	L 0-1	90
	06/02	Czechoslovakia	Sydney	FR	L 0-2	76
1992	26/01	Sweden	Sydney	FR	D 0-0	90
	29/01	Sweden	Adelaide	FR	W 1-0	57
	18/06	Argentina	Buenos Aires	FR	L 0-2	62
	12/07	Croatia	Sydney	FR	D 0-0	90
	10/08	Thailand U19	Jakarta	IC	W 1-0	90
	11/08	Malaysia	Jakarta	IC	L 0-1	90
	13/08	South Korea U23	Jakarta	IC	L 0-1	90
	14/08	Indonesia	Jakarta	IC	W 3-0	90
	11/09	Tahiti	Papeete	WCQ	W 3-0	17
1996	24/04	Chile	Antofagasta	FR	L 0-3	90

FR – *Friendly*, IC – *Independence Cup*, WCQ – *World Cup Qualifier*

Really good football books

Code War$
The Battle for Fans,
Dollars and Survival
by Dr Hunter Fujak

The Australian Youth
Footballer Regulatory Guide
by Peter Paleologos
(Popcorn Press)

The Away Game
by Matthew Hall

Achieving the Impossible
- the Remarkable Story
of How Greece Won
EURO 2004
by George Tsitsonis

Whatever It Takes - The
Inside Story of the FIFA
Way by Bonita Mersiades
(Powderhouse Press)

Surfing for England
Our Lost Socceroos
by Jason Goldsmith

Encyclopedia of Matildas
Revised and Updated
by Andrew Howe
and Greg Werner

Encyclopedia of Socceroos
by Andrew Howe

'If I Started to Cry,
I Wouldn't Stop'
by Matthew Hall

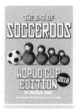

The A-Z of Socceroos -
World Cup Edition 2018
by Andrew Howe (with Ray
Gatt and Bonita Mersiades)

Playing for Australia
The First Socceroos,
Asia and the World Game
by Trevor Thompson

The World Cup Chronicles
31 Days that Rocked Brazil
by Jorge Knijnik

Chronicles of Soccer
in Australia - The
Foundation Years 1859 to
1949 by Peter Kunz

Support Your Local League,
A South-East Asian
Football Odyssey by
Antony Sutton

The Aboriginal Soccer Tribe
by John Maynard

Introducing
Jarrod Black
by Texi Smith
(Popcorn Press)

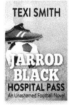

Jarrod Black
Hospital Pass
by Texi Smith
(Popcorn Press)

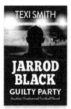

Jarrod Black
Guilty Party
by Texi Smith
(Popcorn Press)

Anna Black
This Girl can Play
by Texi Smith
(Popcorn Press)

The Time of
My Football Life
by David Picken

www.fairplaypublishing.com.au/shop

FAIRPLAY

PUBLISHING